RYTHM OIL
35c

LUCKY MON·GOL MEMPHIS TENN.

RYTHM OIL

A JOURNEY THROUGH THE MUSIC OF THE AMERICAN SOUTH

STANLEY BOOTH

DA CAPO PRESS

For my mother

First published 1991
Copyright © 1991 by Stanley Booth

Some of these pieces were first published elsewhere. For details see under acknowledgments.

Stanley Booth has asserted his right under the Copyright, Designs and Patents Act, 1988 to be identified as the author of this work.

A CIP catalog record for this book is available from the Library of Congress.
ISBN 0-306-80979-6

First Da Capo Press Edition 2000

Published by Da Capo Press
A Member of the Perseus Books Group
http://www.dacapopress.com

1 2 3 4 5 6 7 8 9 10——04 03 02 01 00

Praise ye the LORD. Sing unto the
LORD a new song, and his praise in
the congregation of saints.
Let Israel rejoice in him that made
him: let the children of Zion be joyful
in their King.
Let them praise his name in the
dance: let them sing praises unto him
with the timbrel and harp.
For the LORD taketh pleasure in his
people: he will beautify the meek with
salvation.
Let the saints be joyful in glory:
let them sing aloud upon their beds.

Psalm 149, v. 1-5

CONTENTS

Rythm Oil: An Introduction   1

1   Standing at the Crossroads   3

2   Beale Street's Gone Dry   13

3   Furry's Blues   23

4   Been Here and Gone: The Funeral of Mississippi John Hurt   37

5   A Rainy Night in Memphis   46

6   Situation Report: Elvis in Memphis, 1967   52

7   The Memphis Soul Sound   69

8   Blues Boy   89

9   The Memphis Début of the Janis Joplin Revue   106

10 *The Gilded Palace of Sin*: The Flying Burrito Brothers   111

11 Blues for the Red Man   116

12 Elvis's Women   131

13 Wiregrass   135

14 Garden of Memories   138

15 Psalmist of Soul: Al Green   150

16 That's Why They Call it the Blues: Stax in Atlanta   159

17 The Burden of the Blues: ZZ Top   169

18 Keith Richards at Forty-Five   180

19 Fascinating Changes   190

20 The Godfather's Blues   228

    Acknowledgments   250

    Index   251

Rythm Oil:
An Introduction

I had heard such sounds before, heard them as a little boy lying in bed in the wiregrass country of south Georgia, heard the sounds of animals crying far off in the woods, heard the sounds the black woods hands made having what they called church, far off in the woods, the all-night drums, like the heartbeat of the dark swampy woods, *boom*dada *boom*dada, and heard the sounds I could not identify – the really frightening ones. I had not been so frightened since I was a boy lying slender and white and frail in the dark bed, finding a sound in the night, losing it, waiting for it again, a soft sighing sound that might have been the wind easing through the tops of the long-needle pines, or might have been cattle lowing a long way off, but always came back to sounding most like a simple human exhalation right outside the rusty screen of my bedroom window, the quietly released breath of a man standing quietly, just watching, waiting. I loved the woods but for years I lay awake at night fearing that sound.

The True Adventures of the Rolling Stones

I can still see the cut leather jacket, khaki shirt, and white undershirt, and my grandfather's pale shoulder without a scratch on it. Attacked coming out the door of the small pay-building, one of the frame structures all painted the same shade of green, on the white sand road through the slash pine forest that housed the hundred-odd souls of the Newton Company, he'd fallen away from the blade as it sliced through his clothes.

Frank Porter, the black man who'd tried to stab my grandfather, ran down the building's wooden steps into the early morning fog as my grandfather, pulling a revolver, fired at him, striking Porter's wife, who was coming across the road from the commissary. She lived, and Porter disappeared, never to be heard from again by that particular set of white folk. Until that morning, when the most trusted black man in the turpentine camp attempted to murder my grandfather, the place had seemed to me a paradise, a world of men and women, horses and mules, woods and roads, barns and houses, all larger than life: Jim Johnson wearing my father's blue chalk-stripe in his pine coffin; black women holding up babies with six fingers on each hand. After one man I loved tried to kill another man I also loved, I began to perceive the shadows in paradise and, at last, the dark places within myself.

Rythm Oil is the story of a journey, un voyage au bout de la nuit, from slavery in 1940s south Georgia to murder in 1960s Memphis and back again to savagery in 1990s Georgia, with many laughs along the way: the writer shows up in Louisiana, California, and England, but returns to the place where the bullfrog gets his water. The tradition of romantic poetry, in which artists like the ones considered here surely occupy a place, derives its origin in no small part from Wordsworth and Coleridge's reading of William Bartram, the eighteenth-century American naturalist, on the region and legends of the Okefinokee Swamp. Coleridge's 'Kubla Khan' translates – with a supposed admixture of opium – from Bartram's writing about Salt Springs, in Marion County, Florida. Aside from personal fascination, there is historic precedent for keeping an ear to the American South and Southeast.

'Standing at the Crossroads' presents the pivotal incident in the life of Mississippi bluesman Robert Johnson, the embodiment of Faustian legend. In the 1920s and '30s, the primary entertainment available to such isolated persons as inmates of cotton plantations and turpentine camps was on traveling 'doctor' shows where so-called medicine was sold and the programs included music, comedy, dance, and tableaux and vignettes from classic drama such as Faust. Robert Johnson's world of belief was that of my parents' youth in the South, in which the simplest sensations were laden with prophetic and poetic significance: 'My nose itches – I smell pitches [peaches] – somebody's comin' with a hole in *his britches.' A credulous time. Many watched spellbound as a man sold his soul to the Devil, and some at least, like Robert Johnson in 'Standing at the Crossroads', must have believed.*

The events of Johnson's life, including a short, brilliant, recording career and an early death (according to legend, poisoned by a jealous husband at twenty-six) would remain melodrama if not raised to a tragic power by the qualities of his music and language: dramatic contrasts, exalted diction, poetic imagery Freudian in its pervasive sexuality. Sex, sex as sin, is where this music and these stories live and move and have their being.

> Me and the Devil was walkin' side by side
> I'm going to beat my woman until I get satisfied
>
> Everything I do, you got yo' mouth stuck out
> And the hole where I used to fish, you got me posted out

The following sketch, cast with an eye to the form of the minstrel comedies of the 1830s, can do no more than provide a possible prelude to a play about a genius among barbarians, a lost, tortured, tormented soul.

1

STANDING AT THE CROSSROADS

Midnight. A deserted crossroads in the Mississippi Delta. Beside the white sandy roads (in the actual place represented in this scene) weeds grow rank, bitterweed, gallberry, dogfennel. The clear redbrown water running in the ditches looks stained with old blood. In the woods beyond tower stark slash pines and cypresses, wild gray tresses of Spanish moss in their branches stirring in the wind.

A small open shed of rough pine two-by-fours and tin roofing slumps near the crossroads. Onto the road, coming through the dark swampy woods, hurtles an Old Black Man. He is wearing dress trousers of faded brown or blue, very dusty to the waist and wet below the knees. Also wet is the tail of his long gray coat – it looks like (and possibly is) a Confederate Army officer's overcoat. The shoulders and back of the coat and spots on the man's trousers, soiled plaid shirt, and red bill cap with the initials B.P.O.E. are spattered with tar. Stuck in the gunk are downy white feathers, giving him the appearance of a large molting bird – something perhaps that should be extinct, like an albino pterodactyl, only he is, except for the feathers, very black. He is also barefoot. Wet from the knees down, festooned with tar and feathers, lugging a guitar-case, he crosses the road, puffs of dust rising with each lurch. The moon is full, but clouds keep passing over it, and swift shadows in odd rectangular shapes checker the silver light.

Before the shed he stops, listens, looks up and down each road, then drops the guitar-case and begins plucking feathers.

OLD BLACK MAN: Damn! Damn! Damn! Too Close! Peckerwoods like to kilt me!

He takes off the cap, picking feathers from his hair. From a pocket he produces a very old handkerchief, mops his face and spits out a few more feathers.

OLD BLACK MAN (still breathing hard): *Have* mercy! Done got *ole* — seen a nigger eat a snake — monkey fuck a football — and now I got to be bustin' thoo de gators' bedroom!

He removes the overcoat, plucks at the feathers, gives up, puts the coat back on and, having now the leisure to notice that his feet hurt, picks up the guitar, hobbles to the shed and sits down. First he inspects his feet, making faces as he touches wounds and pulls out splinters.

OLD BLACK MAN: 'Take dey shoes so dey cain't run' — Dey wahn't doin' nothin' but givin' me a head start. (Grimaces with foot pain.)

Next he opens the guitar-case. Two or three quarts of water pour out.

OLD BLACK MAN: One mo' night like this put me out of bidness.

Reaching into the guitar-case, he begins removing and examining certain articles in small, red-flannel pouches.

OLD BLACK MAN: Lodestone. Madstone, Devil's Snuff. *Ruint.* (Dumps it out.) Devil's Shoestrings. Wet as a rat. Dragon Blood powder. Maybe I can dry it out. Black cat bone. Be Together powder. Dragon Blood Stick. Black cat ashes. Love Me powder. Five finger grass. Asafidity. (Sniffs.) *Phew.* Rattlesnake dust. (Shakes his head.) John the Conqueror root. Wonder of the World root. Mojo hands. Tobys. Cunyun jacks. Graveyard dirt. (Dumps the latter and refills the bag with roadside sand, then replaces the flannel bags and takes out a small brown bottle.) Dr. Whitlow's Soothin' Syrup and Savory Tonic. Pore ole doc. I wonder did he get away. Man, them peckerwoods was *mad.* (Holds up bottle.) Sure cure for cancer, clap, and piles, two for a dollar, it'll make you smile. (Drinks, smiles, frowns.) Didn't make them pecks smile. 'Specially dat one wid de rope. Doc never should of tole dem pecks to give it to dey stock. Ever hog, cow, mule, dog, cat, and chicken in Cogdell, Missippi, stone dead or in a coma. (Laughs.) Mercy, mercy. (Looks around, becomes solemn.) Down in de *low*-ground, barefoot as a *yard*-dog, lost as a *by*-God. (Drinks again, hears something.) Hsst!

In the distance, coming nearer, out of a direction different from the one the old man followed, there are noises, branches snapping, water splashing. Soon onto the road stumbles, collapsing at the crossroads, a Young Black Man in a black suit. He too has a guitar (slung neck down across his back on a piece of plowline) and is wet from the knees down, but he is hatless and wearing black-and-white spectators.

YOUNG BLACK MAN: Lord have mercy –

He is quickly on his feet and hurrying away (without seeing the old man) but the old man has had time to see the shoes.

OLD BLACK MAN (not too loud): Hey! Lil ole boy! Wait up!

YOUNG BLACK MAN (stopping, barely onstage): Who it is?

OLD BLACK MAN: Po' traveler. Rest a spell. (He tilts his cap at a nonchalant angle, puts on a pair of shades, lights a cigarette, leans back and crosses his legs. He looks coldblooded, smart, evil, and totally cool, like the late Lightnin' Hopkins.) Look like you been rode hard and put up muddy.

YOUNG BLACK MAN: I got to go.

OLD BLACK MAN: Where you headed dis evenin'?

YOUNG BLACK MAN: Down to the ferry.

OLD BLACK MAN: Which ferry?

YOUNG BLACK MAN: 'Bout half a mile down yonder. (points) Five cent one way.

OLD BLACK MAN: You in trouble?

YOUNG BLACK MAN: Not if her ole man don't catch me. He had a .44 Colt. Nickle-plated.

OLD BLACK MAN: It don't do no good to run. She may done put salt in his shoes and he be fast asleep.

YOUNG BLACK MAN: He was wearin' 'em.

OLD BLACK MAN: Or maybe he salted yo' tracks and you bein' led right back to stare down dat .44 barrel. Sit down, boy. You need help.

YOUNG BLACK MAN: What you doin' here?

OLD BLACK MAN: Waitin' for you, boy. What took you so long?

YOUNG BLACK MAN: Where you come from?

OLD BLACK MAN: All over. *Travelin'*, son. I ain't slept for two nights hand-runnin' in de same town since I was thirteen years old. I been everwhere and seen everbody. Been in thirty-eight states and nine foreign countries, countin' Oklahoma. I seen President Roosevelt when he wahn't nothin' but a govner. I shaken hands with Jack Johnson. I seen his white wife.

YOUNG BLACK MAN (coming closer): You travel barefoot?

OLD BLACK MAN (without hesitation): Never wear shoes. Shoes tilt de spine and alter de constituent of de human brain. Black *and* white. I done studied it. Worked for years with a doctor, white man, medical doctor. Fack, me an' him just parted.

YOUNG BLACK MAN: You a musicianer?

OLD BLACK MAN: Musicianer, root doctor, rain maker, water witch, card dealer, crap shooter, spiritual adviser. I am de seventh son of de seventh daughter of a seventh son. Who are you, boy, where's yo' home?

YOUNG BLACK MAN: Robert Johnson. I ain't got no home. (He offers his hand. The old man looks at it, takes it and squeezes it briefly.)

OLD BLACK MAN: Mine is, ah, Taylor. Cyclone Taylor.

ROBERT: Cyclone. Like a big wind.

CYCLONE (looks, eyebrows raised, at Robert, who appears innocent of sarcasm): I done some fighting as a younger man. Bare knuckle bouts. But I found a Greater Power –

   Not far away in the darkness a screech owl makes the plummeting, petulant cry that sinks the heart in its descent.

CYCLONE (loudly): *Oak* tree! That'll shet him up. That's how you hesh a screet-owl, name de tree he sottin' in. Co'se you *can* squeeze yo' lef' wrist in yo' right hand to *choke* 'm off. Or you can turn yo' pockets inside out – (pauses, regarding Robert) – to *pay* him off. You know de screet-owl cry spoze to proceed a deaf. Mmm, hmm, if sump'm don't change, somebody bound to die. Sho is. You want a cigarette?

   Robert says nothing. Cyclone lights a cigarette. The screech owl cries again.

ROBERT: He still there.

CYCLONE: Dat ain't him. Dass anudden. Dat ain't de same one. I can charm a billygoat. I haves cunyun jacks and mojo hands of all types and kinds. I can give you graveyard dirt that make hounds from hell chase dey tails. I can turn de evil eye of a jealous husband – (pauses, looking down). You ought to consider goin' barefoot, son. Make a world of difference to yo' health.

   Robert says nothing but, taking off his guitar, sits on the bench beside the old man.

CYCLONE: Hmp. (little disdainful snort) *You* a musicianer?

ROBERT: I been tryin' to learn guitar.

CYCLONE: Do better to learn doctorin' or dealin' cards. Dese yere field (pron. *feel*) niggers don't like musicianers. I seed de time, comin' past cotton fields, I'd stop under a tree at de water jug – go to pickin',

terreckly dere be four-five women and me in de shade, all dem men niggers sweatin' in de field. Dey come up for water, I say, 'Hi, how you
doin',' dey say, 'Go to hell,' you know. Scairt dey lose dey women. Dey
lose 'em, too. I was a grown man when I was fifteen, didn't have to
work, carried money to de bank. Didn't have no worriess. Didn't hit a
lick at a snake. I seen it all. You don't know how dese guys is, fella. Two
of my best friends was kilt dead for playin' music. Poisoned one and kilt
de yuther. You try it. Drop a button on you, boy, 'fore you can be sure.
You ought to be a doctor. You a seventh son?

ROBERT: No – I was the tenth child – I was my mama's bad luck child.
My mother and father parted over me. My father had cut a dago and
been hid out two years when I came along –

CYCLONE: It wahn't yo' mama fault, boy. It's like de cow – it's de
nature of de beast to be brindle. Next time you see a woman walkin'
barefoot, you watch her. She don't walk like you and me. We picks our
foots *up* – She go *slidin'* along, heels go *shpp shpp shpp*, you know what
she doin'?

ROBERT: Ah, no sah.

CYCLONE: Whisperin', man, her heels is whisperin', carryin' on dat
conversation wid de Devil. Women is de weak vessel. It wahn't yo'
mama's fault.

ROBERT: No, it wahn't her fault. My stepfather – ah, father – good to
her. I just wahn't spoze to come along. I never could fit in – too little to
work hard and too low-down to preach – and that's all my daddy and
mama knows. I ain't no good and I can't be good. They say me playin'
blues caused my wife and son to die when he was borned.

CYCLONE: What is yo' age, Robert?

ROBERT: Nineteen.

CYCLONE: *Can* you play?

ROBERT: Not a whole lot.

CYCLONE: Play me something.

Robert tunes his guitar in the conventional manner and plays 'No Place Like Home'. It sounds as much like Jimmie Rodgers as Charlie Patton, but it is sung in a fervent (but underplayed) manner that makes it moving.

CYCLONE: Robert Johnson. Po' Bob. Who you been hearin'?

ROBERT: You know Son House?

CYCLONE: *Sho.* I know all them old thugs. Me and Charlie Patton was in the same jail cell in Belzoni. Tommy Johnson –

ROBERT (realizing as he speaks the significance of his words): Tommy Johnson sold his soul to the Devil. At a crossroads. In the full moon. (He is now standing.)

CYCLONE: Yeah, I heard dat. (Chuckles deeply. Robert looks at him in terror.)

ROBERT: *Where did you come from?*

CYCLONE: Just come from Cogdell, Missippi. Doc Whitlow and I had our stay cut short. Some folks dere was tryin' to get us to stay a while longer when I got – when I left. I hadn't been in South Missippi in years, but dey never did have much sense of good humor.

ROBERT: I know who you is.

CYCLONE: I been called by many names.

ROBERT: Teach me the blues.

CYCLONE: Sit down, boy. (Robert sits.) Fust and fo'most, you already know de blues. Everybody do, even white people, 'cos everybody had some hard times. Black or white, rich or poor, man or woman. Hard times been all over. De blues ain't no sin. People blame de blues. De blues is a lot like church. When a preacher's up dere preachin' de Bible, he's honest to God tryin' to tell de truth, and so is a blues singer. Bein' a blues singer is a whole lot like bein' a preacher. I have preached, and I ain't too good to do it again. Tell de truth, I have been close to God.

ROBERT: You was throwed out of Heaven.

CYCLONE: I was certainly thrown out of Cogdell.

ROBERT: Teach me the blues.

CYCLONE: Got any money?

ROBERT: Not a cent.

CYCLONE How you goin' on de ferry?

ROBERT: I don't know. Sometime a person will do something for a song.

CYCLONE: Come on, boy, de last fair deal's goin' down.

ROBERT: You can have my soul.

CYCLONE: Yo' what? What I want wid dat?

ROBERT: I know you done got most of 'em. Teach me, I been lookin' for you all my life.

CYCLONE (humoring Robert): If so be I mus', w'y den I shill. (Cyclone stands.) Stand up, Robert.

Robert stands and follows Cyclone's directions.

CYCLONE: Walk to de center of de crossroads. (Cyclone goes along, keeping his distance.) Close yo' eyes. Turn around three times to de lef'. Now three times to de right. Keep yo' eyes shot. Now step out of yo' shoes.

ROBERT: My shoes?

CYCLONE: Hush yo' mouf, boy. Dis de mos' impo'tant part. Step backwards out yo' shoes. Now open yo' eyes.

Cyclone is standing in front of Robert, holding a red flannel bag. Muttering to himself, he circles Robert, sprinkling dust from the bag.

CYCLONE: Dis is graveyard dirt, taken in de moon-dark by a cross-eyed, red-head, bluegum nigger from de grave of Jesse James. Dis bring confusion to yo' enemies. Now raise up yo' lef' hand. (Pours dust into Robert's hand). Now wid yo' right hand sprinkle it into yo' shoes. Leave de shoes right in yo' tracks, or yo' enemies can trail you. Now close yo' eyes. Shemanyeye, shemanyeye, shemanyeye. Step backwards. No, wait a minute. I almost forgot. Drink dis here. (Hands Robert Dr. Whitlow's tonic bottle).

ROBERT: Tommy Johnson didn't say nothing about drinkin' nothin'.

CYCLONE: Who doin' dis, me or you?

ROBERT: You is.

CYCLONE: Drink it down. (Robert drinks.) All of it. Hand me the bottle. All right. Now. Step backward out de circle. Come on back over and sit down.

They sit in the shed.

CYCLONE: Take yo' guitar. Play dat same piece you was playin'.

Robert starts to play 'No Place Like Home'. Cyclone takes out his guitar and starts to play very strongly in another key.

CYCLONE: You need to change that tuning, son. This song spoze to be in Spanish, and I b'lieve you in Mexican.

Cyclone takes Robert's guitar and changes the tuning.

CYCLONE: Now before long, boy, you goin' to sleep. And when you wake up this will all be like a dream. You will be able to learn anything you want to play on the guitar, and yo' shoes will be waiting for you in Hell.

Together they play 'No Place Like Home'. Robert falls asleep. Cyclone, picking up his guitar-case, walks to the center of the crossroads and puts on the shoes. Passing the shed he drops a nickel into Robert's guitar.

CYCLONE: So long, Po' Bob. Here's a nickel for de ferry. Me and yo' shoes will see you in Hell.

2

BEALE STREET'S GONE DRY

My own enlightenment came in Cleveland, Mississippi. I was leading the orchestra in a dance program when someone sent up an odd request. . . Would we object if a local colored band played a few dances?

. . . We eased out gracefully as the newcomers entered. They were led by a long-legged chocolate boy and their band consisted of just three pieces, a battered guitar, a mandolin and a worn-out bass.

The music they made was pretty well in keeping with their looks. . . The strumming attained a disturbing monotony, but on and on it went, a kind of stuff that has long been associated with cane rows and levee camps. Thump-thump-thump went their feet on the floor. Their eyes rolled. Their shoulders swayed. And through it all that little agonizing strain persisted. It was not really annoying or unpleasant. Perhaps 'haunting' is a better word, but I commenced to wonder if anybody besides small town rounders and their running mates would go for it.

The answer was not long in coming. A rain of silver dollars began to fall around the outlandish, stomping feet. The dancers went wild. Dollars, quarters, halves – the shower grew heavier and continued so long I strained my neck to get a better look. There before the boys lay more money than my nine musicians were being paid for the entire engagement. Then I saw the beauty of primitive music.

W.C. Handy,
Father of the Blues

Cotton-makers' Jubilee, Beale Street, Memphis, 1957 (© Ernest C. Withers)

At the first Rock and Roll Hall of Fame Banquet, in January 1986, some months after Cleveland had been chosen as the site for the Rock and Roll Museum, Sam Phillips, whose Sun Records had made known to the world the music of Elvis Presley, Jerry Lee Lewis, Charlie Rich, Johnny Cash and Roy Orbison – among many others – introduced Carl Perkins with the words, 'It's a late date to be saying it, and I mean no disrespect to the people of Cleveland, who I'm sure are a fine people and spirachul *people – but Cleveland ain't ever gonna be Memphis.'*

He was booed by an audience too young and ignorant to know or care what Memphis, the Mississippi Delta, the South, have meant to music.

Before the first ten years of the twentieth century were over, W.C. Handy had started writing and publishing songs based on the blues he heard on Memphis's Beale Street. In the '20s and '30s, the original blues performers themselves, men like Will Shade, Gus Cannon, Robert Wilkins, Furry Lewis and Robert Johnson, set the tone: 'Cocaine habit is mighty bad, it's the worst old habit that I ever had.' The '40s found Memphians Jimmy Lunceford, Buster Bailey, and the elder Phineas Newborn, the latter two side-men with Duke Ellington and Lionel Hampton, carrying the tradition forward with swing and boogie-woogie. It has been suggested that Carl Perkins's 'Blue Suede Shoes' – the first record to reach the top of the pop, rhythm and blues, and country charts – represents one of the most important steps in the evolution of American consciousness since the Emancipation Proclamation. Perhaps it was an even more important step, because the Proclamation was an edict handed down from above, and the success of 'Blue Suede Shoes' among Afro-Americans represented an actual grassroots acknowledgment of a common heritage, a mutual overcoming of poverty and lack of style, an act of forgiveness, of redemption.

At a distance of thirty-five years, a generation, it can be seen as the prelude to a tragedy, the murder of Martin Luther King, one of the '60s assassinations from which the country still has not recovered.

In 1959, having graduated from Sidney Lanier High School for (white) Boys in Macon, Georgia, I moved with my family to Memphis. I knew little about the place other than that it was on the Mississippi river and had an association with the kind of music I liked. I soon learned that Memphis was, if anything, even more 'Southern' and puritanical than Macon, with no liquor served by the drink and almost no integration. Restaurants, taxis, hotels, parks, libraries, movies, all were segregated. Blacks still sat in the back of the buses. Whites who wanted to hear black music went to an all-white club called the Plantation Inn across the river in West Memphis, Arkansas, and listened to a singing group called the Del Rios or to Loman Pauling and the Five Royales. My first experience on Beale Street was being thrown out of a Ray Charles concert at the Hippodrome for sharing a table with some black classmates from newly integrated Memphis State University. There were tables for blacks and tables for whites, but no mixing allowed. 'What you mean, pattin' these nigger girls on the ass?' a cop asked me. 'I haven't patted anybody on the ass yet, sweetheart,' I said, finding myself seconds later face to face with the gravel in the alley. Living in Memphis, off and on, for twenty-five years, learning the blues, I would come to know those alleys, that downtown gravel, well.

An essay I wrote in the mid-1970s for Beale Street Saturday Night, *a documentary album by James Luther Dickinson, provides a snapshot, now fading, of Memphis as it was then. Beale Street these days is not exactly thriving, but you can go there on certain nights and hear great music from the likes of Herman Green and Calvin Newborn. The following, though, is how it used to be.*

Once a friend came to dinner at my house in Memphis, Tennessee, bringing two girls on holiday from London, new friends he had met on his way across town. Some people, I hear, have rules about mealtimes, banning serious conversation and the throwing of food, but at my house the only rule is that there are no rules. So while we were eating and getting drunk I asked my friend's English friends if they were enjoying Memphis. The girls, who were paying for their holiday by working as waitresses in a bad Memphis-Italian restaurant, were enjoying Memphis hardly at all, and what they enjoyed least was their customers telling them how good life is down among the magnolias on the Mississippi.

It took some time to describe the disgusting ignorance of people who don't know how bad their lives are. By the time the girls had finished answering the question, I had finished dinner and was about three-fourths done getting drunk. Maybe more than three-fourths. I told them that in this century, Memphis, Tennessee, has changed the lives of more people than any other city in the world. I used, I regret to report, the phrase 'cultural influence'. The girls, one of whom kept falling asleep from some pills some of the benighted people of Memphis had given her, wanted to know whether I preferred Memphis to Paris, London, Rome, and then left to wait tables. I never had a chance to tell them that, like it or not, they had shopped at supermarkets, eaten at drive-in restaurants, slept in Holiday Inns, and heard the blues because people in Memphis had found ways to convert these things into groceries.

I know now, because I am more sober, that none of us can say what city has in our time most affected people's lives. Los Alamos, New Mexico, and Los Angeles, California, both have been influential, and so have St. Louis, Missouri, and Peking, China. But after the yellow fever plagues that all but destroyed Memphis at the end of the last century, people there created from the shell of an antebellum southern town a new city with new traditions.

The ninth-century tradition among the Indians, the first inhabitants we know about in the place that would one day be called Memphis, was to live in small villages and hunt with spears and clubs in forests of giant chestnut, elms, many kinds of hickory and oak, for buffalo, deer, plentiful game, birds and fish. The sixteenth-century tradition among the Spanish in the same place was to feed the Indians alive to dogs. There were too many Indians then for that tradition to last, but in the end there were too many white men, Spanish, French, English and American, killing as they came. The Chickasaws sold the land in 1818 to the United States government for 5 cents an acre. The next year, Generals Andrew Jackson and James Winchester and Judge John Overton, land speculators from Nashville who were already the *de facto* owners of most of the land before the government bought it, laid out plans for the city of Memphis. Jackson had granted squatters' right on his land to many of his old troops, and he sold out before the old soldiers learned that their land was to be incorporated and Jackson's gift to them would be taxed. Jackson went on to be President and to send the Indians to Oklahoma.

In the next twenty-five years, Memphis grew from a flatboat town, a collection of waterfront shacks, to a steamboat town with strange grand houses built away from the river beside huge magnolia trees. On Front Street, a mule could still step in mud up to his shoulders.

During the Civil War, after the heroic, twenty-minute Battle of Memphis, the Union Army was headquartered on Beale Street, where local blacks, most of them freed slaves who feared the local whites,

Phineas Newborn, Snr. on drums (date and photographer unknown)

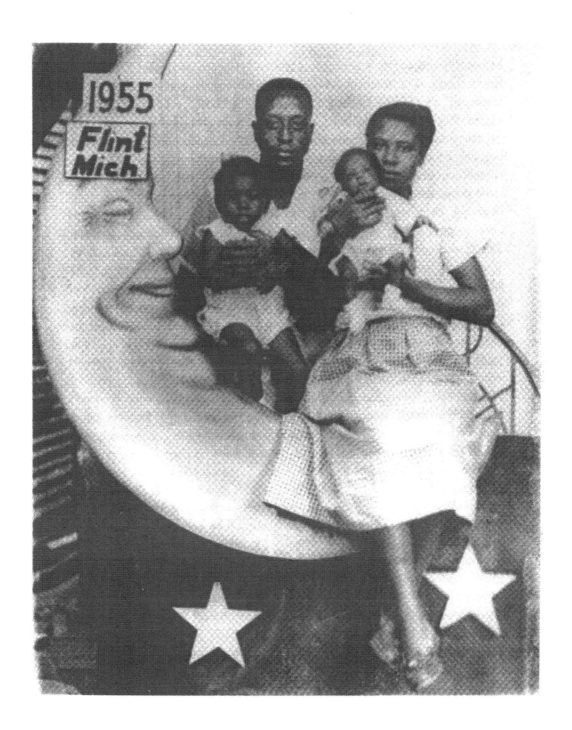

Dr. Ross, Sun Records publicity photograph, Memphis, 1955

began to gather. The war did not destroy Memphis, as it did other cities, like Atlanta. The fine old houses were untouched, but the city became stagnant. The rich felt little in common with poor whites, less with blacks. No sewers were built; why should the rich buy indoor plumbing for the poor? So there came the yellow fever, again and again, like the plagues of white men on the Indians, until the land was once more worthless enough to arouse greed.

In 1878, when yellow fever struck Memphis for the third time, most of its 55,000 people left. About 6,000 whites and 14,000 blacks stayed; only 30 per cent of the whites, but 90 per cent of the blacks, survived. There was considerable weight of opinion, especially amongst the writers of newspaper editorials in river towns to the north, that Memphis should be burned as a breeder of pestilence. Memphis did surrender its city charter, recovering it in 1893, after building sewage disposal and running water systems.

Memphis was a town again, but just the shell of one, a blank page on which Clarence Saunders wrote *Piggly Wiggly*. Like Thomas Edison, who after the war developed a means of transmitting electric current to kill the roaches in the Main Street rooming-houses where he lived, Saunders with the supermarket was a man with a plan. Fortune's Jungle Garden, a restaurant too small to hold the crowds after the opera, took food out to customers who would eat and drink in their carriages under the trees late at night. When Ed Crump came to Memphis from Holly Springs, he was just one more speculator, another man with a plan. W.C. Handy and a number of other people around this time began writing down and publishing blues songs. These men and their plans prospered. Crump became Mayor of Memphis in 1909, and the melody lingers on. Through the 1920s Crump controlled West Tennessee, had great power in the state legislature and disproportionate influence in the United States Congress. When asked for whom they would vote, Memphians said, 'I'm not sure – Mr. Crump hasn't made up my mind.' The depression of the 1930s helped few people anywhere, but it was Franklin Roosevelt's hostility to city bosses, along with the efforts of brave locals like Lucius Burch and Edward Meeman, that made certain Mr. Crump's decline. By then Crump was past his prime, and no politics was local.

Beale Street was also past its prime, but it wasn't local, either. There was enough left in 1956 that Count Basie, playing in town, could hear Phineas Newborn, Jr., at the Hippodrome. The street had lost its bloom, but there were still a lot of stores, most of them pawn shops. In the years since, 'urban renewal' has erased the black parts of the surrounding neighborhood. The path of Martin Luther King from the Clayborn Temple African Methodist Episcopal Church to Beale Street has been scraped clean, bound by curbs, and planted with grass.

What happened to King in Memphis was murder, but what is the word for the fate of Eli Persons? In 1917 Persons was charged in Memphis, on what evidence no one knows, with the rape and beheading of a sixteen-year-old white girl. Law officers gave him to a crowd of more than a thousand whites, who decided not to lynch Persons, since hanging was too good for him and not enough to satisfy the girl's mother. They built a bonfire with Persons tied to the central log, burned him to a crisp, cut out his heart and rolled his head down Beale Street.

Memphis is called The Bluff City because it is on the highest spot on the Mississippi river between the Ohio river and Natchez, but the bluff is near its lowest point at the foot of Beale Street. The *Kate Adams*, the *Viney Swing*, the other great steamboats, are gone, but the river is still wet, a witness, never silent, which never accuses but sometimes condemns. Beale Street begins at the river, struggles up the bluff, across the I. C. tracks and Front Street, past empty sockets and dry rot of urban blight. The quiet voices of men down the street trading for cotton do not reach our ears, and even the ghosts of the girls of the original Gayoso Hotel seem to be asleep.

The grand old Orpheum Theatre, with its resident phantom, stands at Beale and Main, just beyond the killer Mall. Across Main Street both sides of Beale have been bulldozed, a new bank and a new public utilities building have been constructed, and all traces of the past have been destroyed up to Lansky's Men's Wear, the place where Carl Perkins and Elvis Presley learned how to dress cool. In Lansky's window are striped shoes and a lemon-yellow suit with scalloped lapels.

Crossing Second Street, coming to pawn shops where mesh screens protect empty, boarded-up display windows, you notice that no one else is on the street. Passing the place that used to be a Chinese opium den, you see no one. A. Schwab's department store, Art Hutkin's hardware store, the Engelbergs' pawn shop, are about all that survive of human commerce to Third Street, the beginning of the blocks that made Beale Street 'the greatest place on earth', Thomas Pinkston said, 'until they ruint it.'

In the early decades of this century, before Beale Street was ruint, Memphis was the murder capital of the country, and Beale Streeters did more than their part to secure the title. One night in 1909 a saloon-keeper named Wild Bill Latura walked into Hammitt Ashford's black saloon, announced that he was going to turn the place into a funeral parlor, and with six bullets shot seven patrons of the establishment, killing five. Beale Street was dangerous, but there were no Beale belles and no cocaine down on the old plantation. That same year Sam Zerilla opened the Pastime Theatre, soon followed by the Palace Theatre, built by Antonio Barrasso and the Pacini brothers. On Thursday nights the Palace presented special shows for whites.

Now not only is the Palace gone but also the Monarch, Hammitt Ashford's, P. Wee's, and all the whorehouses of Gayoso Street. At Myrtle Street, near the end of Beale, you can throw a half-empty beer bottle through the window of 706 Union Avenue, where Sam Phillips made the first recordings of Elvis Presley, Jerry Lee Lewis, Johnny Cash, Charlie Rich, and Howling Wolf, and chances are no one will even see you. It is a short walk across Nathan Bedford Forrest Park to the University of Tennessee medical school, where many people from Beale Street have been dismantled by students to be buried in three-foot boxes. They don't get many Beale Street cadavers now, because most people from Beale Street are dead or gone, or both. The hotel and office buildings of downtown Memphis that once looked down on Beale Street do not see even the little that is left, because all the old downtown hotels and many other buildings are empty. Through the wisdom of its civic leaders, Memphis is once again nearing the point of being worthless enough to attract money. When that happens, watch out. As Sleepy John Estes said, Memphis has always been the leader of dirty work in the world.

3

FURRY'S BLUES

In one of those downtown Memphis alleys, or just off it, I found Furry Lewis, and we adopted each other. 'Me and him just like brothers,' Furry would say, pointing at me, and it was true, though he never allowed me to forget which brother was the older and wiser.

In the fall of 1963, I had gone to New Orleans to do graduate work in art history at Sophie Newcombe College, part of Tulane University. I attended school for about six weeks and stayed in New Orleans nearly a year. When I came back to Memphis, I went to work for the Tennessee Department of Public Welfare, leaving it in 1966 to write a novel about poor people that ended with mass demonstrations and tanks on Main Street. A day or two after I finished (I'd written a chapter a day for eighteen days) I ran into Charlie Brown and asked him to take me to see Furry Lewis. We stopped by Charlie's flat, he picked up a .38, and we went to Fourth and Beale.

When we came into the alley, the children stopped playing. They stood poised, watching us. There were two-storey brick buildings on both sides, with wooden stairways that shut out all but a thin blue strip of sky. Filthy rags and broken bottles lay on the concrete pavement. There were women sitting on the doorsteps, some of them together, talking, but most of them alone, sitting still, ignoring the heat and the buzzing flies.

'How are you?' Charlie Brown spoke to one of them.

'I ain't doin' no good,' she said.

She did not look up. The children's gaze followed us as we walked on. The women talking would stop as we came near and then, as we went past, would start again.

Close by, a fat woman was holding a small brown-and-white dog to her bosom.

'What you got there?' Charlie asked her.

'Little spitz,' she said. 'Look how dirty he is. He pretty when he clean.'

'Nice dog,' he said. 'Is Furry home?'

'De up deah. De ain't been long gone up.'

We climbed the back stairs of the building on our left and went down a bare, dusty hall to a door with a metal number 3 over the cloth-patched screen. Charlie started to knock, and then we heard the music and he waited. 'Got a new way of spellin',' a quiet musing voice sang. 'Memphis, Tennessee.' A run of guitar chords followed, sceptical, brief: 'Double M, double E, great God, A Y Z.' Then two closing chords, like a low shout of laughter, and Charlie knocked.

The door swung open. There, sitting next to a double-bed, holding a guitar, was Furry Lewis.

During the heyday of Beale Street, when the great Negro blues artists played and sang in the crowded, evil blocks between Fourth and Main, Furry, a protégé of W.C. Handy, was one of the most highly respected musicians. He was also one of the most popular, not only in the saloons and gambling dives of Memphis but in the medicine shows and on the riverboats all along the Mississippi. In Chicago, at the old Vocalion studios on Wabash Avenue, he made the first of many recordings he was to do, both for Vocalion and for RCA Victor's Bluebird label. But Beale Street's great era, and the young Furry Lewis's recording career, ended at the close of the 1920s; Furry would not record again until 1959. Nor, since the Depression, has he performed regularly, even in his home town. He makes his living as a street-sweeper. When he does play, it is usually at the Bitter Lemon, a coffee house that caters mainly to the affluent East Memphis teenage set, but whose manager, Charlie Brown, is a blues enthusiast and occasionally hires Furry between rock and roll groups.

Charlie, a tall, blond young man, bent to shake hands with Furry.

Furry did not stand. One leg of his green pajamas hung limp, empty below the knee.

The boy wearing gold-rimmed spectacles who had got up from a chair to let us in said, 'I'm Jerry Finberg. Furry's been giving me a little guitar lesson.' We shook his hand, then Charlie introduced me to Furry and we all sat down. The room held a sizable amount of old, worn furniture: the bed, a studio couch, three stuffed chairs, a chifforobe and a dresser. Beside the bed, there was a table made from a small wooden crate.

'It's good to see you, Furry,' Charlie said.

'You too,' said Furry. 'You hadn't been here in so long. I thought you had just about throwed me down.'

Charlie said that he could never do that and asked Furry if he could come out to the coffee house for a couple of nights in the coming week. Furry picked up a pair of glasses from the bedside table, put them on, then took them off again. He would like to, he said, but his guitar was at Nathan's. 'This here belongs to this boy, Jerry.' He put the glasses back on the table. It held aspirin, Sal Hepatica, cigarette papers and a Mason jar full of tobacco. Charlie said not to worry, he'd get the guitar.

'Will you, sure 'nough?' Furry asked, looking at Charlie with serious, businesslike, gray eyes.

'I'll get it tomorrow. What's the ticket on it?'

'Sixteen dollars.'

'I'll get it tomorrow.'

'All right,' Furry said, 'and I'll come play for you.' He reached out and shook hands solemnly with Charlie.

'Could you play something now, or don't you feel like it?' Charlie asked.

Furry smiled. 'I may be weak, but I'm willing,' he said. He took a small metal cylinder from his pajama pocket and picked up the guitar. 'I believe I'll take you to Brownsville.' He slipped the cylinder over the little finger of his left hand and started to play, his short leg crossed over the longer one, his bare narrow foot softly patting the plain brown boards as he sang. 'Well, I'm goin' to Brownsville, I'm goin' take that right-hand road'; the cylinder slid, whining, over the treble strings.

'I was in Brownsville, Tennessee,' Furry said, 'working on a doctor show, and I met a little girl I liked; but her parents wouldn't let me come around to see her, 'cause I was showfolks, and they was respectable. So I wrote this: 'And the woman I love's got great long curly hair.' The guitar repeated the line, added a delicate, punctuating bass figure, and then, as if it were another voice, sang the next line with Furry, staying just behind or slightly ahead of the beat: 'But her mother and father do not allow me there.'

As he played, I looked around the room. The brown-spotted wallpaper was covered with decorations: over the bed were a few sprigs of artificial holly, an American flag, hanging with the stripes vertical and the stars at the bottom left, three brightly colored picture postcards and an ink sketch of Furry. On the wall behind the couch, there was a child's crayon drawing in which Jesus, dressed in handsome red and blue robes, held out his arms to an enormous white rabbit.

Furry's right hand swooped and glided over the guitar, striking notes and chords in what looked, but did not sound, like complete random. At times, he slapped the guitar-box with two fingers or the heel of his hand as, in the same motion, he brushed the strings. 'Call that spank the baby,' he said. The guitar was both an echo of his voice and a source of complex and subtle accents. He sang, 'Don't you wish your woman was long and tall like mine?' then repeated the line, leaving out, or letting the guitar speak, half the words. 'Well, she ain't good-lookin', but I 'clare, she takes her time.' The bass figure followed, then one amused, final chord. Furry laid the guitar down.

'You play beautiful guitar,' Charlie said.

'Yes, it is,' Furry said, holding up the instrument. 'Believe I'll be buried in this one.'

'Was that Spanish tuning?' asked Jerry, who had been leaning forward, elbows on his knees, listening intently.

'They some beer in the icebox,' Furry said.

Jerry sighed and stood up. 'Come on,' he said to me. 'Help bring the glasses.' We went into the kitchen. It was almost as large as the front room, with a stove, a refrigerator, a good-sized table and, in one corner, another double bed. A cabinet held gallon jars of flour, sugar, lima beans and an assortment of canned goods: Pride of Illinois white sweet corn, School Days June peas, Showboat pork and beans, Lyke's beef tripe, Pride of Virginia herring, Bush's Best black-eyed peas and turnip greens.

Jerry took a quart of Pfeiffer's beer out of the refrigerator. I found four glasses on a newspaper-lined shelf, rinsed them in the square metal sink ('They clean,' Furry called, 'but no tellin' what's been runnin' over 'em') and we went back into the other room. We had just finished pouring when there was a knock at the door.

'That's my wife,' Furry said, sliding the latch open. 'Come in, Versie.'

She came in, a compact, handsome woman. I introduced myself and the others said Hello. Versie, in a pleasantly hoarse voice, told us that only that morning, she had been asking Furry what he had done to make his boyfriends stay away so long.

'They all throwed me down,' Furry said, then laughed and told Versie he was going out to play at the Bitter Lemon. She smiled and asked if she could get us anything to eat. We all said No, thank you, and she sat down.

'My wife loves to see after folks,' Furry said. 'Do anything in the world for people. Feed 'em, give 'em something to drink; if they get too drunk to go home, got a bed in there to put you to sleep on. And I'm the same way. But you know, there's one old boy, I see him every day at work, and every time I see him, he bum a cigarette from me. Now, it ain't much, but it come so *regular*. So the other day, I told him, "Boy, ain't but one difference 'tween you and a blind man." And he said, "What's that?" And I told him, "Blind man beg from everybody he hear, you beg from everybody you see." '

'Well,' Versie said, from her chair on the other side of the room, 'it's a pleasure to do things for people who are so nice to us. We tried and tried to find out Furry's age, so he could get this Medicare, and Jerry went out to Furry's old school and made them look through the records and find out when he was born. He spent several days, just to help us.'

'Found out I was born 1893,' Furry said. 'March the 6th, in Greenwood, Mississippi. But I moved to Memphis, with my mother and two sisters, when I was six. My mother and father were sharecroppers and they separated before I was born. I never saw my father, never even knew what he looked like.' He took a drink of beer.

'Where did you live when you came here?' I asked.

'My mother had a sister lived on Brinkley Avenue,' he said. 'Call it Decatur now. We stayed with her. They a housing project there now, but I could still show you the spot.' He took another drink, looked at the glass, then emptied it. 'I was raised right there and walked a few blocks to the Carnes Avenue School. Went to the fifth, and that's as far as I got. Started going about, place to place, catching the freights. That's how I lost my leg. Goin' down a grade outside Du Quoin, Illinois, I caught my foot in a coupling. They took me to a hospital in Carbondale. I could look right out my window and see the ice-cream factory.'

He took a cigarette from a pack of Pall Malls on the bedside table. 'That was 1916,' he said. 'I had two or three hundred dollars in my pocket when that happened, too; I had just caught a freight 'cause I didn't feel like spending the money for a ticket.' He struck a match, but the breeze from the window-fan blew it out. Charlie took the cigarette, lit it and handed it back. 'Love you,' Furry said. 'Goin' put you in the Bible.'

He stuck the cigarette in the corner of his mouth, picked up the guitar and played a succession of slow, blues-drenched chords that seemed to fill the room. 'I'm doing all right,' he said. 'What you want to hear?'

'Do you remember "Stagolee?" ' I asked.

'What song?'

'One you recorded a long time ago, called "Stagolee".'

'Long time ago – I wasn't born then, was I?' He quickly changed tunings and started to sing the song. He did one chorus, but it went off after the second, which began, 'When you lose your money, learn to lose. . . '

'What was that last?' Charlie asked.

Furry repeated the line. 'That means, don't be no *hard* loser. That's what this song is about.' He began again, but after a few bars, he lost the tune. He was tired.

Charlie stood up. 'We've got to go, Furry.'

'No,' Furry said. 'You just got here.'

'Got to go to work. I'll pick you up Tuesday night.'

'I'm so glad you came by,' Versie told Charlie, in the hall. 'Sometimes Furry thinks everybody has forgotten him.'

It had rained while we were inside, and the air in the alley smelled almost fresh. The women were gone now and only a few of the children were still out. It was nearly dark. We walked back to the car and drove down Beale Street, past the faded blocks of pawn shops, liquor stores and poolrooms. The lights were coming on for the evening.

After the Civil War, many former slaves came in from the country, trying to find their families. There were only about 4,000 Negroes in Memphis in 1860, but by 1870 there were 15,000. Beale Street drew them, it has been said, 'like a lodestone'.

The music the country Negroes brought, with its thumping rhythms, unorthodox harmonies and earthy lyrics, combined with the city musicians' more polished techniques and regular forms to produce, as all the world knows, the Beale Street blues. Furry cannot remember when he first heard the blues, nor is he certain when he started trying to play them.

'I was eight or nine, I believe,' he said, 'when I got the idea I wanted to have me a guitar.' We were at the Bitter Lemon now, Furry, Versie, Charlie and I, waiting for the crowd to arrive. The waitresses, pretty girls with long straight hair, were lighting candles on the small round tables. We sat in the shadows, drinking bourbon brought from the liquor store on the corner, listening to Furry talk about the old days.

He was coatless, wearing a white shirt with a dark blue tie, and he was smoking a wood-tipped cigar. 'I taken a cigar box, cut a hole in the top and nailed a piece of two-by-four on there for a neck. Then I got some screen wire for the strings and I tacked them to the box and twisted them around some bent nails on the end of the two-by-four. I could turn the nails and tune the strings like that, you see. I fooled around with it, got so I could make notes, but just on the one string. Couldn't make no chords. The first real guitar I had, Mr. Cham Fields – who owned a roadhouse, gambling house – and W.C. Handy gave it to me. They brought it out to my mother's and I was so proud to get it, I cried for a week. Them days, children wasn't like they are now.' His cigar had gone out; he relit it from the candle on our table, puffing great gray clouds of smoke. 'It was a Martin and I kept it twenty years.'

'What happened to it?' Charlie asked.

'It died.'

Furry put the candle down and leaned back in his chair. 'When I was eighteen, nineteen years old,' he said, 'I was good. And when I was twenty, I had my own band, and we could all play. Had a boy named Ham, played jug. Willie Polk played the fiddle and another boy, call him Shoefus, played the guitar, like I did. All of us North Memphis boys. We'd meet at my house and walk down Brinkley to Poplar and go up Poplar to Dunlap or maybe all the way down to Main. People would stop us on the street and say, "Do you know so-and-so?" And we'd play it and they'd give us a little something. Sometimes we'd pick up fifteen or twenty dollars before we got to Beale. Wouldn't take no streetcar. Long as you walked, you's making money; but if you took the streetcar, you didn't make nothing and you'd be out the nickel for the ride.'

'That was Furry's wild days,' Versie said. 'Drinking, staying out all night. He'd still do that way, if I let him.'

Furry smiled. 'We used to leave maybe noon Saturday and not get back home till Monday night. All the places we played – Pee Wee's, Big Grundy's, Cham Field's, B. B. Anderson's – when they opened up, they took the keys and tied them to a rabbit's neck, told him to run off to the woods, 'cause they never meant to close.'

I asked Furry whether he had done much traveling.

'A right smart,' he said. 'But that was later on, when I was working with Gus Cannon, the banjo player, and Will Shade. Beale Street was commencing to change then. Had to go looking for work.' He rolled his cigar ash off against the side of an ashtray. 'In the good times, though, you could find anything you could name on Beale. Gambling, girls; you could buy a pint of moonshine for a dime, store-bought whiskey for a quarter. We'd go from place to place, making music, and everywhere we'd go, they'd be glad to see us. We'd play awhile and then somebody would pass the hat. We didn't make too much, but we didn't need much back then. In them days, you could get two loaves of bread for a nickel. And some nights, when the people from down on the river came up, we'd make a batch of money. The roustabouts from the steamboats, and Kate Adams, the Idlewild, the Viney Swing – I've taken trips on all them boats, played up the river to St. Louis, down to New Orleans – white and colored, they'd all come to Beale. Got along fine, too, just like we doing now. 'Course, folks had they squabbles, like they will, you know. I saw two or three get killed.'

There were enough squabbles to make Memphis the murder capital of the country. In the first decade of the century, 556 homicides occurred, most of them involving Negroes. Appeals for reform were taken seriously only by those who made them. When E. H. Crump ran for mayor on a reform ticket, W. C. Handy recorded the Beale Streeters' reaction: 'We don't care what Mr. Crump don't allow, we goin' barrelhouse anyhow.'

But as the self-righteous Crump machine gained power, the street slowly began to change. Each year the red-light district grew smaller; each year, there were fewer gambling houses, fewer saloons, fewer places for musicians to play.

Then came the Depression. Local newspapers carried accounts of starving Negroes swarming over garbage dumps, even eating the clay from the river bluffs. Many people left town, but Furry stayed. 'Nothing else to do,' he said. 'The Depression wasn't just in Memphis, it was all over the country. A lot of my friends left, didn't know what they was goin' to. The boy we called Ham, from our band, he left, and nobody ever knew what became of him. I did have a little job with the city and I stuck with that. I had been working with them off and on, when there wasn't anyplace to play. They didn't even have no trucks at that time. Just had mules to pull the garbage carts. Didn't have no incinerator; used to take the garbage down to the end of High Street, across the railroad tracks, and burn it.'

Before Beale Street could recover from the Depression, World War Two brought hundreds of boys in uniform to Memphis; and, for their protection, Boss Crump closed the last of the saloons and whorehouses. It was the final blow.

Furry sat staring at the end of his cigar. 'Beale Street really went down,' he said after a moment. 'You know, old folks say, it's a long lane don't have no end and a bad wind don't never change. But one day, back when Hoover was president, I was driving my cart down Beale Street and I seen a rat, sitting on top of a garbage can, eating a onion, crying.'

Furry has been working for the City of Memphis Sanitation Department, since 1923. Shortly after two o'clock each weekday morning, he gets out of bed, straps on his artificial leg, dresses and makes a fresh pot of coffee, which he drinks while reading the Memphis *Press-Scimitar*. The newspaper arrives in the afternoon, but Furry does not open it until morning. Versie is still asleep, and the paper is company for him as he sits in the kitchen under the harsh light of the ceiling bulb, drinking the hot, sweet coffee. He does not eat breakfast; when the coffee is gone, he leaves for work.

The sky is black. The alley is quiet, the apartments dark. A morning-glory vine hanging from a guy-wire stirs like a heavy curtain in the cool morning breeze. Cars in the cross alley are covered with a silver glaze of dew. A cat flashes between shadows.

Linden Avenue is bright and empty in the blue glare of the street lamps. Down the street, St. Patrick's looms, a sign, 100 YEARS WITH CHRIST, over its wide red doors. Furry, turning right, walks past the faded, green-glowing bay windows of an apartment house to the corner. A moving-van rolls past. There is no other traffic. When the light changes, Furry crosses, heading down Hernando. The clock at Carodine's Fruit Stand and Auto Service reads, as it always does, 2:49.

The cafés, taverns, laundries, shoe-repair shops and liquor stores are all closed. The houses, under shading trees, seem drawn into themselves. At the Clayborn Temple A.M.E. Church, the stained-glass windows gleam, jewel-like against the mass of blackened stone. A woman wearing a maid's uniform passes on the other side of the street. Furry says good morning and she says good morning, their voices patiently weary. Beside the Scola Brothers' Grocery is a sycamore, its branches silhouetted against the white wall. Furry walks slowly, hunched forward, as if sleep were a weight on his shoulders. Hand-painted posters at the Vance Avenue Market: CHICKEN BACKS 12 1/2c LB.; HOG MAWS, 15c; RUMPS, 19c.

Behind Bertha's Beauty Nook, under a large, pale-leafed elm, there are twelve garbage cans and two carts. Furry lifts one of the cans on to a cart, rolls the cart out into the street and, taking the wide broom from its slot, begins to sweep the gutter. A large woman with her head tied in a kerchief, wearing a purple wrapper and gold house slippers, passes by on the sidewalk. Furry tells her good morning and she nods hello.

When he has swept back to Vance, Furry leaves the trash in a pile at the corner and pushes the cart, with its empty can, to Beale Street. The sky is gray. The stiff brass figure of W. C. Handy stands, one foot slightly forward, the bell of his horn pointing down, under the manicured trees of his deserted park. The gutter is thick with debris: empty wine bottles, torn racing forms from the West Memphis dog track, flattened cigarette packs, scraps of paper and one small die, white with black spots, which Furry puts into his pocket. An old bus, on the back of which is written, in yellow print, LET NOT YOUR HEART BE TROUBLE, rumbles past; it is full of cotton choppers: their dark, solemn faces peer out the grimy windows. The bottles clink at the end of Furry's broom. In a room above the Club Handy, two men are standing at an open window looking down at the street. One of them is smoking; the glowing end of his cigarette can be seen in the darkness. On the door to the club, there is a handbill: BLUES SPECTACULAR, CITY AUDITORIUM: JIMMY REED, JOHN LEE HOOKER, HOWLIN' WOLF.

Furry pushes the garbage onto a flat scoop at the front of the cart, then goes to the rear and pulls a jointed metal handle, causing the scoop to rise and dump its contents into the can. The scoop is heavy; when he lets it down, it sends a shock from his right arm through his body, raising his left leg, the artificial one, off the ground. Across the street, in a chinaberry tree, a gang of sparrows are making a racket. Furry sweeps past two night clubs and then a restaurant, where, through the front window, large brown rats can be seen scurrying across the kitchen floor. A dirty red dog stands at the corner of Beale and Hernando, sniffing the air. A black soldier in a khaki uniform runs past, heading toward Main. The street lamps go off.

When Furry has cleaned the rest of the block, the garbage can is full and he goes back to Bertha's for another. The other cart is gone and there is a black Buick parked at the curb. Furry wheels to the corner and picks up the mound of trash he left there. A city bus rolls past; the driver gives a greeting honk and Furry waves. He crosses the street and begins sweeping in front of the Sanitary Bedding Company. A woman's high-heeled shoe is lying in the sidewalk. Furry throws it into the can. 'First one-legged woman I see, I'll give her that,' he says and, for the first time that day, he smiles.

At Butler, the next cross street, there is a row of large, old-fashioned houses set behind picket fences and broad, thickly leafed trees. The sky is pale blue now, with pink-edged clouds, and old men and women have come out to sit on the porches. Some speak to Furry, some do not. Cars are becoming more frequent along the street. Furry reaches out quickly with his broom to catch a windblown scrap of paper. When he gets to Calhoun, he swaps cans again and walks a block – past Tina's Beauty Shop, a tavern called the Section Playhouse and another named Soul Heaven – to Fourth Street. He places his cart at the corner and starts pushing the trash toward it.

From a second-storey window of a rooming-house covered with red brick-patterned tarpaper comes the sound of a blues harmonica. Two old men are sitting on the steps in front of the open door. Furry tells them good morning. 'When you goin' make another record?' one of them asks. 'Record?' the other man, in a straw hat, says. 'That's right,' says the first one. 'He makes them big-time records. Used to.'

Furry dumps a load into the cart, then leans against it, wiping his face and the back of his neck with a blue bandanna handkerchief.

Down the stairs and through the door (the old men on the steps leaning out of his way, for he does not slow down) comes the harmonica player. He stands in the middle of the sidewalk, eyes closed, head tilted to one side, the harmonica cupped in his hands. A man wearing dark glasses and carrying a white cane before him like a divining rod turns the corner, aims at the music, says cheerfully, 'Get out the way! Get off the sidewalk!' and bumps into the harmonica player, who spins away, like a good quarterback, and goes on playing.

Furry puts the bandanna in his pocket and moves on, walking behind the cart. Past Mrs. Kelly's Homemade Hot Tamales stand, the air is filled with a strong odor. Over a shop door, a sign reads: FRESH FISH DAILY.

Now the sky is a hot, empty blue, and cars line the curb from Butler to Vance. Furry sweeps around them. Across the street, at the housing project, children are playing outside the great blocks of apartments. One little girl is lying face down on the grass, quite still. Furry watches her. She has not moved. Two dogs are barking nearby. One of them, a small black cocker spaniel, trots up to the little girl and sniffs at her head; she grabs its forelegs and together they roll over and over. Furry starts sweeping and does not stop or look up again until he has reached the corner. He piles the trash into the can and stands in the gutter, waiting for the light to change.

For the morning, his work is done. He rolls the cart down Fourth, across Pontotoc and Linden, to his own block, where he parks it at the curb, between two cars. Then he heads across the street toward Rothschild's grocery, going to try to get some beer on credit.

While we were talking, people were coming in, and now the tables were nearly filled. Charlie looked at his watch, then at Furry. 'Feel like playing?' he asked. 'I always feel like playing,' he said. He drank the last of the bourbon in his glass. 'Yes, sir. *Always* feel like that.'

'I'll announce you,' Charlie said. He carried a chair onto the stage, sat down, and repeated the lecture he uses whenever he hires an old-time musician. It begins, 'Without the tradition of American Negro music, there would be no rock music.' The lecture's purpose is to inspire the rock generation with love and respect for the blues. However, the audience, none of whom looks older than twenty, seems more interested in each other than anything else.

When the speech ended, with 'I am proud to present . . .' Furry, carrying his battered Epiphone guitar, limped onto the stage. The applause was polite. Furry smiled and waved. 'Ladies and gentlemen,' he began, 'I'm very pleased to be here tonight to play for you all. I've been around Memphis, playing and singing, for many years. My wife is with me tonight; we've been married many years. When we got married, I only had fifteen cents and she had a quarter.' I looked at Charlie. He avoided my eyes.

'And then one day,' Furry went on, his tone altering slightly, 'she upped and quit me, said I had married her for her money.'

Furry laughed, Versie laughed, the crowd laughed, and Charlie and I looked at each other and laughed and laughed, shaking our heads. 'I love him, the old bastard,' Charlie said. 'Sorry, Versie.'

But Versie, watching Furry proudly, had not heard.

He had begun to play a slow, sad blues, one that none of us had ever heard, a song without a name: 'My mother's dead,' he sang, the guitar softly following, 'my father just as well's to be. Ain't got nobody to say one kind word for me.'

The room, which had been filled with noise, was now quiet. 'People holler mercy,' Furry sang, 'don't know what mercy mean. People . . .' – and the guitar finished the line. 'Well, if it mean any good, Lord, have mercy on me.'

When, after nearly an hour, Furry left the stage, the applause was considerably more than polite. But I knew that it was only the third time Furry had heard public applause during the year, and that in this year, as in most of the years of his life, his music would probably bring him less than $100. Soon, we would take him home and he would change clothes and go out to sweep the streets. I wondered, as Charlie and Versie were congratulating him and pouring fresh drinks, how he had managed to last, to retain his skill.

Furry was sitting back in his chair, holding a drink in one hand and a new cigar in the other, smiling slightly, his eyes nearly closed. I asked him if he had ever been tempted to give up, to stop playing. 'Give out but don't give up,' he said. He tasted his drink and sat straighter in the chair. 'No,' he said, 'all these years, I kept working for the city, thinking things might change, Beale Street might go back like it was. But it never did.'

'But you went on playing.'

'Oh, yes, I played at home. Sometimes, nothing to do, no place to play, I'd hock the guitar and get me something to drink. And then I'd wish I had it, so I could play, even just for myself. I never quit playing, but I didn't play out enough for people to know who I was. Sometimes I'd see a man, a beggar, you know, playing guitar on the sidewalk, and I'd drop something in his cup, and he wouldn't even know who I was. He'd think I was just a street-sweeper.'

4
Been Here and Gone: The Funeral of Mississippi John Hurt

One night in 1966, planning to go along with Furry Lewis as he swept the streets the next morning, I took a Placidyl and went to bed about 9.00. Before I fell asleep, Charlie Brown called to say that Mississippi John Hurt was at the Bitter Lemon. Thinking it might be my only chance to hear Hurt, I got up and went to the club. As it turned out, I was right. Hurt was on his last trip to California for his last recording session. What folklorists call a 'songster' – a performer of set pieces rather than a great improvisor – Hurt was a pleasant man whose music contained a gentle, bawdy humor. I met him in the summer, and in the winter he was dead.

On Fourth Street in Memphis, just south of Beale, around the corner from the place where, in 1909, Wild Bill Latura shot Leslie Williams, Long Charley, and two men named Speck and Candy, Furry Lewis is waiting. He sits on the edge of his bed, leaning forward, his chin resting on the crooked handle of his walking stick. He is wearing black wing-tip shoes, blue suit-pants, a white shirt, and a grey Countess Mara necktie with a black-and-white design of a doctor's bag and stethoscope. The television set is on, and he stares at whatever is playing at a little after eleven on Sunday morning, 'Face the Nation' or old cartoons.

I am coming up the worn, warped stairs between Rothschild's grocery and Stewart's tavern, down the long dingy hall, with its buckled floor that rolls like the swell of the sea, to knock at Furry's door. 'Come in, then,' he calls.

Inside, because I am late, I say, 'I'm sorry, Furry.'

'They postpone the funeral?' he asks, afraid that he has got dressed up only to be disappointed.

But Mississippi John Hurt, another blues player of Furry's time, is at the Century Funeral Home in Greenwood, where he has been lying for the past eleven days. The funeral, I tell Furry, will take place on schedule.

'Yes,' Furry says, 'they need to get him in the ground.' He puts on his blue coat, takes two Hav-A-Tampa cigars from a Mason jar beside the bed, fixes his hat, a pale gray unblocked beaver, square on his head, and we set out.

Downstairs, waiting in her yellow Mustang, was my girlfriend Christopher. When she saw us coming, she got into the back seat, so that Furry, with his wooden leg, could sit in the front.

'Hi, Furry,' Christopher said.

'Hey, little miss,' said Furry, fulfilling his self-image as a Dignified but Playful old Gentleman.

It was a bright, cool, November morning. We drove out on the new expressway, Interstate 55. Not only is it a faster route, it also keeps you out of the tiny, mean towns where you see the signs: Bob-Ann Café and Tourist Court (Private Club). However, you almost regret not seeing them, those quiet explosive towns in the isolated stretches of the Delta, where the Sound was born from moans, cries, and hollers. By taking the expressway, we missed Hernando, birthplace of the tambourine-playing Reverend Robert Wilkins, blues singer turned sanctified preacher. South of Hernando, past Love and Coldwater, is a place named Como, where Fred McDowell, the best of the younger (under sixty) men still playing in the old Delta blues guitar style, is pumping gas at Stuckey's Candy Store. Previously, Fred was a sharecropper, but the last year he paid his boss man off for his outfit (land, seed, fertilizer, rent on a house and mule) and came out with $30, so he went to Stuckey's, where he makes a little better, and where there is a telephone handy for when he gets calls to appear at places like the Newport Folk Festival.

Fred, like John Hurt, is one of the few who stayed. Mississippi is the soul brothers' Old Country, a wonderful place to be from. The farther the better. It is remarkable how many seminal figures on modern

American music have left the central part of the Mississippi Delta. If you describe on a map a circle with its center at Moorhead, Mississippi, the place where the Southern cross the Yellow Dog, lying within a hundred-mile radius are not only Como and Hernando, but also Red Banks, Helena, Lyon, Leland, Rolling Fork, Corinth, Ruleville, Greenville, Indianola, Bentonia, Macon, Eden Station, West Point, Tupelo, Tippo, Scott, Shelby, Meridian, Lake Cormorant, Houston, Belzoni, Bolton, Tunica, Yazoo City, Lambert, Vance, Burdett and Clarksdale, whence come Gus Cannon, Roosevelt Sykes, Son House, Jimmy Reed, Muddy Waters, Fat Man Morrison, Charlie Patton, B.B. King, Albert King, Skip James, Bo Diddley, Emma Williams, Howlin' Wolf, Elvis Presley, Mose Alison, Big Bill Broonzy, Willie Brown, Jimmie Rodgers, Robert Johnson, Bukka White, Otis Spann, Bo Carter, James Cotton, Tommy McClennan, Jasper Love, Sunnyland Slim, Brother John Sellers, and John Lee Hooker. Also within this radius are Greenwood, where Furry Lewis was born, and Grenada, where John Hurt died.

'Did you and Miss'ippi John ever play together?' I asked Furry.

'No, me and him never saw one another but once or twice. One time on Beale Street, and another time he was coming out of the Peabody Hotel when I was going in. White fellow from Chicago was there recording us.'

'I loved him,' Christopher said. 'He was such a sweet little man, and he was a wonderful guitar player.'

'Yes,' said Furry, who is convinced, and not altogether without reason, that he is the best blues guitarist who has ever lived, 'but he was sho ugly. I swear 'fore God he was.'

On both sides of the wide, divided highway there was nothing but barren countryside and fields the color of winter straw. Occasionally we saw tiny unpainted shacks, and once in a while a filling station with the gas pumps resting on the ground. It is not hard to understand the fierce chauvinism of Mississippi patriots. To stay there, you would have to convince yourself that you loved it.

In Grenada, where the expressway ends, we stopped for lunch. I was traveling with the girl I loved and one of my country's finest folk musicians, both of them more than deserving of the best food the town had to offer, and to hell with this race nonsense. What could one do but seek out the nicest restaurant in town? Well, one could sneak around and park in the back of a Dixie Burger Broil, which is what I did. Come to think of it, this may have *been* the nicest restaurant in town. At any rate, I left Christopher and Furry in the car and went to the front of the place, where I ordered cheeseburgers and root beer through a screen window.

The Burger Broil, in case you're ever in Grenada and looking for a meal, stands on a corner next to the railroad track. As I waited for the cheeseburgers, a white Thunderbird with two teenaged couples in it came past. They were all very handsome, blond hair, brown hair, fine complexions, the pleasantest kind of Southern youth, cruising through Grenada on a Sunday afternoon. At the corner there was a stop sign and the brake lights came on just for a second, as a little Negro boy on a bicycle rolled into the intersection. The honey-haired girl driving stepped on the gas, the car jumped forward, the little boy braked, swerved, skidded, almost toppled over. One of the Thunderbird's handsome youths, curling his lips back to reveal his fine white Southern teeth, yelled 'Watch it, nigger!' He seemed oddly lazy, as if the performance were obligatory, and he was giving it a perfunctory reading. But as the car sped off, bucking and raising dust over the railroad track, the Negro boy followed it with a look of pure, beautiful, ten-year-old hatred. Then, catching himself unwary, he glanced around, saw me – a white man in a three-piece suit – and the mask went back on. His face was blank, impassive, as he pedalled away. The lunch cost two dollars and thirty-five cents.

State Highway Eight, between Grenada and Greenwood, is a narrow, crumbling, asphalt strip. It led us through more of the brown decaying fields and past thin stands of pines. There were two or three towns of a few scattered houses. Then we came to a sign that said Avalon. John Hurt was born in Teoc, Mississippi, a town so small that it doesn't appear on my Esso three-state map, but Avalon is where he lived and farmed nearly all his life. He left for short periods in 1928 and '29, when he made his first recordings and appearances, and after 1963, when he was 'rediscovered'. But he always came back. I had wondered what it would be like. First there was a long, empty stretch of fields. Somewhere around the middle, a wide, dusty clay road crossed the highway. Then, on the far side, there was another sign, just like the first one, facing away.

'That was Avalon,' I told Furry.

'Sho was,' he said.

The next town was Greenwood, which Furry left, with his mother and sisters, at the age of six, and had not seen for sixty-eight years. Christopher asked him if he remembered it, and he said he remembered how he'd wanted to get out of it. The slum apartment Furry lives in looks hardly any better than the shanties you pass coming into Greenwood, but Furry, seeing them, said 'Man, I wouldn't live here! Nosir!'

It took us twenty minutes to find the Century Funeral Home, a small white frame house with a cyclone fence around it, down in what used to be called the quarters, and the funeral procession had already started for St. James's Baptist Church in Avalon. A short, fat man, shiny black, wearing a short-sleeved white shirt, black bow-tie, and black straw hat, told me I couldn't miss it: 'Just take a right at the road.'

We did not catch up with the procession, hurrying out of Greenwood past the shacks that had ushered us in, but when we reached Avalon we could see the pink dust still hanging in the air over the clay road. We followed the road through the gray, plowed-under fields till we came to the long line of cars, where we parked and started walking. The cars were old, but most of them had been spruced up with decorations: reflector mud-flaps, plastic Jesuses, dangling monkeys, even a few flying foxtails. The sky was becoming overcast; the muted sun was glowing like a plum over a wooded ridge that rose behind the fields to our left. On a small plot almost in the center of the immense flatness was the church, a one-room, wood-frame building, wrapped in brick-veneer tarpaper, roofed with tin. The hearse, a pale blue '55 Cadillac, was parked on the grass by the front door. The wooden box which would contain the coffin was lying beside it.

The church looked as if it might hold 200 people, and there were more than that outside. They were all country Negroes, dressed in funny old clothes, but they wore them with a kind of grace and even hipness, as if their shiny garbardine suits and brown ventilated shoes, nylon dresses and hats with veils, were equal in style to the Italian sweaters and sharp-toed slip-ons, the miniskirts and blonde wigs, of their city cousins. No one seemed to mind that the majority of the crowd was forced to remain outside. We saw three elderly sisters, clucking to each other, come up the road and across the yard to the front door, where a man who had been standing on the top step trying to see over the heads of the people jammed in the doorway (he was a big man, perfectly bald, wearing a chalk-striped blue suit that was creased from being folded away) turned to them, smiling broadly, and said, 'B'lieve yawl done got far as yawl gone *get!*'

It was definitely a festive occasion. Mississippi farm workers are as poor as any people in this country. The bleakness of their lives must be a match for the landscape, and any diversion, even a funeral, is a pleasure.

On the far side of the church there was a group of men, such as you see at country funerals, all shouldered together as if in a football huddle, breaking at intervals into shaking, knee-slapping laughter. We had been standing in the yard for about ten minutes when a man left the group, came over, and asked if we would like to go inside. I thanked him, and said that it looked too crowded for us to try.

'Well,' he said, speaking very slowly and precisely, 'we could certainly find room for you. I suspect you all have come a long way to be at Uncle John's funeral. I am his nephew, Theodore Roosevelt Hurt.'

I told him who I was, that Christopher was a friend of mine and a fan of John Hurt, and that Furry was Furry Lewis, the famous Memphis blues player. Theodore Roosevelt Hurt said that he was the one who took Uncle John home from the hospital. 'Aunt Jessie called me – I live in Greenwood, and I had just got in from work – and said, "T.R., Uncle John passed this evenin'." I couldn't hardly believe it. They all call me T.R. Except Uncle John, he called me Tudderman. We were very close, almost like father and son. We used to sit up and sing together for hours in the evenings.'

I asked if he were a musician, and he said, 'Uncle John used to try to show me how to pick guitar, but my fingers just wouldn't make the stops.' He held up his hands, which were short and so thick that they appeared to be swollen. 'But I do sing. I have a little quartet that appears on the radio in Greenwood every Sunday morning.'

We talked a little more, and then he asked again if we'd like to go inside. 'We would be *proud* to have you,' he said, and I began to see that we were Visiting Dignitaries.

'All right,' I said. 'Later on we'll try to sneak in for a minute.'

'Fine,' said T.R. 'Now when the time come, *you* –' (pointing to me) 'shall go in, you *wife* –' (pointing to Christopher) 'shall go in, and –' (jerking his thumb as he turned away) 'this colored fellow can go in with you.' Then he went back to the huddle.

As the sky grew darker, the wind increased, and now it was getting chilly. The whole scene seemed like a painting, the low, dull, sky, broad gray fields, the little crowd around the church, so picturesque that it was in danger of being cute; but so lonesome and empty that the painting was saved from becoming a Norman Rockwell illustration, even when the dark speck I had watched moving across the row of fields to the left became a boy in a black suit, with red socks and a wide, expectant grin. He had almost reached the fence when T.R. came back.

'We can go in now,' he said.

'Do you think so?' I asked. 'I haven't seen anyone come out.'

T.R. answered, but the sound of his voice was lost in a series of shrieks from inside the church. He gestured for us to follow him around to the back. As we started, two men came out the front door, one holding up the other, who was swooning and sobbing, 'Daddy's dead.' From my experience attending the funerals of my relatives in south Georgia, I assumed he was someone who had never known John Hurt. The two of them came down the steps and went to sit in the Cadillac.

We followed T.R. through the dried, weedy grass. Cockleburs stuck to my pant legs, and when I bent to brush them off, T.R. went almost to his knees, plucking the spiny burs with his thick fingers. 'Hey, let me –' I said. 'I can –' But he would not stop.

The front wall of the outhouse, deep in the far corner of the yard, was only about four feet high. Inside it a man was standing with his back to us. A woman leading a little girl got about halfway to the outhouse before she saw the man. Then she stopped and began looking around casually, as if she had not been going anywhere in particular. In a moment (T.R. and I had just finished picking my pants clean) the man came out, and as he passed by them he smiled and tipped his hat.

The back steps had collapsed on one side. T.R. climbed them first, to give Christopher a hand, then I helped push Furry up, so I was last to see that once we were inside, we were standing in the pulpit, behind the altar.

A thin, hawk-nosed man with white hair clipped down almost to his dark skull was preaching in the classic call-and-response pattern: 'Now John Hurt – went to Chicago. He went – to New York. *Detroit.* California. But he came *back* –' (Praise God!) 'to his neighbors. Why? Because *he* – was a neighbor.' (Amen!) 'The evidence,' he said, cueing one side of the room, then the other, 'is on the right hand –' (Yes, Lord!) 'and on the left.' (Hallelujah!)

He was working into a nice groove, but T.R. went over, laid a hand on his shoulder, whispered in his ear, and he stopped and stepped back. Then T.R. spoke to the congregation: 'Some of Uncle John's friends from out of town are here, and they would like to say a few words.' Furry and I swapped double takes, as T.R. offered us the stand. 'After you,' I said.

With his hat in one hand, his cane in the other, Furry stepped up to the pulpit, and said he was glad to be there. 'This is Furry Lewis talking,' he said. 'We come clean from Memphis to be with you today. I knew John Hurt from the old days. Me and him used to play together on Beale Street, and seem like I just got kind of filled up inside, and had to come down here to be with you.' (Tell it!)

He went on for some time, faking beautifully, and then he said, 'Now John Hurt is gone, and we miss him. But you know,' he said, ringing the final changes, 'we love – but God love best.' (That's *say*in' it!)

As I went to the front of the pulpit, I saw the coffin, a fine-looking metal one, lying before the altar. Seated in a crowded pew down front were two white couples – boys with moustaches, girls with long, straight hair – stone folk hippies come from God knows what northern spot. They were not looking at each other nor at anyone else, all of them obviously freaked out by finding in the heart of the Delta, not Blacks but Darkies.

I don't remember what I said. The last time I saw John Hurt I bought whiskey for him, and he played the blues for me, so our accounts were as even as they would ever get. I think I told the people that though this was a sad day, we should remember all the joy he had given us through his music – something like that. I may even have gotten an amen or two.

Then I turned away, Christopher declined to speak, and we started out. On the other side of the pulpit there was an old upright piano. It looked as if it had sat in the unheated church, freezing in the winter, baking in the summer, since it was new. As we left, the plump sister who played it struck the driest, most soulful chord (all the stiff, dusty strings having stretched and shrunk and grown brittle to create a new harmony, more complex, more expressive than that of any conventional music), and the congregation sang: 'Near the Cross, oh, near the Cross, be my Glory ever, and my weary soul shall find, oh, rest beyond the river.'

Down the slanting, broken-down steps, and we were outside again. We had not been in the church for long, but the light had changed, and now the whole countryside, the churchyard, the fields, and the ridge where they would bury John Hurt, all lay in a pale red haze.

We would not stay for the burying, because we wanted to be out of Mississippi before dark. Coming back around the church, I heard someone crying, and hesitated; I had forgotten the man who had been led out earlier. T.R., at my side, said 'That's Uncle John's son.'

'He's gone, he's gone,' the man was wailing. As we came past the Cadillac, through the open window we could hear the other man, whose patience must have been wearing a bit thin, say 'Hush, boy. Yo' daddy's better off than we are now.'

5

A RAINY NIGHT IN MEMPHIS

I once walked down Beale Street with two men who had written books about Elvis Presley. We stopped at Lansky Brothers' window, which displayed among its procurers' habits an early photograph of Presley looking characteristically greasy. We looked at the portrait for a moment in silence and then one of the writers said, 'Like a creature from another planet.' But the writer was from Berkeley, where I am an alien.

I was one month past my first year as a teenager when I saw Presley for the first time, on a television program called 'The Tommy and Jimmy Dorsey Stage Show', dressed in a white suit that would have looked at home on an Afro-American man of the cloth.

I lived in a small town, Thomasville in south Georgia, attended the ninth grade at the all-white high school (that was the year I skipped PE a hundred and seventy-eight consecutive days) and Sunday School at an all-white Methodist church. My father sold insurance. Music made with fiddles and guitars was impolite, just as it was impolite to call black people Mr. and Mrs.

However – my best friend's father was a fireman who played guitar in a rockabilly band, though nobody called it that. It was his own band. My friend played clarinet and saxophone in it, and his mother played the drums. His father had a Harley-Davidson and a Buick hardtop convertible with a slate-gray body and cream top. And sideburns.

It was 1956, and for the past couple of years we had been hearing on the radio performers such as Fats Domino, Little Richard, the Platters, Jackie Brenston, Hank Ballard and the Midnighters, Ray Charles, Chuck Berry and Bo

Diddley. Soon there were so many white performers doing the same kind of music as the black rhythm and blues artists – Elvis, Carl Perkins, Jerry Lee Lewis, Charlie Rich, Gene Vincent, Roy Orbison, Johnny Cash, Bobby Charles – that even if we didn't remember that Al Jolson and Jimmie Rodgers had appeared in blackface, we knew that race was irrelevant.

In Memphis I got to know many associates of Elvis, including Sam Phillips, Elvis's first record producer, and Dewey Phillips. This piece is about the decade when Sam and Dewey made up the rest of the twentieth century.

One rainy evening in September 1948, a mole-colored 1937 Plymouth churns down Main Street in Memphis, heading north toward the cheap rent. Inside are a dark-haired woman with dark circles under her dark eyes, her shifty-faced, handsome blond husband, and in the back seat looking out the window, eyes hungry like his mother's, their son, Elvis Presley, who watches uncomprehending as they pass Grant's dime store where a sandy-haired young man, walking sideways across the street, passes into and out of the Plymouth's headlights.

'Hey! Dewey!' A black policeman calls to the young man from the sidewalk.

'Let's go down to Sunbeam's.'

'Goin' to the Chisca. WHBQ's hirin' me to play records on Red Hot and Blue.'

'When you start?'

'Soon's I talk them into it.'

'When you do, play something for me.'

'"Call the Police",' Dewey Phillips says, crossing Beale Street.

A year earlier, there were no black police in Memphis. In September 1947, Lloyd Binford's censor board banned *Annie Get Your Gun* because its cast included a black railroad conductor, and, as Binford said, 'We don't have any negro [*sic*] conductors in the South.' In November, the American Heritage Foundation, sponsors of the Freedom Train, a real train on a real trip across the United States, symbolic of the progress of freedom and brotherhood, took Memphis off their route because Memphis officials required that the train be segregated. 'A custom of a hundred and fifty years can't be sidetracked in a day or year. . .', E. H. Crump said.

But in 1948, after what may have been his most serious political setback, Crump softened enough to permit black police, though they were not allowed to arrest whites – they could detain a white person until a white officer arrived. Crump, a lifelong Democrat, had refused to support Truman for the presidency, and his candidates for governor and US senator were defeated. The Republican Party platform denounced segregation in the military services (though Dwight Eisenhower among others argued in its favor), and Harry Truman removed the issue with an executive order ending military segregation. The Dixiecrats deserted, but to no end. The times were changing. Jackie Robinson was in his second season as a Brooklyn Dodger, and Memphis had, in Nat D. Williams, its first black radio announcer. Still, a black man in Vidalia, Georgia, was lynched for voting.

Memphis in 1948 was only seventy years – one human lifespan – from the desolation of the plague. At the mid-century point the new generation of Memphis entrepreneurs, including Sam Phillips, Dewey Phillips, Kemmons Wilson and Elvis Presley, was preparing (unbeknownst to some of its members) another cultural explosion.

Dewey Phillips first achieved distinction in Memphis by getting fired for causing/inspiring the entire workforce at the Taystee Bread Bakery on Madison Avenue, where he wore his baker's hat cocked at an angle, to stop making loaves of bread and make little men, like gingerbread men. Moving on to Main Street, Dewey literally stopped traffic by playing records and talking over the intercom at Grant's Dime Store. He then pestered the staff at WHBQ radio, just across the street in the Hotel Chisca, until they let him take over the fifteen-minute popular music show, Red Hot and Blue.

In those days a radio announcer was a man with a trained, or at least cultured, voice. Dewey sounded like what he was, a country boy with the boogie disease. He couldn't read copy, he couldn't cue records without scratching them, but as Sam Phillips said, he had a platinum ear. Dewey also had a warm, loving nature and a brilliant line of dopey jive. 'Take a wheelbarrow full of goober dust –' (they made him stop saying 'pissants') 'they got beautiful plate glass doors, just run right through 'em and tell them Phillips sent you – from Red Hot and B-L-E-W Blue.' He appealed to most Memphians, regardless of race. 'Dewey was not white,' Rufus Thomas once said. 'Dewey *had* no color.' In its first year, Dewey's show expanded by popular demand from fifteen minutes to three hours daily.

Dewey used to say that he and Sam were half-brothers, which was a lie, but some lies are truer than fact. Sam and Dewey were from different families, but their relationship was close. They met while Dewey was working at Grant's and Sam was announcing on WREC and engineering broadcasts from the Peabody Hotel's Skyway Ballroom, shaking his earphoned head nightly, saying, 'There has to be something better than this.' ('They had some great bands,' Sam said, 'but some of those guys had been reading the same charts every night for ten years, and they're still turning the pages.')

As a boy on his family's farm in Alabama, Sam Phillips had listened to a man he called Uncle Silas, a thin, ancient black man dying of syphilis, who sang, 'Didn't he ramble, he rambled until the butcher cut him down.' Sam's response to the old man's songs was so deep that it caused him to question who and what he was, where he came from, the nature of spirit and matter in reality.

The quality of Uncle Silas's voice remained in Sam Phillips's mind like a beacon. In 1950 he started the Memphis Recording Service, doing mostly weddings and funerals at first, then recording artists as diverse as Phineas Newborn, Jr., B.B. King, Walter Houston, Jackie Brenston and Howling Wolf for other labels. After a couple of years he began releasing records on his own Sun label. He kept saying that if he could find a white man who could sing with the black man's individuality and conviction, he could make a billion dollars. The money was important both in itself and as a symbol. Sam Phillips was saying that with such a singer he could change history. He did just that.

Between 1948 and 1953, Elvis Presley, living with his parents in cheap apartment buildings and the Lauderdale Courts federal housing project, listened every night to Dewey Phillips, hearing artists like Louis Jordan, Wynonie Harris, Rosetta Tharpe, Roy Brown, Big Boy Crudup. Sun had its first successful releases in 1953, the year Elvis went to the Memphis Recording Service to make, as most of the world must know by now, a record for his mother. At this time Sam would make acetate copies of records he was thinking of releasing, take them to Dewey, who would play them on air, and if the listeners liked them, Sam would press them up. Sam had had small hits with Rufus Thomas, the Prisonaires, and Little Junior Parker before the epochal night when Elvis, Scotty Moore and Bill Black cut 'That's All Right, Mama'.

The year was 1954. The first Holiday Inn was two years old. Hank Williams, the finest flower of redneck music, died the year before. This year, Boss Crump would die, the Supreme Court would outlaw school segregation, and a 'hillbilly cat' would appear who sang like a black man, who bought his clothes at Lansky's on Beale Street, where the black pimps traded, who had been regarded as 'different' at all-white Humes High School and who broke through America's color line so that its popular culture would never be the same again.

There were so many strong Sun artists – Carl Perkins, Jerry Lee Lewis, Johnny Cash, Charlie Rich, Billy Lee Riley – that there wasn't enough time to record jazz artists like Phineas Newborn, Jr., and gospel artists like the Rev. Herbert Brewster. When RCA Victor offered $35,000 for Elvis Presley's recording contract, Sam Phillips, thinking of what he could do with his label with that much money (back then it seemed like a lot), asked Kemmons Wilson (Sam was an early investor in Holiday Inns) whether he would sell Elvis. 'I wouldn't hesitate,' Wilson said. 'That boy isn't even a professional.'

Sam Phillips says that he has never regretted selling Elvis, but that is because he is a man who does not allow himself to feel regret. Selling Elvis was a monumental human and artistic error. But Sam could not have known that Carl Perkins would have a near-fatal car wreck, or that Jerry Lee Lewis would marry his thirteen-year-old cousin. Dewey might have known, if he had been the kind of man who thought in tactical terms, that a new kind of radio – Top Forty – was coming in to replace him. Even if his apeman sidekick Harry Fritzias hadn't attacked the life-sized Jayne Mansfield cut-out, the days of the personality announcer were numbered.

Almost before it had started, it was over, the decade 1948–58. In August 1958 Elvis's mother was dead, lying in state at Graceland on the pool-table. Dewey, out of work, was in the kitchen making a sandwich,

Sam and Elvis were out back by the pool, Sam telling a grief-crazed Elvis to let the undertakers bury his mother. 'I'll never forget it,' Sam said later. 'The dead leaves all round the pool.'

Elvis was wearing an army uniform that day. When he heard that Elvis had died, John Lennon said, 'Elvis died the day he went into the Army.'

Ten years, more or less, before the start of this decade, the Depression had reduced some Memphians to eating clay. Ten years after the end of the decade, in 1968, Martin Luther King would be killed in Memphis, and who knows when Memphis and the country will recover from that. Later that year Dewey would die, still unemployed.

But in these years, the late '40s to late '50s, lives changed all over the world because of the dreams and dedication of a few Memphis mavericks. In the next three decades, with Stax, Goldwax, Sonic, Royal, American, Fre-Tone, Onyx, Ardent, and other studios, similar things would happen again and again. There's no telling whose paths might cross on a rainy night in Memphis.

6

SITUATION REPORT:
ELVIS IN MEMPHIS, 1967

My Memphis friend John Fergus Ryan, who once said, 'Room service? Would you send up a jar of molasses and an anthill?' told me the name of an editor he knew at Esquire, *to whom, late in 1966, I sent 'Furry's Blues'. In December I entered a form of marriage with my mentor, Christopher. We went on our honeymoon to New York City, where we stayed out all night listening to people like Miles Davis and slept until late the next afternoon. Daily I'd call the* Esquire *editor, Robert Sherrill, but never heard from him. The day before we left New York I phoned one last time, and told Sherrill's secretary that I was leaving town so if he wanted me he'd better get in touch. Then I took a shower, in the midst of which Sherrill called. Having heard that* Esquire *wanted an Elvis Presley profile, I reminded him of 'Furry's Blues' and suggested that I could provide the Presley piece.*

'Why don't you come over,' Sherrill said, 'I ain't got anything to do this afternoon. We can go to the Chock Full and talk about it.'

'Where you from?' I asked.

'North Carolina.'

Sherrill turned out to be a fine editor and one of the smartest men I've ever met. (He predicted in 1967 that the era of peace and love would end in violence and bloodshed, as I recalled at Altamont.) I told him stories about Elvis I'd heard from my mother, who saw Priscilla at the beauty parlor, and Charles Clarke, my family's physician, who'd been Gladys Presley's doctor. Sherrill laughed at the stories and told me to go ahead with the piece. That's how hard it was to do business with Esquire *in 1967.*

Doing business with Elvis Presley was another matter. John Ryan, attempting to do a Presley story after four or five other writers had failed, drafted a request to Colonel Parker, Presley's manager, saying in essence, 'Presley is loved by everyone except the intellectuals. Let me write a piece about him and make the intellectuals love him.' Colonel Parker, aware that there are at most three or four dozen intellectuals on earth, declined the honor. I didn't approach the Colonel; I started looking for Dewey Phillips. He had been, a dozen or so years before, maybe the most famous and influential character in the Mid-South. By 1967 he had vanished.

Milton Pond, who worked at Poplar Tunes record store, located a number for Dewey at a business in Millington, Tennessee, a suburb of Memphis. The man who answered said he might not see Dewey for a week. Ten minutes later my phone rang. 'Hello! Elvis?' Dewey would always call me Elvis or Birdbrain.

In Millington I found Dewey alone in a furniture store that contained nothing but a desk, a folding chair and a phone. God knows what went on there. Dewey and I had been talking for a while about some of our favorite singers, such as Wynonie Harris and Percy Mayfield, recalling the designs of certain record labels, when he looked out the plate-glass window, made a characteristic palm-against-chest neck-stretching gesture, and gave me the lead of a lifetime. I knew that anyone who saw the first four words would finish reading the piece, hoping that it contained more of the same. I also knew Esquire *wouldn't print it, so I double-spaced after the first paragraph and started over.*

'. . . Talkin' about eatin' pussy, me and Sam Phillips used to make old Elvis sick with that stuff. We'd sit around the studio, down at Sun Records, and talk about how good it was, and he'd get so sick he'd go out back and puke. Then he went to Hollywood, made all them movies and come back, and one night we're all down at the studio, Elvis and Sam and me, and Jerry Lee Lewis, whole bunch of us there, and Elvis says, "Mister Sam, you remember when yawl used to make me sick talkin' about eatin' pussy?" Sam says, "What about it?" "Well," Elvis says, "I eat me some the other night. But man, now I'm in trouble." So Sam asks him, "Who was it you eat?" because we thought right off that Elvis had eat somebody's wife and got caught. But he says, "Natalie Wood," and Sam says, "Well, hell-fire, boy, what's your trouble?" and Elvis said, "Damn if I didn't fall in love with it."'

Between Memphis and Walls (you turn right a bit past a big sign saying 'Church of God, Pastor C. H. Brantley, DRINK DR. PEPPER'), there is a small ranch, 160 green and gently rolling acres, a prettier spread than you'd expect to see in the poor, bleak land of north Mississippi. The owner, at thirty-three, has been a millionaire for more than ten years. He has other, more elegant homesteads, but these days he prefers the ranch. Behind the formidable chain-link fence and the eight-foot picket walls that hide his neat red-brick house, he finds a degree of privacy to share with his pretty new wife. The privacy is also shared by twenty-two pure-bred horses, counting colts, and nine hired hands, counting guards. (There were twelve hands, but the number was reduced recently, so the story goes around the ranch, at the request of the owner's wife.) Then, too, there are the continual visitors – the ones who are allowed inside (some driving Cadillacs given them by the owner as Christmas or birthday presents) and the ones who must stay outside, peering over or through the fences. At times, such as when the owner is out riding, the roadside is solidly lined with sightseeing cars. Privacy – the privacy in which to enjoy his leisure time – is extremely valuable to the ranch's young owner, especially since he works less than half the year. Taxes would make more work pointless; his annual income is about $5 million.

And yet, not too many years ago, he was living in a Federal low-rent housing project, working as a truck-driver, movie usher, sometimes forced to sell his blood at $10 a pint. Elvis Presley, a Great American Success Story.

By the ranch's main gate, in an air-conditioned hut, sits Elvis's Uncle Travis, a small, grinning man, with hair as black and skin as dark as an Indian's. A straw cowboy hat rests on his knee. He wears black Western pants and a white shirt with E. P. monogrammed in black Gothic script across the front. Travis likes to reminisce about the girls he has captured and ejected from his nephew's premises. 'I dragged one out from under the old pink Cadillac. She must have heard me comin' and hid under there, and all I saw was her feet stickin' out. I said, "Come on out of there," and she didn't move, so I reached down, took ahold of her feet, and pulled. She had a coat of motor oil a inch thick.' Travis belches.

'Slip in. Jump a fence like a billygoat. If they can't climb over, they'll

opposite: Elvis Presley and B. B. King, Memphis, 1955 (© Ernest C. Withers)

crawl under. If the gate ain't locked they'll drive right through. I had a carload slip past me up at Graceland. Hell, I didn't even go after them, I just locked the damn gate. They made the circle in front of the house, come back down the drive, and when they seen they couldn't get out, the one drivin' says, "Please op'm the gate." I told her "Yes, ma'am, soon's the sheriff's got there." Made out I was real hot, you know. She says, "Please don't call the sheriff, my mama will kill me." I said, "Not till you get out of jail, I don't reckon." She like to died. Then I started laughin', and they seen it was all right, and asked me if they could come back after a while and talk. So I told them yeah, but while they was gone I got to thinkin', Why'd they have to leave, why couldn't they just stay and talk? But one of they mamas came back with them, and she told on them. I'd scared her daughter so bad she'd peed her pants.'

Travis pitches his head back and laughs, displaying a strong white set of uppers. Parked in the drive is a shiny red Ford Ranchero with his name, T.J. Smith, on one door under the ranch's Circle G brand, actually a flying Circle G. I asked what the 'G' stands for.

'Could be Graceland,' Travis says, 'or it could be his mother's name. He meant it to stand for her name.' Travis's expression becomes serious when he speaks of Elvis's dead mother, his own sister. 'He still keeps that old pink Cadillac he bought for her. Don't never drive it, just keeps it as a keepsake. He's got all the cars he needs. Had a Rolls-Royce up on blocks four or five years. Bought a hundred thousand dollars' worth of trucks and trailers right after he got this place. Money ain't nothing to him. Ole boy from Hernando was down there the other evenin' workin' on the fence, and Elvis drove down in one of his new pickups to take a look. Feller says, "Shore do like that truck. Always wanted me one of them." So Elvis says, "You got a dollar?" Feller says, "Yeah, I got one," and gives it to Elvis. "It's your truck," Elvis says.'

Next Travis tells how Priscilla, the new wife, likes Elvis to take her for rides in one of his souped-up go-karts (top speed, more than 100 m.p.h.) around the driveway at Graceland, tantalizing the squealing girls outside the fence.

Then he spits. 'I sit down here, keepin' people out, seven in the mornin' till six in the evenin', five days a week, and I'm about wore out. I think I'll go in the hospital for two or three weeks, take me a rest.'

'Maybe you could get a television set to watch while you're working,' I suggest.

'Yeah, I believe I will get me one. Either that, or some funny books.'

Just outside the gate, in a rented green Impala, are two girls who have come, so they tell me, all the way from New Zealand. 'Is he home?' they ask.

'Who?'

One sneers, one ignores. 'Did you talk to him? What did he say?'

I look away, trying to select a representative quote. On the roof of the house across the road a man is kneeling behind a camera, snapping pictures of the Circle G. 'Let's ride up to Rosemark tomorrow and look at that mare,' I tell the girls.

'Pardon?'

'That's what he said.'

'What, is that all?'

'You should have been here yesterday. He said, "Would somebody please bring me a Pepsi?"' Pepsi-Cola, I would have explained to the girls, is Elvis's favorite drink, just as his favorite snack is peanut-butter-and-mashed-banana sandwiches; but the Impala roars away, leaving a cloud of dust to settle on my shoes.

Sometime ago, before I saw for myself what Elvis is like, I asked a mutual acquaintance about him. 'He's all right,' I was told. 'Pretty interesting guy to talk to.'

'Really? What's the most interesting thing he's ever said to you?'

My friend sat and thought, pulling the hair on his chin. Finally he said, 'Well, once he told me, "Like your beard. How long'd it take you to grow it?" I said it took about three months, and he said, "I'd like to grow me one sometime, but I don't think I could get away with it. Y'know?" And he sort of winked.'

Another friend, whose relation to the Presley household was for a time unique, told me that Elvis is a very straight guy, who uses neither grass nor acid. In Hollywood, Elvis never goes to night clubs or premières. Except for work, he hardly leaves his Bel-Air mansion. 'He's afraid he wouldn't know how to act,' says one of his oldest friends. 'And he wouldn't.'

Even in Memphis, his recreational activities have been, for a millionaire, unpretentious. In the early days at Graceland (the large, white-columned estate, rather like an antebellum funeral parlor, which Elvis bought in 1957), the big kick was roller-skating. After a local rink closed for the evening, Presley and his entourage would come in, skate, eat hot dogs and drink Pepsi-Cola till dawn. When skating palled, Elvis started renting the entire Fair Grounds amusement park, where he and his friends could ride the Tilt-a-Whirl, Ferris wheel, roller coaster, dodgem cars (Elvis's favorite), and eat hot dogs and drink Pepsis till dawn. Until quite recently, Presley has been in the habit of hiring a local movie theatre (the Memphian) and showing rented movies, favoring the films of actresses he has dated. The Memphian has no hot dog facilities, but provides plenty of popcorn and, of course, Pepsis. Now that he is married and an expectant father, he does not get out so much at night, but the daytime is as glamorous, as exciting, as ever.

On a day not so long ago, when Presley happened to be staying at Graceland, the house was crowded with friends and friends of friends, all waiting for old El to wake up, come downstairs, and turn them on with his presence. People were wandering from room to room, looking for action, and there was little to be found. In the basement, a large, divided room with gold records hung in frames around the walls, creating a sort of halo effect, they were shooting pool or lounging under the Pepsi-Cola signs at the soda fountain. (When Elvis likes something, he *really* likes it.) In the living room boys and girls were sprawled, nearly unconscious with boredom, over the long white couches, among the deep snowy drifts of rug. One girl was standing by the enormous picture-window, absently pushing one button, then another, activating an electrical traverse rod, opening and closing the red velvet drapes. On a table beside the fireplace of smoky molded glass, a pink ceramic elephant was sniffing the artificial roses. Nearby, in the music room, a thin, dark-haired boy who had been lying on the cloth-of-gold couch, watching Joel McCrea on the early movie, snapped the remote-control switch, turning off the ivory television set. He yawned, stretched, went to the white, gilt-trimmed piano, sat down on the matching stool and began to play. He was not bad, playing a kind of limp, melancholy boogie, and soon there was an audience facing him, their backs to the door.

Then, all at once, through the use of perceptions which could only be described as extrasensory, everyone in the room knew that Elvis was there. And, stranger still, nobody moved. Everyone kept his cool. Out of the corner of an eye Presley could be seen, leaning against the doorway, looking like Lash LaRue in boots, black Levis and a black silk shirt.

The piano player's back stiffens, but he is into the bag and has to boogie his way out. 'What is this, amateur night?' someone mutters. Finally – it cannot have been more than a minute – the music stops. Everyone turns toward the door. Well I'll be damn. It's Elvis. What say, boy? Elvis smiles, but does not speak. In his arms he is cradling a big blue model airplane.

A few minutes later, the word – the sensation – having passed through the house, the entire company is out on the lawn, where Presley is trying to start the plane. About half the group has graduated into the currently fashionable Western clothing, and the rest are wearing the traditional pool-hustler's silks. They all watch intently as Elvis, kneeling over the plane, tries for the tenth time to make the tiny engine turn over; when it splutters and dies, a groan, as of one voice, rises from the crowd.

Elvis stands, mops his brow (though of course he is not perspiring), takes a thin cigar from his shirt pocket and peels away the cellophane wrapping. When he puts the cigar between his teeth a wall of flame erupts before him. Momentarily startled, he peers into the blaze of matches and lighters offered by willing hands. With a nod he designates one of the crowd, who steps forward, shaking, ignites the cigar and then, his moment of glory, of service to the King, at an end, he retires into anonymity. 'Thank ya very much,' says Elvis.

They begin to seem quite insane, the meek circle proffering worship and lights, the young ladies trembling under Cadillacs, the tourists outside, standing on the roofs of cars, waiting to be blessed by even a glimpse of this young god, this slightly plump idol, whose face grows more babyish with each passing year.

But one exaggerates. They are not insane, only mistaken, believing their dumpling god to be Elvis Presley. He is not. One remembers – indeed, one could hardly forget – Elvis Presley.

The time is the early '50s, and the scene is dull. Dwight Eisenhower is president, Perry Como is the leading pop singer. The world has changed (it changed in 1945), but the change is not yet evident. Allen Ginsberg is a market researcher for a San Francisco securities company. William Burroughs is in New Orleans, cooking down codeine cough syrup. Malcolm X, paroled from Massachusetts's Charlestown Prison, is working in a Detroit furniture store. Stokely Carmichael is skinny, insolent, and eleven years old.

It is, let us say, 1953. Fred Zinnemann rehashes the past with *From Here to Eternity*, and Laslo Benedek gives us, in *The Wild One*, a taste of the future. This is a movie with good guys and bad guys, and the good guys are the ones who roar on motorcycles into a town which is small, quiet, typically American, and proceed to take it apart. Their leader, Marlon Brando, will be called an anti-hero. But there is no need for the prefix. He is a new, really contemporary hero: the outcast.

Soon James Dean repeats the theme with even greater success. But Dean's career was absurdly short. 'You know he was dead before he knew who he was,' someone said. The outcasts of America were left without a leader.

Then, one Saturday night early in 1956 on a television variety program, a white singer drawls at the camera: 'Ladies and gentlemen, I'd like to do a song now, that tells a little story, that really makes a lot of sense – Awopbopaloobop – alopbamboom! Tutti-frutti! All rootie! Tutti-frutti! All rootie!'

Though nearly all significant popular music was produced by Negroes, a white rhythm-and-blues singer was not an entirely new phenomenon. Bill Haley and the Comets had succeeded with such songs as 'Shake, Rattle and Roll', and 'Rock Around the Clock'. But the pudgy Haley, in his red plaid dinner jacket, did not project much personal appeal. This other fellow was something else.

He was not quite a hillbilly, nor yet a drugstore cowboy. He was a Southern – in that word's connotation of rebellion and slow, sweet charm – version of the character Brando created in *The Wild One*. Southern high-school girls, the 'nice' ones, called these boys 'hoods'. You saw them lounging on the hot concrete of a gas station on a Saturday afternoon, or coming out of a poolroom at three o'clock of a

Monday afternoon, stopping for a second on the sidewalk as if they were looking for someone who was looking for a fight. You even see their sullen faces, with a toughness lanky enough to just miss being delicate, looking back at you out of old photographs of the Confederate Army. They were not named Tab or Rock, nor even Jim, Bill, Bob. They all had names like Leroy, Floyd, Elvis. All outcasts, with their contemporary costumes of duck-ass haircuts, greasy Levis, motorcycle boots, T-shirts for day and black leather jackets for evening wear. Even their unfashionably long sideburns (Elvis's were *furry*) expressed contempt for the American dream they were too poor to be part of.

No one writing about Presley should forget the daring it took to be one of these boys, and to sing. A hood might become a mechanic or a house painter or a bus-driver or even a cop, but nobody would expect him to be a singer. If he tried it at all, he would have to have some of his own crowd playing with him; he'd have to sing some old songs his own people had sung before him; and he would have to sing them in his own way, regardless of what people might say about him.

'Mama, do you think I'm vulgar on the stage?'

'Son, you're not vulgar, but you're puttin' too much into your singin'. Keep that up and you won't live to be thirty.'

'I can't help it, Mama. I just have to jump around when I sing. But it ain't vulgar. It's just the way I feel. I don't feel sexy when I'm singin'. If that was true, I'd be in some kinda institution as some kinda sex maniac.'

These days, when asked about the development of his career, Elvis either ignores the question or refers it to 'my manager'. Generally speaking his manager is the person standing closest to him at the time. This is often Alan Fortas, officially the ranch foreman, a young man only slightly less stocky than a bull, with a history of hostility to reporters. When the Beatles visited Elvis in Hollywood, Fortas, not troubling to remember their names, addressed each of them as, 'Hey, Beatle!' They always answered, too: nobody wants to displease Alan.

A more voluble source of information is Dewey Phillips. During Elvis's early career Phillips was probably as close to him as anyone except his mother, Gladys. Now retired, Phillips was then one of the most popular and influential disc jockeys in the nation. He still speaks the same hillbilly jive he used as a broadcaster.

'Nobody was picking up on the ole boy back then. He was a real bashful kid, but he liked to hang around music. They'd chase him away from the switchboard at WMPS, and he'd come hang around Q. That's WHBQ, where I was doing my show, Red Hot and Blue, every night. Weekends, he'd come down to Sun Records – he'd cut that record, "My Happiness", for his mother, paid four dollars for it himself – and Sam Phillips, President of Sun, finally gave him a session. Tried to record a ballad, but he couldn't cut it. Sam got Bill Black, the piano player, and Scotty Moore, the guitarist, to see if they could work anything out with him.

'After a couple of tries, Elvis, Bill and Scotty fixed up a couple of old songs, "That's All Right, Mama," and "Blue Moon of Kentucky" so they sounded a little different. When Elvis began to cut loose with "That's All Right", Sam came down and recorded these son-of-a-guns. One night I played the record thirty times. Fifteen times each side. When the phone calls and telegrams started to come in, I got hold of Elvis's daddy, Vernon. He said Elvis was at a movie, down at Suzore's number two theater. Get him over here, I said. And before long Elvis came running in. Sit down, I'm going to interview you, I said. He said, "Mr. Phillips, I don't know nothing about being interviewed." Just don't say nothing dirty, I told him.

'He sat down, and I said I'd let him know when we were ready to start. I had a couple of records cued up, and while they played we talked. I asked him where he went to school, and he said "Humes". I wanted to get that out, because a lot of people listening had thought he was colored. Finally I said, All right, Elvis, thank you very much. "Aren't you gone interview me?" he asked. I already have, I said. The mike's been open the whole time. He broke out in a cold sweat.'

According to Phillips, Elvis at this time considered himself a country singer. 'Sam used to get him, Roy Orbison, Jerry Lee Lewis and Johnny Cash down at Sun and play Big Bill Broonzy and Arthur Crudup records for them, trying to get them on the blues thing, because he felt like that was going to be hot. One of Elvis's first public appearances was at a hillbilly jamboree at the downtown auditorium. Webb Pierce was there, and Carl Smith, Minnie Pearl, a whole houseful of hillbillies. Elvis was nervous, said he wanted me with him. But Sam and I were out at my house, drinking beer, or we had something going, and I missed the afternoon show. Elvis came looking for me, mad as hell. I asked him what he'd sung and he said, '"Old Shep" and "That's How My Heartaches Begin".'

What happened? 'Nothing.'

'So that night I went along with him and told him to open with "Good Rockin' Tonight" and not to sing any hillbilly songs. I introduced him and stayed onstage while he sang. He went into "Good Rockin'," started to shake, and the place just blew apart. He was nobody, didn't even have his name on the posters, but the people wouldn't let him leave. When we finally went off we walked past Webb Pierce, who had been waiting in the wings to go on. I smiled at him and he said, "You son of a bitch."'

The sales of Elvis's records enabled him to get more bookings, and Dewey Phillips bought him an old Lincoln sedan for $450 so he could play out-of-town jobs. Appearing in Nashville at a convention of the Country and Western Disc Jockeys' Association, he was seen – 'discovered', by talent scouts for RCA Victor. In a moviehouse matinée in Texarkana, he was discovered by Thomas Andrew Parker, a latter-day Barnum out of W.C. Fields by William Burroughs. Parker, an illegal immigrant from Holland, had created a fictional carny background for himself: he had worked in his uncle's 'Great Parker Pony Circus', dipped candied applies, shaved ice for snow cones, operated merry-go-rounds, even put in a stretch as dog-catcher in Tampa, Florida.

Astute techniques in these businesses had enabled Parker to rise in the world to a position of some prestige. The title 'Colonel' had been conferred upon him by, as he put it, 'a few governors'. He was managing the careers of such big-name country entertainers as Hank Snow and Eddy Arnold. But in all his years as a promoter, he had never found so promotable a commodity as Presley. He had seen Elvis at, for his purposes, just the right time. The demand for Elvis's records prompted RCA to offer $35,000 for Presley, lock, stock, and tapes. Sam Phillips accepted.

'Elvis knew he was going big time,' Dewey Phillips remembers, 'and he needed a manager. That was late spring of '55. He was the hottest thing in show business, and still just a scared kid. He had got his mother and daddy a nice house, they had three Cadillacs, and no phone. He asked me to be his manager. I told him I didn't know anything about managing. Then Colonel Parker came to town. He knew what he was doing. He didn't talk to Elvis. He went out to the house and told Gladys what he could do for the boy. That Parker is a shrewd moo-foo, man.'

Elvis's first appearances on network television, on the Tommy and Jimmy Dorsey Show in January and February 1956, changed him from a regional phenomenon into a national sensation. This might not have happened, the American public might simply have shuddered and turned away, had there not been a new group among them: teenagers, the enemy within. When the older generation, repelled by Presley's lean, mean, sexy image, attacked him from pulpits and editorial columns, banned him from radio stations, the teenagers liked him more than ever, and went out and bought his records. Entrepreneurs could not afford to ignore Presley. As one radio producer asked: How can you argue with the country's number-one recording star? Reluctantly, almost unwillingly, show business accepted Elvis. Ed Sullivan, who only a couple of months before had condemned Presley as 'unfit for a family audience', now was obliged to pay him $50,000 for three brief appearances. However, Elvis was photographed only from the waist up, and his material was diluted by the addition of a ballad, 'Love Me Tender', which oozed syrup.

Such attempts to make Elvis appear respectable were very offensive to the good old boys back in Memphis. Steve Allen, involved in a ratings battle with Sullivan, booked Presley, but assured the audience that they would see only 'clean family entertainment'. Elvis appeared and sang, standing still, wearing white tie and tails, with top hat and cane, but without a guitar. Just after the show went off the air, Dewey Phillips's telephone rang.

'Hello, you bastard,' Dewey said.

'How'd you know it was me?' asked Elvis.

'You better call home and get straight, boy. What you doing in that monkey suit? Where's your guitar?'

So when Elvis made his next hometown appearance (it was on July 4, 1956) he reassured his people. The occasion was a charity benefit and Colonel Parker had turned down paying engagements so that Elvis could be part of the show. His was the closing spot, and he was preceded by more than a hundred performers, including the orchestras of Bob Morris and Aaron Bluestein, the Admiral's Band of Navy Memphis, a barbershop quartet called the Confederates, Charlotte Morgan's dancing Dixie Dolls, and innumerable singers, by no means the least of which was one Helen Putnam, founder of Fat Girls Anonymous, who dedicated 'A Good Man Is Hard to Find' to Elvis.

After nearly three hours, with the audience so bored that it was on the point of having a religious experience, Dewey Phillips, who was master of ceremonies, said 'All right. Here he is,' and there he was, his hair hanging over his forehead, a wad of gum in his jaw. He wore a black suit, black shoes, black shirt, red tie, and red socks, clothes with so much drape and flash that they created a new sartorial category, somewhere on the other side of corny. He sang all the old songs in the old way, from 'That's All Right' to 'Blue Suede Shoes' to 'Heartbreak Hotel'. He sang until he dripping with sweat, and when at last he spoke, his words were a promise to his friends, a gift of defiance to his enemies: 'I just want to tell y'awl not to worry – them people in New York and Hollywood are not gone change me none.'

Then his voice became a growl, an act of rebellion: 'You ain't nothin' but a houn' dog,' he sang, and proceeded to have sexual intercourse with the microphone.

> They told me you was high class
> Well, that was just a lie –

If the police had not been there, forming a blue wall around the stage, the audience might have eaten Elvis's body in a eucharistic frenzy. They were his and he was theirs, their leader: it was an incandescent moment.

And the same time it was a climactic one. For as he stood there singing defiance at his natural enemies – those with power, prestige, money – the Humes High School hood, the motorcycle jockey, was gone, and in his place there was a star, with power, prestige, money. A few months from now at about three o'clock one morning, he would be standing with one of his hired companions outside the Strand Theatre on Main Street in Memphis when a couple of his high-street classmates would drive past, not going much of anywhere, just dragging Main. They would slow their car as they came alongside the Strand; they would see it was Elvis; and then, without a word, they would drive on. 'A few years ago,' Elvis said, 'they would have spoken to me.'

Elvis had tried to go on being himself. When Paramount offered him a movie contract with a clause forbidding him to ride motorcycles, he said 'I'd rather not make movies.' They let him keep his motorcycles. All that was really necessary was that he stop doing his thing and start doing theirs. His thing was 'Mystery Train', 'Milkcow Blues Boogie'. Theirs was 'Love Me Tender', 'Loving You', 'Jailhouse Rock', 'King Creole'.

Then he was drafted. The Army cut his hair, took away his fancy clothes, and Elvis let them. His country had served him well and he was willing to serve his country. He is nothing if not fair-minded.

While he was stationed in Fort Hood, Texas, Elvis moved his parents to a rented house in the nearby town of Killeen. His mother, who had been doing poorly for more than a year, worsened, and on August 8, 1958, Elvis put her on a train to Methodist Hospital in Memphis and requested the customary special leave.

It was refused. When Gladys's doctors, at Elvis's request, advised his command of the seriousness of his mother's illness they were told, in effect, 'If it were anybody else, there'd be no problem. It's standard procedure. But if we let Presley go everybody will yell special privilege.'

Days passed while Gladys Presley sank lower and lower. In spite of constant urging from Elvis and the doctors, the leave still was not granted. Finally, on the morning of August 12, Elvis decided that he had had enough. 'If I don't get a pass by two o'clock this afternoon,' he said, 'I'll be home tonight.'

The doctors reasoned with him, urged him to remember that he set an example for millions of other boys. But Elvis had made up his mind. A Humes High boy can be pushed only so far. They could only advise the command of Elvis's plans.

So naturally, the pass came through. The Army is not that dumb. Elvis had the same rights as any other American boy.

Back in Memphis Elvis fought his way through the crowds of newsmen outside the hospital. He was in his mother's room for only a few minutes; then he came out, walked down the hall to an empty waiting room, sank into a chair and cried.

His mother had been the one, perhaps the only one, who had told him throughout his life that even though he came from poor country people, he was just as good as anyone. His success had not surprised her, nor had it changed her. Shortly after Gladys Presley was buried, her husband and son were standing on the magnificent front steps at Graceland. 'Look, Daddy,' Elvis sobbed, pointing to the chickens his mother had kept on the lawn of the hundred-thousand-dollar mansion. 'Mama won't never feed them chickens no more.'

He never really got over his mother's death. He treasured for many years, in his office at Graceland, a lighted, fully decorated, artificial Christmas tree, a souvenir of the last Christmas the family spent together. He had the tree cared for all the time he was in Germany, where the Army had put him safely away.

Elvis liked Germany and both he and his father found wives there. When his tour of duty was ended, he came out with sergeant's stripes. The whole thing was fictionally celebrated in *G.I. Blues*, a happy movie with a multi-million-dollar gross. One Elvis Presley film followed another: *Flaming Star, Wild in the Country, Blue Hawaii, Girls! Girls! Girls!, Kid Galahad, Follow That Dream, It Happened at the World's Fair, Fun in Acapulco, Viva Las Vegas, Kissin' Cousins, Roustabout, Girl Happy, Tickle Me, Harem Scarem, Frankie and Johnny, Paradise – Hawaiian Style, Spinout, Easy Come, Easy Go, Double Trouble, Speedway, Clambake.* They all have two things in common: none lost money, none is contingent at any point upon reality.

But this is not quite true; there is one reality which they reflect. In *Fun in Acapulco*, Elvis walks into a bar which is full of Mexicans, all of whom have good teeth. A mariachi band is playing. Elvis comes in on the chorus, and carries away the verse. Everyone applauds. The men smile and the girls turn on to him. They all think he is a hell of a fellow. One expects that at any moment he may produce a model plane and lead them out on to the lawn.

Elvis has fulfilled the American dream: he is young, rich, famous, adored. Hardly a day passes in Memphis without a politician wanting to name something after him. So far nothing has been found worthy of the honor. Presley has become a young man of whom his city and his country can be truly proud.

And he may not even know whether he misses the old days, the old Elvis. At Graceland, through the powder-white living-room, past the gilded piano, there is a door that looks out onto the swimming pool. If you had been standing there on a recent afternoon, you would have seen Elvis, all alone for a change, riding his motorcycle around the pool, around and around and around.

7

THE MEMPHIS SOUL SOUND

The Esquire *piece stung Presley, as I'd intended. 'Elvis asked me about it,' Dewey told me. 'I said I didn't know nothin'.' A few months later, Presley was working before a live audience for the first time in eight years, making 'The Boxing Ring Special', broadcast in December 1968. Maybe he would have done it anyway.*

While writing 'Furry's Blues' I had begun to envision a book about older blues artists, men like Bukka White, Gus Cannon, Fred McDowell. Writing about poor old black men seemed safe – the Uncle Remus syndrome, I suppose. I sent the Furry piece to many magazines, all of whom said nice things but declined to publish it. The New Yorker*'s rejection slip read, 'The enclosed has a pleasant tone, we felt, but does not appear to be our peculiar kind of nonfiction piece.'*

Publishing the Elvis story in Esquire *made me a professional journalist, something I'd never wanted to be. After a conference with a sub-literate editor at the* Saturday Evening Post, *a periodical that symbolized much of what I hated about America, I found myself doing a piece for them about the music created in such Memphis studios as Stax and American. I went to these places, as I had gone to see John Hurt, at the right time, and for the same reason. I began to specialize in funerals.*

Before the altar at the Clayborn Temple African Methodist Episcopal Church in Memphis, Tennessee, there are three white coffins. Outside, in a freezing drizzle, hundreds of people with umbrellas are trying to shove past the ones who have stopped at the church entrance to buy the glossy 8 × 10 photographs being sold there. The photographs show six teenaged boys, one of them white, the rest Negro, looking like a team of bright young pool hustlers in silk suits with short, double-breasted jackets and black shirts with long roll collars. The name of the group is printed at the bottom: THE BAR-KAYS.

The photographs cost a dollar, but inside you are given an eight-page illustrated Programme. 'OBSEQUIES', the cover announces in gothic print, 'of the late Carl Cunningham, Jimmy Lee King, Matthew Kelly.' Then there is another of the Bar-Kays' promotional pictures, with no indication which of them is which. Everybody knows that Carl is the one smiling in the center, and Jimmy is the one with glasses, kneeling down front. Matthew is not in the picture, because he was not a Bar-Kay, but the Bar-Kays' valet.

James Alexander, the plump boy standing at the left, was not on the plane that crashed a week earlier, killing several people, including the Bar-Kays' employer, singer Otis Redding. Ben Cauley, with a lip goatee, kneeling opposite Jimmy King, was the only survivor. The other two Bar-Kays are in Madison, Wisconsin. Phalon Jones, with the nicely processed hair, is at a local funeral parlor, and Ronnie Caldwell, the lanky white boy, is still in Lake Monona, where the crash occurred.

Inside the Programme, on facing pages, there are individual photographs and biographical sketches of Jimmy King and Carl Cunningham. Jimmy, the group's guitarist and leader, 'constantly sought to produce the degree of excellence in his performance that would bring kings to their feet and comfort and solace to men of lowest degree'. Carl was a drummer, and 'the music which poured from his soul reached the hearts of thousands of souls around the world. The rhythm of his drums still beats out a melody which lingers on and on.' Matthew, the valet, is not pictured, but does receive his own, rather stark, biography: 'His formal education began in the Memphis School System and continued until God moved in heaven and pronounced that his pilgrimage through life had ended.'

The old-fashioned church, with tall stained-glass windows and an overhanging semicircular balcony, is packed to the walls with mourners. A very fat nurse is on duty, and pretty girls in ROTC uniforms are

The Bar-Kays, 1969 (Volt Records publicity photograph)

acting as ushers. As the white-gloved pall-bearers come down the center aisle, the Booker T. Washington High School Band, seated up in the choir-loft, begins a slow, shaking rendition of 'When Day Is Done', and all the relatives, friends and fans of the Bar-Kays stand in silent tribute.

In a square on Beale Street, just a block away, the figure of W.C. Handy, molded in brass, stands in the rain. Since the Civil War there have been many funerals of young men who died in the pursuit of their music. In the old days they died of train wrecks, shooting scrapes, or unmentionable diseases. Now there are other hazards, but the ritual, the honor, remains the same. At the Clayborn Temple, an usher with creamed-coffee skin dabs at her long-lashed eyes, and somehow you cannot help thinking that the Bar-Kays might have lived out their lives and become old men without achieving anything to equal this glorious traditional celebration.

The official eulogy is presented by one of the church elders, a white-haired gentleman who speaks briefly and eloquently, and closes with a memory: 'When I was a boy on Beale Street, we had no electric streetlamps. It was the era of the gaslight, and every evening towards dark the lamplighter would come along in his cart. Frequently night would overtake him as he proceeded slowly down the street, so that as you looked after him, he would vanish in the blackness, and you could not see where he was, but by the glowing light of the lamps, you could see where he had been.

'Now these boys have gone from us into the darkness where we can no longer see them. But when we hear a certain melody and rhythm, when we hear that *soul sound* – then we will remember, and we will know where they have been.'

The early blues musicians were relatively unsophisticated performers, playing unamplified guitar, harmonica, and such primitive instruments as the jug and the tub bass. Professional songwriters, like W.C. Handy, and early recording companies, such as Vocalion and RCA Victor, capitalized on the initial popularity of the blues. But the Depression brought an end to the profits, and the Memphis music business did not revive until after World War Two, with another generation of blues men. They played amplified instruments and for the first time attracted a sizable white audience. A record producer has labelled the early blues 'race' music, but the wider appeal and newly added heavy back beat caused the music of Muddy Waters, John Lee Hooker and Howlin' Wolf to be called rhythm and blues.

Elvis Presley in his earliest recordings combined the music of the country whites with rhythm and blues, and therefore probably deserves to be remembered as the first modern soul singer. As one contemporary soul musician has said, 'Country and western music is the music of the white masses. Rhythm and blues is the music of the Negro masses. Today soul music is becoming the music of all the people.'

Presley's reign was followed by a period of weak, derivative rock and roll, lasting from the late '50s through the early '60s, until the advent of the Beatles. The Beatles themselves, in the beginning, were not essentially different from the better white pop groups, such as Dion and the Belmonts. But the progress of their music toward greater complexity prepared the way for public acceptance of the candid lyrics and experimental techniques that have always been part of the Memphis sound.

The 'new freedom' enjoyed by the pop community was present on the 1920s' recordings of Furry Lewis and Cannon's Jug Stompers; it was there on the early Sun records of Elvis Presley and Howlin' Wolf; and it exists now on the Stax/Volt recordings of Sam and Dave, Otis Redding, and the Mar-Keys. The Mar-Keys, whose rhythm section records alone under the name Booker T. and the MGs (Memphis Group) work as the Stax/Volt house band. The Bar-Kays were hired and trained by Stax to be the road band, because the Mar-Keys, almost constantly busy recording with the company's artists, limit their public engagements to weekends and special occasions, such as Otis Redding's appearance last summer at the Monterey Pop Festival.

At the festival, that celebration of the psychedelic/freak-out/blow-your-mind pop culture, it was sometimes difficult to tell the musicians from the dervishes. The Who exploded smoke bombs and demolished their instruments onstage. Jimi Hendrix, having made a variety of obscene overtures to his guitar, set fire to it, smashed it, and threw the fragments at the audience. But, as one journalist put it, 'the most tumultuous reception of the Festival' went to Otis and the Mar-Keys, all of them conservatively dressed and groomed, succeeding with nothing more then musicianship and a sincere feeling for the roots of the blues.

These basic qualities have characterized Memphis music from the beginning, but they had never before raised it to such a position of leadership. In the next few months, Otis would be voted the world's leading male singer by the British pop music journal *Melody Maker*. The same poll would rate Steve Cropper, the Mar-Keys' guitarist, fifth among musicians. *Billboard* magazine named Booker T. and the MGs the top instrumental group of the year, as did the National Academy of Recording Arts and Sciences (NARAS), and the National Association of Radio Announcers, which also selected the MGs' hit single, 'Hip Hug-Her', as the year's best instrumental recording. NARAS voted Carla Thomas, a Stax vocalist, the most promising female artist of the year. The US armed forces in Vietnam named her their favorite singer.

Earlier in the year, Otis, the Mar-Keys, Sam and Dave, Carla Thomas and other Stax/Volt artists had completed a successful European tour, out of which came a series of powerful live recordings. The Beatles wanted to record an album at the Stax/Volt studios, but security problems made it impossible. The album was to have been produced by guitarist Cropper, who, according to George Harrison, is 'fahntahstic'.

The technical ability possessed by the Memphis musicians can be acquired, but their feeling of affinity with the music seems to be inbred. The Memphis soul sound grows out of a very special environment.

The Mar-Keys, and Booker T. and the MGs, are listed as honorary pall-bearers on the Programme, along with the Heat Waves, the Tornadoes and the Wild Cats. The Bar-Kays were protégés of the Mar-Keys, and the relationship was like that between older and younger brothers. Carl Cunningham had grown up at Stax, having been a fixture in the place since the day he came in off the street with his shoeshine kit. Stax bought him his first set of drums.

Now Booker and two of the MGs were sitting down front in a side pew, just behind the families of the dead Bar-Kays. I had seen none of them since the crash, and when the eulogy ended and the band began to play the recessional, I slipped down the aisle to where they were seated. Booker, at the end of the pew, saw me first. Booker has a college degree and drives a Buick. One gets the impression that he has never made any sort of mistake, not even an inappropriate gesture. As I approached, he extended his hand, the one nearest me and nearest his heart. We squeezed hands silently, and then he passed by, followed by Steve Cropper. Steve looks like a very young Gary Cooper. He produced the records of Otis Redding, who was to be buried the next day. Steve is an enigma. He shook my hand briefly but warmly and said, 'How's it going?' He is white, as is bassist Donald 'Duck' Dunn. Duck, short and plump, seems more of a good ole boy than anyone at Stax, but he is the only one who has been influenced by the hippies. When he came back from Monterey he let his red hair and beard grow, and now, with his little round belly and cherry-like lower lip, he looks like a blend of Sleepy, Happy and Dopey. We shook hands and walked together up the aisle. At the front door Duck reached into his pocket for a cigarette and said, in the manner of Southern country people who express their greatest sorrow as if it were an annoyance hardly worth mentioning, 'Been to one today, got to get up and go to another one tomorrow.'

Two weeks before, Otis Redding and Steve Cropper had been sitting on folding chairs, facing each other, in the dark cavern-like grey-and-pink studio at the Stax/Volt recording company. Stax is located in a converted movie theater in McLemore Street in Memphis, next to a housing project. The marquee is still there, with red plastic letters that spell 'Soulsville, USA'. The sign was changed once to read 'Stay in School', but the kids from the project threw rocks at it, so it was changed back again.

Otis Redding grew up in a housing project and left school at fifteen, but now when he came to the studio he was in a chauffeured Continental. Still, he had not forgotten who he was, where he had come from. The boys from the project knew this, and called Otis their main man. When he got out of the long white car and started across the sidewalk, he took the time to say, 'What's happening?' to the boys in bright pants, standing at the curb.

'I was born in Terrell County, Georgia, in a town called Dawson. After I was one year old we moved to Macon. I've stayed in Macon all my life.

First we lived in a project house. We lived there for about fourteen years. Then we had to move out to the outskirts of the city. I was going to Ballard Hudson High School, and I kind of got unlucky. My old man got sick, so I had to come out of school and try to find some kind of gig to help my mother. I got a job drilling water wells in Macon. It's a pretty easy job, it sounds hard but it's pretty easy. The hardest thing about it is when you have to change bits. They have big iron bits that weigh 250 pounds, and we'd have to change them, put them on the stem so we could drill – that was the hardest thing about it.

'I was almost sixteen at this time, just getting started singing. I used to play gigs and not make any money. I wasn't looking for money out of it then. I just wanted to be a singer.

'I listened to Little Richard and Chuck Berry a lot. Little Richard is actually the guy that inspired me to start singing. He was from Macon, too. My favorite song of his was "Heebie Jeebies". I remember it went, "My bad luck baby put the jinx on me." That song really inspired me to start singing, because I won a talent show with it. This was at the Hillview Springs Social Club – it's not there any more – I won the talent show for fifteen Sunday nights straight with that song, and then they wouldn't let me sing no more, wouldn't let me win that five dollars any more. So that . . . really inspired me.

'Later on I started singing with a band called Johnnie Jenkins and the Pinetoppers. We played little night-club and college dates, played at the University of Georgia and Georgia Tech. Then in 1960 I went to California to cut a record, "She's All Right". It was with Lute Records, the label the Hollywood Argyles were on. It didn't do anything. I came back to Macon and recorded a song I wrote called "Shout-bama-lama". A fellow named Mickey Murray had a hit off the song recently, but it didn't sell when I did it. It kind of got me off to a start, though, and then I came to Memphis in November 1961.

'Johnnie Jenkins was going to record, and I came with him. I had this song, "These Arms of Mine", and I asked if I could record it. The musicians had been working with Johnnie all day, and they didn't have but twenty minutes before they went home. But they let me record "These Arms of Mine". I give John Richbourg at WLAC in Nashville a lot of credit for breaking that record, because he played it and kept playing it after everybody else had forgot about it. It took nine months to sell, but it sold real good, and – and I've just been going ever since.'

Otis is playing a bright red dime-store guitar, strumming simple bar chords as he sings:

'Sitting' in the mornin' sun,
I'll be sittin' when the evenin' comes –'

The front of the guitar is cracked, as if someone has stepped on it. As he sings, Otis watches Steve, who nods and nods, bending almost double over his guitar, following Otis's chords with a shimmering electric response.

'Sittin' in the mornin' sun –'

'But I don't know why he's sittin',' Otis says, rocking back and forth as if he were still singing. 'He's just sittin'. Got to be more to it than that.' He pauses for a moment, shaking his head. Then he says, 'Wait. Wait a minute,' to Steve, who has been waiting patiently.

'I left my home in Georgia,
Headed for the Frisco bay –'

He pauses again, runs through the changes on his fractured guitar, then sings:

'I had nothing to live for,
Look like nothing's gonna come my way –'

'I write music everywhere, in motels, dressing rooms – I'll just play a song on the guitar and remember it. Then, usually, I come in the studio and Steve and I work it out. Sometimes I'll have just an idea, maybe for a bass line or some chord changes – maybe just a feeling – and we see what we can make out of it. We try to get everybody to groove together to the way a song feels.'

When Steve and Otis have the outlines of a song, they are joined by the rest of the MGs. Booker and Duck come in first, followed by drummer Al Jackson. Duck is telling Booker about his new stereo record player. 'I got me a nice one, man, with components. You can turn down one of the speakers and hear the words real clear. I been listening to the Beatles. Last night I played *Revolver*, and on "Yellow Submarine", you know what one of 'em says? I think it's Ringo, he says, "Paul is a queer." He really does, man. "Paul-is-a-queer", bigger'n shit.'

Booker sits at the piano, Duck gets his bass, which has been lying in its case on the worn red rug, and they begin to pick up the chord patterns from Steve and Otis. Al stands by, listening, his head tilted to one side. Duck asks him a question about counting the rhythm, and Steve looks up to say, 'In a minute he'll want to know what key we're in.' Duck sticks out his lower lip. He plays bass as fluently as if it were guitar, plucking the stout steel strings with his first two fingers, holding a cigarette between the other two. Booker sits erect, his right hand playing short punctuating notes, his left hand resting on his left knee. Otis is standing now, moving around the room, waving his arms as he conducts these men, his friends, who are there to serve him. He looks like a swimmer, moving effortlessly underwater. Then something happens, a connection is made in Al Jackson's mind, and he goes to the drums, baffled on two sides with wallboard. 'One, two,' he announces. 'One-two-three-four.' And for the first time they are all together, everyone has found the groove.

The Mar-Keys drift into the studio and sit on folding chairs behind another baffle, one wall of which has a small window. They listen, sucking on reeds, blowing into mouthpieces, as Otis and the rhythm section rehearse the song. When Steve calls, 'Hey, horns! Ready to record?' they are thrown into confusion, like a man waked in the middle of the night. They have nothing to record; there are, as yet, no horn parts. Steve and Otis develop them by singing to each other. 'De–de–da–dee,' Steve says. 'De–de–da–*daaah*,' says Otis, as if he were making a point in an argument. When they have the lines they want, they sing them to the Mar-Keys, starting with the verse part, which the Mar-Keys will forget while learning the parts for the chorus. After a few tries, however, they know both parts, and are ready to record. 'That feels good, man, let's cut it.'

During the rehearsal, one of the neighborhood kids, wearing blue jeans, an old cloth cap, and Congress basketball sneakers with one green and one yellow lace, has slipped into the studio. He sits behind a cluster of microphones, unnoticed by Otis, who passes directly by him on his way to the far corner of the room, where he strikes a wide, flat-footed stance facing a wallboard partition. Otis can hear but cannot see Al Jackson, holding one stick high as if it were a baton, counting four, then rolling his eyes toward the ceiling and starting to play.

After 'Dock of the Bay' was recorded, Steve and Booker added guitar and piano fills. The song boomed into the studio from a speaker high on the rear wall, and Booker played precise little bop, bop-bop figures, while Steve followed the vocal with a quivering blues line. The speaker went dead, then the engineer's voice came: 'Steve, one note's clashing.'

'Sure it is,' Steve tells him. 'It was written to clash.' Which, in point of fact, is not true, since nothing has been written down so far. 'Let's do it once more,' Steve says. 'We can do that bridge better. I can. First part's a groove.'

Inside the control room, Otis and Duck are talking. 'I wish you all *could* go with me to the Fillmore on Christmas,' Otis says.

'Man, so do I. I got some *good* fren's in San Francisco. We could rent one of them yachts.'

'I *got* one already. Three bedrooms, two baths, sumbitch is nice, man.'

'My ole lady's kill me,' Duck says.

When the recording is finished, Steve and Booker come into the control room, followed after a moment by the little boy in Congress sneakers. The tape is played back at a painful volume level. Steve and Otis stare deep into each other's eyes, carrying a kind of telepathic communication. The little boy, looking up at the speaker the music is coming from, says, 'I like that. That's good singin'. I'd like to be a singer myself.'

'If you got the feelin', you can sing soul. You just sing from the heart, and – there's no difference between nobody's heart.'

'That's it,' Otis says when the record ends.

'That's a mother,' says Booker.

Nearly every man at Stax dresses in a kind of uniform: narrow cuffless pants, Italian sweaters, shiny black slip-on shoes. But now, standing in the lobby, there is a tall young Negro man with a shaved head and full beard. He is wearing a Russian-style cap, a white pullover with green stripes, bright green pants, black nylon see-through socks with green ribs, and shiny green lizard shoes. In a paper sack he is carrying a few yards of imitation zebra material, which he intends to have made into a suit, to be worn with a white mohair overcoat. His name is Isaac Hayes. With his partner, David Porter, Hayes has written such hit songs as 'Soul Man' and 'Hold On, I'm Comin'' for Stax singers Sam and Dave. Porter, dressed less spectacularly in a beige sweater and corduroy Levis, is sitting at a desk in the foyer, not making a phone call.

'Come on,' says Hayes. 'Let's go next door and write. I'm hot.'

'I can't go nowhere till I take care of this chick.'

'Which chick is this?'

'You know which chick. You think I ought to call her?'

'What the hell do *I* care? I want to go write.'

'Well, she's occupying my mind.'

'Let's go, man, let's go. I'm hot.'

Porter shrugs and follows Hayes to an office next door where there are three folding chairs, a table littered with old issues of *Billboard* and *Hit Parader*, and a baby grand piano with names and initials carved into it. Hayes sits down at the piano and immediately begins to play church chords, slow and earnest. As he plays he hums, whistles, sings. Porter hums along. He has brought with him a black attaché case, and now he opens it, takes out a ball-point pen and several sheets of white typing paper, and begins writing rapidly. After about three minutes he stops, takes a pair of shades from his pocket, puts them on, throws back his head, and sings: 'You were raised from your cradle to be loved by only me –'

He begins the next line, then stops. 'Don't fit, I'm sorry.' He rewrites quickly and starts to sing again. Then Hayes stops playing, turns to Porter, and says, 'You know what? That ain't exactly killing me right there. Couldn't we get something going like: "You can run for so long, then you're tired, you can do so and so –"'

'Yeah,' Porter says. 'Got to get the message in.'

The door opens, and a small man wearing a black suit, black hat and black mustache comes in, leading a very thin girl in an orange wig. 'You got to hear this,' the man says, nodding toward the girl, who is visibly shaking. 'Are you nervous?' Hayes asks her. 'Just relax and enjoy yourself. Don't worry about us. We just two cats off the street.' The girl smiles weakly and sits down.

Porter is writing 'Forever Wouldn't Be Too Long' across the top of the page. Then,

> My love will last for you
> Till the morning sun finds no dew
> 'Cause I'm not tired of loving you –

He stops, puts down the pen, and yawns: 'Naw, I had something flowin' in my mind.'

'How long you be working?' the man in the black suit asks.

'How do I know?' Hayes says. 'We don't observe no time limits.'

'Yes,' says Porter, 'Hayes will probably be here all night. He don't observe no time limits.'

Hayes laughs, Porter stomps his right foot once, twice, Hayes strikes a chord, Porter closes his eyes and shouts: 'Cross yo' fingers.' He sings, bouncing, the chair squeaking, getting louder and faster, as if he were singing a song he had heard many times, and not one he was making up in an incredibly fluent improvisation. The girl smiles, then breaks into a giggle. When Porter stops, he groans. 'Man, we should've had a tape-recorder, I'll never get that feeling again. Damn! That's a hit! "Cross Yo' Fingers!" That's a hit title!' He turns back to his writing paper and begins to reconstruct the lyrics.

Hayes looks at the girl. 'So you're a singer?' She gulps and nods. The wig, high heels, a tightly belted raincoat only make her seem thinner and more frightened. 'Would you like to sing something for us?'

She swallows and nods again. They pick a song, a key (Hayes asks, 'Can you sing that high?'), and she begins to sing. At first her voice trembles, but as she sings it grows stronger. She shuts her eyes and moves softly back and forth, as her voice fills the room. Porter stops writing to watch her. She is so frail looking that one expects her to miss the high notes, but she hits them perfectly each time, as her voice swells, blossoms. Finally she stops, on a long, mellow, vibrating note, opens her eyes, and gulps.

Porter applauds. 'Wasn't-that-beautiful,' he says.

'Where did you go to high school?' Hayes asks the girl.

'Manassas.'

'Man – I went to Manassas. How'd you escape the clutches – When did you graduate?'

She looks away and does not answer.

'Haven't you graduated? How old are you?'

The girl mumbles something.

'What?'

'Seventeen,' she whispers.

'Seventeen? A voice like that at seventeen? Old Manassa. Damn, you can't beat it.' Hayes begins singing the Manassas Alma Mater song. Porter joins in. They get up and start to dance. Porter takes the girl's hands, and she joins him, singing and dancing. They all whirl around the room, as the man with the mustache closes his eyes and smiles.

Stax's only current rival in success is American Studios, on Thomas Street in North Memphis. American has recorded hits by artists as various as Wilson Pickett, the soul singer; Sandy Posey, the country-pop singer; King Curtis, the funky tenor player; Patti La Belle and the Blue Belles, a girls' singing group; Paul Revere and the Raiders, a white rock group; and the Box Tops, a band of Memphis teenagers whose first record, 'The Letter', outsold even the 'Ode to Billy Joe' to become the year's number one pop single.

There is no sign outside American, but no one seeing the long sweep of charcoal-gray exterior would expect the place to be anything but a recording studio. American was created in 1962, when a Stax engineer, Lincoln 'Chips' Moman, left and formed his own company with Donald Crews, a farmer from Lepanto, Arkansas. Moman, who started out as a house painter, has been described as 'the living embodiment of the Memphis Sound'. He has tattooed on his right arm the word 'Memphis', on his left a big red heart. Although he produces most of the records cut at American, he has a reputation for never being at the studio. Donald Crews, who has never produced anything that could not be grown in rows, is almost always there, and he greeted me as I came in. 'Used to be a receptionist around here,' he said, 'but she took to singin', and now we don't have one any more.' With a wave he indicated two gold records on the wall. They had been awarded to Sandy Posey, the ex-receptionist, for her first two recordings, 'Born a Woman' and 'Single Girl'.

I told Crews that I was writing about the current revival of the Memphis sound, and I wanted to understand it better. He told me that he wanted to, too. 'The music business is a mystery to me,' he said. 'We've had good luck with it – had more than twenty records in the charts this year – but I don't know how we done it. Only thing I've noticed is, down here we're all independents. All the Memphis studios have been Memphis owned. In New York, or even Nashville, they're spending Warner Brothers' money, or CBS's money, but when we produce a record down here, it comes out of our own pockets. That makes a little difference. Who you ought to talk to is one of our producers. I believe Dan Penn is in his office upstairs.'

I found Penn, a young blond man wearing blue jeans and bedroom slippers, at his desk playing a ukulele. He told me that he had come to Memphis from Vernon, Alabama, after working for a while as staff guitarist in a studio at Muscle Shoals, because he wanted to produce hit rock and roll records. One of his first was 'The Letter'.

'Dan,' I said, 'what is it about Memphis?'

'It ain't Memphis,' he said. 'It's the South.'

'Well, what is it about the South?'

'People down here don't let nobody tell them what to do.'

'But how does it happen that they know what to do?'

He twirled the ukulele by the neck, played two chords, and squinted at me across the desk. 'It ain't any explanation for it,' he said.

Downstairs, I was stopped by a little Negro boy wearing Congress basketball shoes. He looked even scruffier than the one who had been at Otis's session. 'You Wilson?' he asked.

'What?'

'You name Wilson?'

'No,' I said.

'I thought you was Wilson.'

'Sorry,' I said, and started out the door.

'Hey,' the little boy said, 'take this.' It was a small grey business card, with an address and the inscription, 'Charisma Project.'

I was outside before I thought to wonder where the boy had gotten the

card. It was a coincidence, because I was headed for the Charisma
Project, but he could have found the card at any of a dozen places. James
Dickinson, the Project's founder, has worked at nearly all the local
studios. Under his direction the Project has created theater, recordings,
and the annual Memphis Blues Festival, which in recent years has given
work to some of the finest old Delta musicians. Dickinson alone in
Memphis combines the talents of a musician, songwriter, producer and
historian. And it was Dickinson who gave me, at last, a definition of
soul.

The front office of the Charisma Project, located in an old white house
on Yates Road in East Memphis, is crowded with sound equipment and
antique instruments – a zither, a pump organ, a bass recorder, a drum
with one head bearing a hand-painted view of Venice. Dickinson said
that his involvement with Memphis music began after an incident which
took place when he was twelve years old. 'I was downtown with my
father. We came out of the Falls Building into Whiskey Chute, and there
it was – Will Shade, Memphis Willie B., Gus Cannon, and their jug
band, playing "Come On Down to My House, Honey, Ain't Nobody
Home But Me". I had had formal piano lessons since I was five years
old, and all of a sudden here was this awful music. I loved it instantly. I
had never known that music could make you feel so good. I started
seeking out soul musicians, learning what I could from them. My first
teachers were Piano Red, Butterfly Washington and, a little later, Mance
Lipscomb.' By his late teens Dickinson was fronting his own band,
sharing billing with such early giants of rock as Bo Diddley.

He spent several years playing organ, guitar and piano at recording
sessions in Memphis and Nashville, but since the formation of the
Charisma Project he has concentrated on events such as the Blues
Festival and on producing records. 'Memphis is the center of American
popular music,' Dickinson said. 'The market goes away at times, but it
always comes back, because music that is honest will last. You hear soul
music explained in terms of oppression and poverty, and that's certainly
part of it – no soul musician was born rich – but it's more than that. It's
being proud of your own people, what you come from. That's soul.'

> I'm a Soul Man
> Got what I got the hard way
> And I'll make it better each and every day
> I'm a Soul Man

The Porter and Hayes song had just become the nation's number one hit, earning a gold record for Sam and Dave, who would be singing it in Memphis on Saturday night. With Carla Thomas, they were to headline the twentieth edition of the Goodwill Revue, a charity music concert sponsored annually by radio station WDIA.

In 1948 WDIA became the nation's first radio station with programming exclusively for Negroes. WDIA described itself then as 'The Black Spot on Your Radio Dial – 50,000 Watts of Black Power'. Now the station has broadened its focus, and the word 'Soul' has been substituted for 'Black'.

From the beginning WDIA has been involved with projects to aid the community it serves. Proceeds from such events as the Goodwill Revue help to provide and maintain boys' clubs and recreational centers in poverty areas, Goodwill Homes for juvenile court wards, and a school for handicapped Negro children. Perhaps because of its strictly philanthropic nature – many artists perform without pay, and all WDIA employees, even those who perform, must buy a ticket – the Goodwill Revue has become a sort of love feast of the soul community.

In an annual message to the station's friends, the general manager said, 'In sponsoring these shows, WDIA is merely providing you with a means of expressing your own generosity.' But this year the station was also providing the audience with an opportunity to enjoy its own music at a time when there was more reason than ever to be proud of it.

In previous years, the first half of the program, traditionally reserved for gospel music, has been at least as important as the latter, secular half. But the audience has grown steadily younger and less interested in the old-time religion, and now the gospel groups play to a half-empty house. The Revue was being held in the Mid-South Coliseum, and a scanty crowd, sitting on wooden folding chairs, their feet resting on cardboard matting laid out over an ice-hockey floor, listened coldly to the Evening Doves, the Harmonizing Four, the Gabriel Airs and the

Spirit of Memphis Quartet. Only one group, the Jessy Dixon Singers, led by tall, handsome, white-gowned coloratura Adrea Lenox, created much enthusiasm, with rousing, stomping choruses of 'Long As I've Got King Jesus, Everything's All Right'.

During the intermission, nine Negro policemen who had been sitting behind the big, roll-out stage took their folding chairs and went out front, where they could hear better. The Coliseum was nearly filled to its capacity of 14,000 for the opening acts (dancers, minor singing groups) of the Revue's second half, but the audience did not come to life until the appearance of a great figure in the history of soul music – Muddy Waters. Wearing an iridescent aquamarine/sapphire silk suit, huge green-and-white jewelled cuff-links, and matching pinky diamonds, Muddy walked onstage, sang the opening bars of one of his earliest recordings, and was greeted by a roar of welcoming applause.

> I got a black cat bone, I got a mojo tooth
> I got a John the Conqueror root, I'm gone mess with you
> I'm gone make all you girls lead me by the hand
> Then the world will know I'm a hoochie coochie man

The loudspeaker system crackled and spluttered while Muddy was on, but everyone knew the words. During the performance of the next singer, Bobby Bland, the first four rows to the right of the stage began to sway together and to sing, or hum, along with the music, long-held notes in four-part harmony, even anticipating the chord changes. The four rows were filled with the Teen Town Singers, a group of 'about sixty talented youngsters' from high schools and junior colleges in the Memphis area, some of whom each year are given scholarships from Goodwill Revue revenues.

When Carla Thomas was eighteen, she was a Teen Town Singer. That year she wrote and recorded a song called 'Gee Whiz', which made the top ten on the popularity charts, and made her a star. She has seldom been without a hit since, and now as a mature artist she is known as the 'Queen of the Memphis Sound'.

Her material has matured with her, but her first song at the Revue went back to the beginning. She stepped into a pink spot, a big, beautiful, brown girl wearing a white brocade dress flowered with pearly sequins, and sang one of her early successes, 'B–A–B–Y'. The Teen Town Singers sang along on every note, inspired by the knowledge that any of them might become Royalty of Soul.

When Carla's father Rufus Thomas, a WDIA disc jockey with several record successes of his own (his hit, 'Walking the Dog', created one of the dance crazes of the '60s), joined her for a duet, the atmosphere was like that of a family reunion. Rufus and Carla sang, ''Cause I Love You', the first song Carla ever recorded, and the first hit, however small, to come out of the Stax/Volt studios. The audience loved it, clapping on the afterbeat, and they might not have allowed them to leave the stage if Sam and Dave had not been scheduled to appear next.

Sam Moore and Dave Prater, along with Carla and the other Stax artists, had taken soul around the world, and now they were bringing it back as number one, the world's most popular music. Their singing combines all the historical elements of soul music – gospel, blues, rhythm. 'They'll go to church on you in a minute,' a Stax executive has said, and it is an apt description of what they did at the Revue.

With their band, in black pants and turquoise balloon-sleeved shirts, strung out across the stage behind them, Sam and Dave, dressed all in white, singing, dancing, shouting, exhorting the congregation like old-fashioned preachers, created a sustained frenzy of near-religious ecstasy. 'Now doggone it, I just want you to do what you want to do.' 'Put your hands together and give me some old soul clapping.' 'Little louder.' 'Little bit louder.' 'Do you like it?' 'Well, do you like it?' 'I said, Do you like it?' 'Well, then, let me hear you say YEAH!'

It was nearly midnight when, with their coats off, shirts open and wringing with sweat, they got around to the song that seemed to say it all, for soul music's past, present and future.

> So honey, don't you fret
> 'Cause you ain't seen nothin' yet
> I'm a Soul Man

The next night, Otis Redding, the King of Memphis Soul Sound, and the Bar-Kays, who would have helped to shape its future, would be dead. It would be, as the Beatles called it, 'a bitter tragedy'. But the strength of soul music has always been the knowledge of how to survive tragedy. Remembering another great soul star, Otis Redding once said, 'I want to fill the silent vacuum that was created when Sam Cooke died.' Now Otis's death has left an even greater vacuum. But someone will come along to fill it. He may even be here already, walking down some street in Memphis, wearing Congress sneakers.

8

BLUES BOY

I had said goodbye to Otis Redding on Friday night, December 8, 1967; on Sunday night he died.

The 'Memphis Soul Sound' piece appeared in the last issue of the Saturday Evening Post *after 242 years of consecutive publication. I sought refuge from the tribulations of the above-ground press in doing a profile of B.B. King for* Eye *magazine, a Hearst imitation of* Rolling Stone.

I'd gotten the notion of writing about B.B. King while listening to the radio in my grandfather's kitchen in Waycross, Georgia, where I'd gone for the funeral of my grandmother. While I was there, Martin Luther King was killed, and when I returned to Memphis a few days later, there really were tanks in the streets.

The next morning, downtown to march in support of King, I saw Furry Lewis sitting on a cane-bottomed chair in front of his apartment building. Rioting had given Beale Street a bombed-out, shattered quality. Broken glass lay everywhere. Thousands of angry people were marching. 'What do you think about all this, Furry?' someone asked, and Furry said, 'I think it's all right.'

On the evening of June 5, 1968, less than two months after King's assassination, Christopher and I were packing to go to San Francisco for a B.B. King appearance at the Fillmore. As I walked into the bedroom fresh from a shower, clad in a towel, I glanced at the television set and saw the scene, a political rally at a hotel, break into a form of chaos that was by now all too familiar. 'They just shot another one,' I said as Christopher came into the room. The next night, B.B. King dedicated a song to the memory of Robert Kennedy.

The stage at the Fillmore Auditorium in San Francisco, where a jazz combo is now playing 'Up, Up, and Away', is littered with various items left there by the Mothers of Invention, among them a cabbage and an inflated plastic model of male genitals, many times normal size, done in an American-flag motif, the penis striped, the scrotum starred. The auditorium is about the size of your old high school basketball gym, and the Holy See, a light-show outfit, is throwing huge glops and swirls of Jello-colored light down the two side walls; across the back of the stage, stroboscopically alternating with flashes of a milk bottle, is a huge close-up of a woman's naked breasts. At the entrance to the auditorium is a long fluorescent tube glowing with black light, which you may stand beneath to see the color your skin will be three days after you are dead; but no one is looking at these things.

It is still early, not ten o'clock yet, but the Fillmore is crowded – there are hundreds of hippies, remnants of last summer's stories in *Time* and *Newsweek*; dozens of straight California teenagers, suntanned, clean, wearing white Levis; and here and there, looking a trifle grim, a grey-haired Mom and Dad. They are all standing together, shoulder to shoulder, facing the stage (except the ones who have already been overcome by the grass smoke in the air and are stretched out on the grimy floor – no seats at the Fillmore) all staring transfixed at the spot on the stage where, slender, red, slightly arched, the Guitar is waiting. It is not just another hippie guitar with a psychedelic paint job, like Elvin Bishop's or Eric Clapton's (Clapton had his painted by the people who did John Lennon's Rolls-Royce, not long after he had his hair made into an electric fright wig by Twiggy's hairdresser) – none of that fashionable jive – this is a big, bright red, Blues Guitar. In fact, as Clapton, Bishop, Mike Bloomfield or any other young guitarist will tell you, it is *the* Blues Guitar: a Dynamarker tape on the tailpiece reads, 'My Name Is Lucille – My Boss Is B. B. King'.

The B. B. King band, Sonny Freeman and the Unusuals, is now playing a Cannonball Adderley jazz tune. Sonny Freeman is the drummer, and the three Unusuals play organ, trumpet and tenor. They are all black, with natural haircuts, black on black jackets, and white turtlenecks. Each is wearing on a gold chain one of the large junk-jewelry amulets that seem, when worn today by black men, a kind of badge, or insignia. B.B. himself is backstage, upstairs in one of the Fillmore's shabby dressing-rooms, changing clothes. He arrived late, just as the preceding act, Booker T. and the MGs, was going off, and sent the band on to hold the crowd. The traffic was unexpectedly heavy coming over from Oakland, where he was staying at the Holiday Inn, and his driver did not know San Francisco, or B.B. would not have been late. He dislikes being late, and seldom has been in the last twenty years, during which time he has had more chances to be late, since he has had more work, than any other blues performer. He has sold more records than any other blues singer, living or dead, and he is one of a small, select group of artists – including Frank Sinatra and Duke Ellington – who are considered to be, at their distinctive specialties, the best in the world. The people in the business end of the business like to call B.B. 'The King of the Blues'. But occupying such a pre-eminent position is like being the Fastest Gun in the West: everybody wants to take you on.

When B.B. comes downstairs and starts toward the stage (the crowd parting before him, murmuring gentle respect), his smile seems a bit tight around the corners. The Fillmore's manager has announced that Albert King, whom the audience knows as another strong old Guitar Man, is on hand. Albert has flown up from LA for this one night, to play with B.B. and, as everyone including B.B. is aware, to try to cut him.

'A lot of people who have just recently started listening to blues', Elvin Bishop said later, 'hear B.B., Clapton, Bloomers, me, Albert, Buddy Guy, and think we're all very good. They don't realize that twenty years ago B.B. started the whole thing. He created the style of electric guitar playing that makes it possible for all of us to play the way we do.' But twenty years ago, B.B. knows, is not where it's at. Tonight is where it's at, at the Fillmore, with an amplifier that is not working properly, refusing to produce enough volume. The amplifier would not matter so much in a club, but at the Fillmore, ear-splitting volume is *de rigueur*. And in the wings is lurking funky old Albert, ready to come on and play blues which B.B. knows will never match his own for elegance, but which certainly do sound as if they came from the *bad* part of town.

Now, a couple of facts are worth recording. Albert has in recent months taken to calling his guitar 'Lucy', and has also been putting it out in interviews that he and B.B. are half-brothers, sons of the same father.

They are, in fact, not related. But B.B. does not deny Albert's story. 'It can't hurt me,' he has said, in private. 'And if it helps somebody else, then I'm happy to go along.'

So, best wishes to Albert, but still, B.B. does not intend for anyone, not even his *real* half-brother, to come onstage and cut him.

There is, potentially, a lot at stake. B.B. has spent the last twenty years playing night after night in ghetto saloons; the Fillmore is a possible threshold to stardom in the white pop-music world. It is a world which a fortunate few Negro performers fit into naturally; most of those who do not, spend their lives trying to adapt themselves to it. But not B.B. As he steps into a white spot, resplendent in a burgundy dinner jacket and a pleated nylon turtleneck of a remarkably rich, bright color, a kind of electric rose, he greets the cheering audience in his usual way: 'Thanks very much. We hope we can move you tonight, and if you like the blues, I think we can.' *If you like the blues* – because he is not going to play anything else.

His commitment to the blues is as deep as the involvement which he feels the blues has in his own and his people's history. He wants success as much as any man, but acceptance must come on his own terms. It is the one resolute bit of pride in the makeup of an extremely modest man. B.B. feels that if an audience will listen to his music, just give it a chance, they cannot help but respond to it. He occasionally begins sets by simply standing at the rear of the stage, playing several choruses without any introduction, letting the music speak for itself.

Tonight, however, there is not time for such a leisurely approach. Slipping the guitar's white neckband over his head, B.B. begins with one of his best-known songs, 'How Blue Can You Get'. He strikes the guitar strings very hard, forcing a response from the crippled amplifier (which he will not mention onstage, not wanting to be thought of as a man who makes excuses). B.B.'s style, derived in part from such earlier blues men as Elmore James and T-Bone Walker, also owes a great deal to certain musicians of the classic swing era, among them Charlie Christian, the guitarist with Benny Goodman, and tenor saxophonist Lester Young. It is based on long, sweeping lines of single notes (made possible by the development of the modern electric guitar, with its facility for sustaining tones) punctuated occasionally by crisp chords that are reminiscent of another early influence – the gypsy guitarist Django Reinhardt. But the jazz elements are fully amalgamated into the blues. B.B.'s music demonstrates that the blues can absorb influences from sophisticated sources without losing its basic directness and punch. 'How Blue Can You Get', a blues in the familiar accusation-lament pattern, builds from the opening lines, 'I've been downhearted, baby, ever since the day we met', to this pounding climax:

> I gave you a brand-new Ford
> You said, 'I want a Cadillac;'
> I bought you a ten–dollar dinner
> You said, 'Thanks for the snack;'
> I let you live in my penthouse
> You said it was just a shack;
> I gave you seven children
> And now you want to give them back.

The band provides a firm framework, underscoring B.B.'s vocal with obbligatos, punctuating the guitar phrases with concise horn figures. B.B.'s voice perfectly complements his guitar, his passionate falsetto tones equalling the guitar's quivering high notes. Amid shouts ('Tell it!') from the audience, the band goes directly into an uptempo instrumental, which is followed by 'Payin' the Cost to Be the Boss', B.B.'s latest single, at the moment number 33 on *Billboard*'s top 100, the only blues on the chart. The audience is cheering.

Then B.B. asks for a big hand to welcome onstage 'one of the great ones', Albert King. Albert, who is only slightly smaller than a gorilla, lumbers on, his guitar looking like a ukulele in his enormous hands. He plugs it into a huge Showman amplifier, and then he and B.B. start to play, swapping choruses in A. Albert's style, though based on B.B.'s, is much simpler and harsher; it is powerful, however, and a great crowd-pleaser. B.B.'s more relaxed and melodic lines are soon overpowered by Albert's longer, and louder, bent notes, which provoke steadily increasing howls from the audience.

As the contest continues, it begins to seem more and more like a prize fight: a fifteen-rounder, with B.B., the old champion, down by eight rounds. And then, just as it becomes clear that only something as decisive as a knockout can win, B.B., who had been standing idly at the side of the stage while Albert put down riff after driving riff, begins to hit the strings of his guitar, sweet Lucille, as hard as he can, one note at a time, playing a blues chorus so strong and high and wild that the audience, shocked, becomes silent; then he pauses, takes two steps forward to the mike, and sings: 'My brother's in Korea, baby, my sister's down in New Orleans'. The last part of the line is drowned out by the screams of the audience, who had forgotten, in the heat of the guitar duel, that B.B. is not only the master of modern blues guitar, he is also the founder of entire schools of blues singers. Albert must have forgotten this, too; and now the pain of miscalculation is as plain on his face as it had been on Sonny Liston's that night in Miami Beach when he miscalculated his chances against Cassius Clay. As he stands flat-footed, stunned, B.B. turns and, between phrases, finishes him off: 'Where the fiddle, boy?' he asks, and Albert meekly starts to play accompaniment. The horns fall in behind, and B.B. sings three inspired choruses of his most dramatic song, 'Sweet Sixteen', concluding in a stop-time passage in which he is literally overcome by the blues. 'I'm having so much trouble', he sings, 'Baby, I wonder' (Pow! from the horns) 'Yes, I wonder' (Pow!) 'Ohhh' (he sinks toward the floor, only to be lifted to his feet by the horn players for the last, blues-wailing, line): 'I wonder what in the world's gonna happen to me'.

When the noise from the audience subsides, B.B. characteristically ends the set standing aside, giving Albert the spotlight once more. He is a generous man, and his point has been made. No one at the Fillmore could doubt that B.B. is the King of the Blues.

He proves this wherever he goes, and these days he goes a lot of places. After twenty years as a ghetto artist, B.B. in the last eighteen or so months has gotten his first gigs in white rock-clubs, jazz festivals, network television, the movies and Europe. 'It's like riding in the front of the bus for the first time,' he says.

B.B.'s current headquarters is in Memphis, in a one-storey office building at the corner of Beale Street and Danny Thomas Boulevard. I visited him there not long ago. The neighborhood is Negro; Beale Street is shabby, its glittering days long past, and the reception desk in B.B.'s outer office looks out across the four lanes of Danny Thomas Boulevard, named for the comedian, at rows of dilapidated slum apartments. B.B.'s personal office is a large, wood-panelled room with a blue-green carpet, a long black leather couch, a table-topped desk, and a bookcase containing such titles as *The World Book Encyclopedia, High School Subjects Self-Taught, The World's Great Men of Color, Who's Who in America, Female Sexual Anatomy, I Paid My Dues* by Babs Gonzales, *Whitfield's Universal Rhyming Dictionary, Introduction to the Study of Musical Scales, The Key to Winning at Dice,* and *The Function of the Orgasm* by Wilfred Stekel. Sitting atop the bookcase were recorded foreign-language courses in French, German, Spanish and Japanese, as well as a Sears, Roebuck portable TV set. There were various tape-recorders and record-players strewn around the room, and stacks of old 78 r.p.m. recordings. Thumb-tacked to the wall behind the desk was a large sepia photograph of Martin Luther King. B.B., dressed in a gold-colored double-breasted sport coat, black slacks, shoes and socks, a pale yellow shirt, and a heavy silk yellow-gold tie, darker than the shirt but lighter than his coat, offered me a seat in a comfortable Danish wood chair. He sat behind the desk, and we talked for a while about contemporary popular music and how his blues relate to it.

'You take an artist like Aretha, say, or James Brown. When you hear them, you have to stop and pay attention. Their music gets you right away. Now, if I were singing or playing, maybe it wouldn't move you too much at first. But if you were a little blue about something, just anything at all, maybe you're a little downhearted, or it's just a gloomy kind of day, you'd start to listen, and by the time the song or record was over, you might say, "Hey, play that again."' He smiled. B.B. at forty-two is a handsome man, with skin the color of bitter chocolate, wavy black hair, a thin line of mustache and a lip goatee. 'At least, that's what I hope you'd say.

'I'd like to have the kind of appeal other artists have, but I've about come to the conclusion that I should just go on trying to make it my own way. I got started about 1948. My first record, the one that really got me off to a start, was one of Lowell Fulson's songs, "Three O'Clock Blues." From '52 to '56, it looked like I couldn't make a mistake, every record I did was big. But then rock came along, Elvis Presley and all that, and the trend changed. I couldn't ever play rock. I always put too much emphasis on the lyrics of a song and how it feels. Everybody else was just interested in movin', so I kind of got left behind. I had worked so long, and it all seemed to have been for nothing. I got sick and disgusted and even though I kept on playing, my heart wasn't really in it.

'But in the last few months, man, the white kids have come to my rescue. I mean guys like the Rolling Stones, Mike Bloomfield, Elvin Bishop, Al Kooper – all these guys come and sit in with me, and we have a ball together, and it means so much to me. And because they were interested in me, a lot of other people have got interested. After we played San Francisco last year, that led to our playing the Monterey Jazz Festival. KQED television taped four hour-long shows there, and we were in two of them. Since then we've done the Steve Allen show, the Newport Jazz Festival, I did two songs for Sidney Poitier's movie, *For Love of Ivy*, and we went on a concert tour of Europe. I had always been afraid to go to Europe, but over there, seems like everybody knew about us, even more than they do over here. It made us feel real good. I wouldn't want to live there, though. You hear so much about swinging Europe, but a lot of those towns close up at eleven o'clock. Now Paris, we didn't go to bed in Paris, so it reminded me a little of Atlanta, or maybe Memphis. We stayed up all night going from one club to another, so it was a little like home to me, but those other places, the concert would start at seven thirty, and be out by ten – nothing to do after that, everybody goes to bed. Still, they were great to us over there, we did radio shows all over, and a half-hour TV show in Cologne that was syndicated through central Europe. I want to reach as many people as possible. That's why I opened this office, so I can look after business a little more closely. I don't ever want to retire. As long as I'm a man, I want to play. But I want to be able to come back here, one or two days a week. It helps your mind, relaxes you, whether you get much rest or not. Tonight I'll probably go out with some friends and probably some broads. It's good to come back, and have a little fun.'

We made arrangements to meet the next afternoon to talk about B.B.'s early career. I thanked him and left him to his friends, presumably, and his broads. But the next day, when I arrived at B.B.'s office, he told me that he had not left the place since I saw him last. He had changed into a white shirt and black knit cardigan, and he was wearing a pair of horn-rimmed glasses. His desk was clearer of papers than it had been the day before, and he said that he had spent the night putting his business affairs in order, and had gone to bed on the couch at 5.00 a.m. B.B. does not have a home, and he had been too tired to go to a motel.

There was a bottle of Johnny Walker Scotch (red label) open on the desk; B.B. poured us both a drink in Coca-Cola paper cups. In a moment his secretary, Mrs. Polly Walker, a large, good-humored lady, came in, saw the Scotch, and said, 'Sure makes a good breakfast, don't it?' She was carrying a newspaper-wrapped plate with B.B.'s lunch, which consisted of corn bread, pig's knuckles, collard greens with a thick white onion slice, sweet potatoes, and black-eyed peas with fat bacon. 'Soul food,' B.B. said.

On the floor behind the desk a record-player was spinning old blues 78s; a Sonny Boy Williamson record had been playing as I came in. It was followed by an Elmore James record, and then one by Peetie Wheatstraw, the last of the stack. 'I like to carry old records with me on tape wherever I go,' B.B. said. 'It gives me something to listen to on the road, and I'm always trying to learn what I can from somebody that has come along before me.' We waited till the end of the Peetie Wheatstraw record before starting our talk.

'I was born between Indianola and a place called Itta Bena, down in the Mississippi Delta,' B.B. said. 'My mother and father named me Riley B. King. They separated when I was four, and my mother took me to Kilmichael, where we lived with some white people she worked for, Mr. and Mrs. Flake Cotledge. My mother passed when I was nine, and then I lived on with them by myself. I had a little house that I lived in, and I had my little chores, I milked ten cows in the morning, ten in the afternoon, and worked in the fields. I walked to school, three miles away in Elkhorn. The school had only one teacher, and he taught from what we called pre-primer through the twelfth grade, ninety-two pupils in one room.

'I had sung duets at church with my mother when I was five or so, and I can remember listening to records by Gene Autry, Blind Lemon

Jefferson, and Jimmie Rodgers, the old white blues singer, on my aunt's wind-up Victrola, and trying to play her pump organ – but it was at school that I got my first real encouragement to try and do something with music. We had heard of such gospel groups as the Golden Gate Quartet from Memphis, the Jubilaires and the Dixie Hummingbirds, because we'd go to town in Kilmichael every Saturday, and people would play their records on juke-boxes. Nobody had radios except the bosses. So we started a quartet called the Elkhorn Jubilee Boys, and our teacher let us sing at school plays and things.

'But the thing that may have influenced me most was that my uncle married the sister of a sanctified preacher. I would be there sometimes on Sundays, when the preacher, Reverend Archie Fair, would visit his sister. He was a guitar player, and he'd bring his guitar and lay it on the bed, and while they were having dinner, I'd be fooling with that guitar. When it seemed like I was really interested in it, he started showing me things, and I think I learned three chords, but those three have stayed with me through the years.

'I was about twelve then, working for fifteen dollars a month plus my room and board. Which today sounds like nothing, but then it meant a whole lot. One day I talked to my boss, Mr. Cotledge, and told him I'd found this little guitar, and I wanted it. So he got it for me, I think it cost ten or twelve dollars, and he took it out of my pay. It was a little red Stella, and I kept it for years, even after I went back to live with my father.

'I was fourteen when he found me. He had gotten married again and had other children that I didn't know, but when he found out where I was he came for me. They lived in Lexington, Mississippi, and he worked in a place called Kern, driving a tractor on a plantation. I was a little bit shy at first, because to me it was like a different family, even though it was my own father. But I learned to love them.

'I went to Ambrose Vocational High School in Lexington. I kept fooling with the guitar, but I was lonesome because I'd left the guys that I grew up with and had been singing and going to school with. I stayed there nearly three years, though, until I got married. Then I moved back down around Indianola and started another gospel group, called the St. John's Gospel Singers. We worked during the week and sang on weekends. I was picking cotton at 35 cents a hundred pounds, and I think the most I ever picked was 460 pounds in a day.

'On Saturdays and on the Sundays when the group wasn't working, I would take the money I made during the week and get a ticket for as far as I could go, and sing my way back. I'd go to different cities and sing and play on the street, like a blind man. People would see me with my guitar, and ask me to sing a song or two, and give me something for it. And sometimes I'd make more than I had working the whole week, or maybe even two weeks.

'Then the war started, and I was inducted into the Army. I went to Camp Shelby, right outside Hattiesburg. But I was a good tractor driver, and they deferred me out, said I was needed in civilian work. I was only in the Army a few months. It was while I was in, though, that I started singing blues. My people were very religious, and wouldn't have anything to do with blues singers, so when I got back I kind of kept the blues to myself and went on singing with the gospel group.

'As long as the war was on, I had to stay and work, but when it ended, I said, Fellows, now it's time for us to start to move. We had been singing on the radio, WGRM in Greenwood, WJPR in Greenville, and I thought we should start traveling and try to make a name for ourselves. They all had families, but I was married, too. Anyway, they said no. So one day I made up my mind, That is it, I'm leaving. I didn't have any money, so I started walking to Memphis. My father was already there, I think he came in '41, but we're both lazy about writing, and I didn't know where he was staying. So after I got to Memphis – I hitched a ride on a truck to the city limits – I started living with my cousin, Bukka White, the blues singer. He got me a job working with him at the Newberry Equipment Company, where they made underground gas tanks for service stations.

'Now, right across the river in West Memphis, Arkansas, Sonny Boy Williamson was doing a radio show, 'King Biscuit Time', every afternoon. I used to listen to it down in Indianola when we'd come out of the field for lunch. So, after I had been in Memphis for a while, I kind of got my nerve up, and I went over there. I went to the radio station, and talked to Sonny Boy, who was very nice to me, and let me sing a song on the air. It just happened that on this particular day Sonny Boy had two jobs: one where he had been working for a lady that had a, sort of a gambling house. (Things were pretty open in West Memphis at this time.) And he had another job that paid more money, and that was the one he wanted to go to, so he said, I'll tell you what I'm gonna do. I'm gonna let you take this job at Miss Annie's down on 16th Street. So I went down there, and the men liked me, and the ladies liked me, and Miss Annie liked me. I was about twenty-two years old then, pretty well grown up. Miss Annie said, "I want to hire you, but you can't help me get business unless you're on the radio, like Sonny Boy is. If you can get on the radio, I'll pay you twelve dollars a night and give you a room and board."

'I had a quarter at the time, just enough to get back to the bus depot in Memphis. When I got there, I started walking to radio station WDIA, out on Union Avenue, several miles away. It had been a country and western station, but now it was programmed for Negroes. While I was walking over there, it started raining. I was wearing my old army fatigue jacket with a frayed cotton-sack strap, and I had my guitar slung across my back. When I got to WDIA I looked like something out of a POW camp. Soaking wet, I walked to the door, and from inside Nat Williams, who was the first Negro disc jockey in the country, saw me standing there and came out and asked what he could do for me. I said: "I want to go on the radio." So he called the station manager, Mr. Bert Ferguson. Mr. Ferguson had been manager of WJPR in Greenville, and he remembered me, remembered the group and everything. He said, "We've got a new program coming on, and this might be just the thing we want." They were about to start a show advertising Peptikon, a patent tonic that was sort of a competitor to Hadacol, which Sonny Boy was advertising. They put me on the air, and I was on for ten minutes every day. They didn't pay me for it, but I could advertise where I was going to play, and I was paid for every Peptikon commercial I did. Never will forget, one of my jingles was, "Peptikon sure is good, you can get it anywhere in your neighborhood." They called me the Blues Boy from Beale Street. I never played on Beale Street, but that was what they called me. A lot of people, instead of calling me Blues Boy, would just say B.B. And the name stuck.

'I was still a very bad musician. My timing was so bad that in a twelve-bar blues I might play eight bars one time and fifteen the next. But there were a lot of really good musicians in Memphis, and I tried to learn from them. Guys like Hank Crawford, Herman Green, George Coleman, Phineas Newborn – they'd say, "Look, man, here's a pattern, play it like this." And I'd always listen. I got a little trio together, with Earl Forrest on drums and Johnny Ace on piano. We did fifteen minutes live every day. Then the station made me a disc jockey. I had the Sepia Swing Club from 3.00 to 3.55. Some scouts for Bullet Records heard me, and I did one session for them in Nashville. Then the Bihari brothers from California heard about me. They were starting a new label called RPM, and they came and recorded me. I made nine records before we recorded "Three O'Clock Blues" at the YMCA on portable equipment. It was number one on the R & B charts for eighteen weeks. And that was what made B.B. King.'

B.B. has now spent almost twenty years on the road, working an average of over three hundred nights yearly; and 'except for times when we were snowed in or something', he has missed only three performances. He has played big theaters, like the Regal and the Apollo, and one-room beer joints: 'places so hot the moisture in the air condensed on our instruments; so cold we'd have to thaw out our hands with matches before we could play; places with no bathroom, no dressing-room, we'd have to change clothes in the manager's office, or in the car. Once, a long time ago, there was a place in Twist, Arkansas. It was a little wood-frame juke joint with a pot-bellied stove. Cold winter night. Two men started fighting, knocked over the stove, and the whole place caught fire. There was a stampede out when the fire started. I ran, too, but I had left my guitar, so I went back into the burning building to get it. As soon as I got back outside, the roof caved in, and several people were killed. The next day we found out that the two men had been fighting over a girl named Lucille. So I named my guitar Lucille, to remind me never to do anything like that again.' But most of B.B.'s nights have been spent in one kind of place: a lower to middle-class Negro night club. There have been so many of them, like the Zebra Room in Oklahoma City, the Peacock Lounge in Atlanta, the Sir John in Miami, that they have become confused in B.B.'s mind.

In Memphis, B.B. has appeared regularly at the Club Paradise. The Paradise, originally a bowling alley, is in a long, low, brick building on East Georgia Street, across from the Clayborn Homes housing project, next door to a laundromat. In the lobby, on the night I was there, a big, jovial, Negro man in a grey uniform was frisking the customers for weapons. 'It's to everyone's advantage,' he said, smiling, patting me down. 'Look in that box, you'll see what I mean.' It was still early, but a cardboard box at his side already contained eighteen case knives, ranging from a gold dress knife to long pearl-handled frog-stickers, as well as a small dagger and an ice pick.

Inside, the Paradise is a huge, low-ceilinged room, wider than it is long, still very much like a bowling alley, except that where the lanes would be there are dozens of white-clothed tables. Wandering among the tables, carrying a Polaroid camera, was a young man who, if you gave him a dollar, would record your evening for posterity. Another man was selling B.B. King souvenir hats and cigarette-holders. The hats were of blue felt, with a Robin Hood peak and a white feather in the brim. B.B.'s name was written in silver spangles on both the hats and the foot-long holders. Above the crowd there were orange neon lights that made the ends of cigarettes burn pale green.

The bandstand was low, set against the rear wall, flanked by two large artificial potted palm trees. The eight-piece Club Paradise house band was there in its shirt-sleeves, accompanying a lady singer named Big Ella. She was short but very big, with light skin and long Indian-straight hair pulled back in a pony tail. She was wearing a peach-colored silk dress, her feet hidden by its dyed-to-match fur hemline. Around her neck was a tiny gold cross, and she was singing 'Funky Broadway'.

She did it well, in a good-humored, dirty way, and then it was done badly for the next two hours by a long string of preliminary acts, soul singers to left-handed guitar players. They played and sang other songs too, but each of them did 'Funky Broadway' at least once. Then Randy, the dancing, smiling, tambourine-shaking MC, introduced Junior Wells, who shared billing with B.B. Wells came out, a small, thin-shouldered man wearing tangerine pants and shirt and a gold medallion as big as an Aztec calendar, and did a nervous, jerky imitation of James Brown. He apologized to the audience for his last appearance, during which he had fallen off the bandstand on his head, and said that regardless of what people might say about his being too old to jump, if they would just let him warm up with a little of his blues, he'd show them that he could jump with the best. Then Wells, a good blues singer and a virtuoso harmonica player, dedicated a song to Sonny Boy Williamson, who taught him, and played a long, superbly mournful, harmonica solo. He sang a fast novelty blues ('Down in the barnyard pickin' up chips, 'long come a moo-cow shakin' her hips'), then resumed his attempt at the currently popular James-Brown-style soul singing for which his talent is ill suited.

The Paradise audience seemed not to care what he did. They ignored him, as they had ignored the other acts, and went on drinking, eating fried chicken or fish sandwiches from the Paradise kitchen, dancing in the roped-off areas to the side of the bandstand, buying souvenirs. After an intermission, the house band was replaced by Sonny Freeman and the Unusuals, who did 'Funky Broadway' and a lot more songs. The Paradise provides 'the finest in soulful entertainment' till 4.00 a.m., and the time has to be killed somehow.

It was nearly 1.00 when Randy, waving his tambourine, introduced 'the one and only' B.B. King. B.B., dressed in a blue dinner-jacket and soft blue turtleneck, strode onstage into a fast, wake-'em-up version of 'Every Day I Have the Blues', which succeeded moderately; there were shouts and applause. 'We're going to play some good drinkin' music tonight,' B.B. said. 'So if you like the blues, just stick around.'

B.B. is unfailingly gracious and friendly with audiences. 'I've worked hard myself,' he has said, 'and I know what it means to get off work, take a shower, and go out to blow off steam. I'm proud to be able to entertain a guy like that, and give him some of it, because I can remember.' Unfortunately, however, the audiences do not always reciprocate. There have been nights when B.B. has tried as hard as he could to move audiences composed of his own people, 'who should love the blues', and has received no response; and sometimes this has hurt him so badly that he has gone offstage and cried. 'I really do cry. It's emotionally upsetting to see people hate my music who should like it.'

The crowd at the Paradise did not hate B.B.'s music, but they did not sit still waiting for his next note. He got them with two almost brutally loud and funky choruses, and held them through one of his most old-fashioned songs, the one which begins, 'I don't want a soul, baby, hangin' around my house when I'm not at home'. But with the next song, a fast instrumental blues, people began to leave the tables for the dance floor (the girls hanging on to their purses), and the ones who remained seated seemed to realize that they were getting behind on their drinking and eating. The set became a Mexican standoff; B.B. managed to get the crowd's attention repeatedly – with a rocking 'You Upset Me, Baby', and a slow ballad, 'I Don't Even Know Your Name', which he reshaped into a blues – but was never able to keep it long enough to really get into anything. His last song had a jumping, almost Latin, feel.

As the morning dragged on there was another intermission, another tragic waste of Junior Wells's abilities, another long session with Sonny Freeman and his band, and as three o'clock rolled around, another set with B.B.

Second sets are traditionally best, but in the Club Paradise at three o'clock, the prospects did not look so good. Most of the tables were empty. Several of the rest were occupied by sharp-looking young men who had fallen asleep with their heads on the tables, their girlfriends sitting beside them, staring indignantly into space. There were older men asleep too, leaning back, thumbs hooked in pockets. Except for a few drunks wandering aimlessly around the room, the only people awake were the middle-aged ladies: plump, even heavy, sitting chin in hand before a glass of watery bourbon, a B. B. souvenir hat tilted jauntily over a no longer pretty face. Some of them had been listening to B. B. since the days when he played barefoot in the back yard of the Streamlite Café, too young to go inside.

B. B.'s first song, 'Help the Poor', was relaxed and swinging, but not inspired. When B. B. is playing his best, every nuance can be seen in his face, but now his expression was bland and detached. He played a slow blues, followed by 'Heartbreak' done so fast it was almost, but not quite, rock and roll, and cut the tempo back to do a fervent, gospel-tinged 'Need Your Love So Bad'. The audience's response to all this was, at best, sluggish. 'You know we're working hard up here,' B. B. said. 'Let us hear you put your hands together.'

A drunk had moved across the room with short, wobbling steps until he was standing directly in front of B.B., swaying dangerously, as if he might collapse onto the bandstand. After a few uncertain moments he drifted away, but was soon replaced by another, more extraverted drunk, who walked up and grabbed B.B.'s shoulder as he turned to call the next tune. The man handed B.B. a slip of paper with a request written on it. B.B. read the paper, then said, 'Yes, sir, I've been payin' the cost for many moons to be the boss.' He played 'Rock Me, Baby', in a loud, flat tone, as if the sound of his guitar were a wall he could hide behind.

When the song ground to a halt, B.B. stood for a minute or two looking down, as if he were alone in the room. He started playing what seemed to be random phrases and aimless runs of notes, banging the guitar strings like someone curious to hear what noises they would make, while behind him the organ played long, eerie chords. His eyes were closed, and he was shaking his head slowly, side to side. He paused, and then struck one note, held it, twisted it, let it dwindle to a whisper that suddenly became a blurred, roaring chord. 'Now here it is three o'clock in the morning', he sang, 'can't even close my eyes.' The middle-aged ladies squealed. 'I can't find my baby, and I can't be satisfied.' Then he played another single note, his face drawing into a squint as he bent the note into a phrase, tied the phrase into a knot, a nearly unbearable contortion of sound, building in volume and intensity until it became almost painful, ascending slowly toward the note of resolution. And as B.B. hit the high, pure, final note, he smiled, eyes still closed, a wide pink smile of delight and satisfaction. One of the ladies stood on her chair, clapping, her B.B. hat jiggling on her head.

'I just want to make people happy,' B.B. told me, that day as I was leaving his office. 'Black, white, red or green. There are a lot of places I want to go and things I want to do, but if I can just go on playing my music for the people, that's enough. It's all I live for.'

9

THE MEMPHIS DÉBUT OF THE JANIS JOPLIN REVUE

Having written about Furry Lewis, Elvis Presley, Otis Redding and B. B. King, I slowly awoke to the realization that I was describing the progress of something, a kind of sexy, subversive music. At the time, the only menace akin to that which emanated from Presley's early appearances belonged to the Rolling Stones, whom I'd seen in 1965 at the Memphis Mid-South Coliseum, where they did a short but intense set. A bit fearful of writing about them, because they were young, rich and white, I was reassured by Jim Dickinson: 'They bound to be good old boys.' In September of 1968, I went, again for Eye, *to London, chancing to arrive the day before Brian Jones's last drug trial. I spent nearly a month with the Stones, who accepted me because like them I was a freak behind music.*

A couple of people close to the Rolling Stones − publicist Leslie Perrin and the indefinable Jo Bergman − had suggested I write a book about the band, but I was far too serious and high-minded. Once I finished the Eye *piece, however, I decided there was or would be more to the story, and began writing what seemed an endless series of basic-English letters to the Stones requesting a document giving me their co-operation. While waiting for a reply that I would finally have to write myself, I did a few pieces for* Rolling Stone, *the first about Janis Joplin.*

'Janis,' I said, 'I'm going to write a little something for *Rolling Stone* about your new band's début in Memphis, and −'

'*Rolling Stone*? Those shits! They don't know what's happening, they're out in San Francisco feeling smug because they think they're where it's at. This is where it's at, Memphis!'

People say that Janis Joplin is the best white female blues singer of our time, but what other white girl sings blues? The remarkable thing about Janis Joplin is that she is a real blues singer, in 'our' time, when imitations are good enough for most people. She has, like all true originals, a strong sense of tradition, and Memphis is the blues singers' La Scala. (Aretha Franklin cuts in New York, but with musicians flown up from Memphis.)

So it was important to Janis Joplin, the only outside act invited to the Second Annual Stax/Volt Yuletide Thing, that she do well. And did she? Backstage after it was over, she said, 'At least they didn't throw things.'

The Yuletide Thing was scheduled for Saturday night, December 21, at the Memphis Mid–South Coliseum. Miss Joplin had left Big Brother and the Holding Company and was rehearsing with a new group of musicians, but not until three days before, when Mike Bloomfield came from San Francisco, acting on orders from manager Albert Grossman, to help with arrangements, did the Janis Joplin Revue achieve any sort of unity. They rehearsed on Wednesday and Thursday in San Francisco, and on Friday afternoon in the B studio at the Stax/Volt Recording Company in Memphis. They had come to Memphis a day early to attend a Christmas cocktail party at the home of Stax president, Jim Stewart.

It was the smallest and most prestigious Memphis Sound party of recent years, a Stax family affair with just a few carefully selected guests from outside. There were tables laden with great bowls of fat pink shrimp, chafing dishes with bacon-wrapped chicken livers, all sorts of sandwiches dyed red and green for Christmas, and plate after plate of olives, candies and other trifles. In one corner a large Christmas tree was standing, its colored lights blinking off and on. Some of the guests were sitting on the leopard-print couches, some on the thick red rug. Isaac Hayes and David Porter, authors of 'Soul Man', 'Hold On, I'm Comin'', and other Sam and Dave hits, were there, Hayes dressed all in black, Porter in red. Steve Cropper was wearing a black cut-velvet suit and green ruffled shirt. Duck Dunn refused the bar's fine whiskey and drank Budweiser. 'I can drink this till nine in the mornin', and I can't that other,' Duck explained. 'Course, I'll feel this till nine tomorrow night.'

Into this pleasant scene Janis and her band descended, making hardly a ripple. One of the outside guests, somebody's wife, did discover, not who Janis was, but that she was somebody, and asked for an autograph. 'It's for my son, Barney,' the woman said. 'That's B - a - r - n - e - y.' Janis signed a slip of paper and gave it to the woman, who was not satisfied. 'No,' she said. 'It's got to say, "To Barney", B - a - r - n - e - y.' Janis took the paper and started to write. 'That's B - a - r - n - e - y, Barney,' the woman said.

'I know', Janis told her, 'how to spell Barney.'

Memphis had not known what to expect of Janis Joplin, this 'hippie queen'. There was some fear that she might turn out to be blatantly unprofessional, as so many people are in contemporary popular music. It was a relief, then, backstage the next night at the Yuletide Thing, to see that she was wearing make-up and a cerise jersey pants-suit with a burst of cerise feathers at the cuffs. She looked like a girl who was ready to go out and entertain the people.

Bloomfield spent the day working with the band, and Grossman himself was on hand to see how things went. They might have gone beautifully. The Janis Joplin Revue was set to appear after all the other acts except Johnny Taylor, a minor Stax artist whose recent million-selling single, 'Who's Making Love', earned him the closing spot.

I was in a corridor backstage, talking with Bloomfield, Cropper and Dunn, when the first act, the re-formed Bar-Kays, came out of their dressing-room wearing zebra-striped flannel jumpsuits. Bloomfield's eyes widened. It was the first sign of the cultural gap that was to increase as the evening progressed.

The thing is, a stage act in Memphis, Tennessee (or, as the famous Stax marquee puts it, 'Soulsville, U.S.A.') is not the same as a stage act in San Francisco, Los Angeles or New York. These days a lot of people think if a fellow comes on stage wearing black vinyl pants, screams that he wants to fuck his poor old mother, then collapses, that's a stage act; but in Memphis, if you can't do the Sideways Pony, you just don't have a stage act.

The Bar-Kays did the Pony, they boogalooed, stomped, hunched, screwed each other with guitars, did the 1957 Royales act at triple the 1957 speed, were loud, lewd, and a general delight. After three songs they were followed by Albert King and his funky blues, but they came back, now dressed all in red, to boogaloo behind the Mad Lads, William Bell, Judy Clay, and Rufus and Carla Thomas. Rufus, 'The Dog,' and his beautiful daughter, who was wearing a rhinestone-encrusted turquoise gown, sang 'The Night Time is the Right Time', and did a dance that stopped just short of incest. Members of Janis Joplin's Revue watched from the wings, shaking their heads.

After a brief intermission, Booker T. and the MGs appeared and played, as they always do, impeccably. They accompanied the next act, the Staple Singers, who did 'For What It's Worth', and a very moving 'Ghetto'. Then Eddie Floyd, who is not, by a long shot, Otis Redding, but is still a very good soul singer, came on and got the biggest audience response of the night. He opened with 'Knock on Wood', and during his next song, 'I Never Found a Girl', had dozens of girls coming down to the stage to touch his hand. If Janis had come on directly after he left the stage, she might have got the kind of reception she wanted. But that's not the way it happened.

When the Bar-Kays jump around in their zebra suits, and Carla Thomas does the Dog with her daddy, they are hamboning; but then so is Frank Zappa when he belches into the microphone at the Fillmore. The crowd at the Fillmore, East or West, expects to see a band shove equipment around the stage for ten minutes or more, 'getting set up' – not being show-biz, in that context, is accepted show-biz practice.

But in Memphis, this is not what the people come to see. The warmth that Eddie Floyd's appearance had generated was dispelled while Janis's band put their instruments in order. She planned to do three songs and then encore with her specialties, 'Ball and Chain', and 'Piece of My Heart'. Obviously she did not realize that about half the audience, the black people, had no idea who Janis Joplin was, and the other half, mostly teenaged whites, had never heard her do anything except her two best-known songs.

She opened with 'Raise Your Hand', an Eddie Floyd song, and followed it with the Bee-Gees' 'To Love Somebody'. She sang well, in full control of her powerful voice.

The band was not together, but they all seemed to be excellent musicians, and one could predict that, given sufficient rehearsal time, they would make a great back-up band for Janis, if they did not have one basic flaw – none of them plays blues. They come from the Electric Flag, the Paupers, the Chicago Loop, and one is left over from Big Brother and the Holding Company. They can all play, but not blues, and who is there to teach them? Certainly not Mike Bloomfield, whose music, like Paul Butterfield's, is a pastiche of incompatible styles. One Memphis musician suggested that three months at Hernando's Hideaway, the Club Paradise or any of the Memphis night-spots where they frisk you before you go in might give them an inkling as to what the blues is about. Failing that, Janis might start over with some musicians who know already how to do the Sideways Pony.

When she finished her third song and started to leave the stage, there was almost no applause, and so, of course, no encore. A few people went backstage, where everyone from the Revue was in shock, staring at the walls, and tried to tell Janis that she was not to blame for what happened. She had sung well, and the rest had been beyond her control. But she wasn't having any of it, and soon she went back to her room at the Lorraine Motel, where B. B. King and a lot of other blues singers had spent unhappy nights before her.

THE GILDED PALACE OF SIN:
THE FLYING BURRITO BROTHERS

No one told me before the Joplin article came out that she had taken one look at the Lorraine Motel, where Martin Luther King had been shot — Stax had reserved for her a soulful and political room there — and hauled ass to the Rivermont, a high-rise hotel on the bluff more congenial than a black ghetto flop, however historic, to a middle-class white girl from Texas. I thought I'd been très sympathetic to the problems she faced in Memphis, but she didn't like people writing about her problems and died, so I hear, bearing me ill will. Can't please everyone.

The record played most often around the Rolling Stones' office in the fall of 1968 was the Byrds' Sweetheart of the Rodeo. Gram Parsons, a young man I'd never met from my birthplace, Waycross, seemed to have turned the well known folk-rock outfit into a kind of country-rock band.

In spring of 1969, Parsons, who'd left the South Africa-bound Byrds when the Stones told him nobody played there because of its apartheid policies, released an album with his new band, the Flying Burrito Brothers. I was still waiting for a letter from the Stones, and it was pleasant to have the chance to write about something close to home.

Gram Parsons, the head Burrito, stares out of the cover photograph of *The Gilded Palace of Sin* album wearing a suit made by Nudie of Hollywood, who specializes in the outfits with spangled cactuses and embroidered musical notes worn by such traditional country and western performers as Porter Wagoner and Buck Owens. But Parsons's suit is decorated with green marijuana branches, and there are naked ladies on the lapels.

Wonderful as this is, it seems even more of a wonder when you know that Parsons comes from Waycross, Georgia, especially if you happen to know what Waycross, Georgia, is like.

Jerry Wexler of Atlantic Records, sitting around his Long Island house one night with Bert Berns, trying to come up with a real down-home song for Wilson Pickett, suggested that they write one about Waycross. 'I figured there couldn't be any more down-home place than that,' Wexler explained later. 'Waycross, Georgia, would have to be the asshole of the world.'

Waycross, population approximately 20,000, is located 60 miles from the Atlantic Ocean, 36 miles from the Florida state line, about 15 minutes via alligator from the Okefinokee Swamp, close to the heart of Wiregrass, Georgia, a territory which may well be the deepest part of the Deep South. Memphis, Birmingham, Atlanta are Southern; but they are nothing like Waycross. People around Waycross think of Atlanta the way you and I think of the moon – a place which, though remote, might possibly be visited someday by us or our children.

Wiregrass, the territory which includes Waycross, encompasses nearly 10,000 square miles of pine-and-palmetto forest, grading almost imperceptibly into the Okefinokee, in Seminole the Land of the Trembling Earth. The forest floor, carpeted with sweet-smelling dry brown pine needles, laced with creeks and rivers, becomes more unsteady under your feet, until another step, onto land that looks the same as the place where you are standing, will take you too far, the ground gives way, and you are sucked down into the rich peaty swamp, which, though it supports great pines, will not support you. Many men have walked into the Okefinokee, where even the pretty little plants eat meat, never to be heard from again. There is more water than land, and the huge cypresses towering overhead, form the walls of corridors through the brown water, which is clear in the hand and good to drink.

The people of Wiregrass – dealers in, among other things, pine trees, tobacco, peanuts, sugar cane, moonshine whiskey, trucks, tractors, new and used cars, Bibles, groceries, dry goods and hardware; in isolate farms on swamp islands; in turpentine camps deep in the woods, like Dickerson's Crossing, Mexico, the Eight-mile Still; in unincorporated settlements like Sandy Bottom, Headlight, Thelma; in towns like Blackshear, Folkston, Waycross; from banker to bootlegger – all share two curses: hard work and Jesus. Wiregrass must be one of the last places in the world where the Puritan ethic still obtains, making an almost unrelievedly strenuous way of life even more grim. Before smoking tobacco was known to be a health hazard, it was frowned upon by many people there, simply because it gives pleasure. Although Waycross has the Okefinokee Regional Library and once had a world movie première (a swamp picture called *Lure of the Wilderness* starring Jeffrey Hunter), culture exists there only in the anthropological sense. The social life of the community has two centers, with, in general, mutually exclusive clientele: churches and roadhouses. There is violence, illicit sex, drunkenness – in a word, sin – in south Georgia, but they have not become behavioral standards. The ideal still is to be a hard-working, God-fearing, man or woman, boy or girl.

So here we have Gram Parsons, from Waycross, Georgia, with shoulder-length hair, and dope and pussy on his jacket. Parsons's first record, as far as I know, was *Safe at Home* by his earlier group, the International Submarine Band. The album, 'a Lee Hazlewood Production, produced by Suzi Jane Hokom', included songs associated with Johnny Cash, Merle Haggard, Big Boy Crudup and Elvis Presley, as well as a couple of country classics ('Miller's Cave' and 'Satisfied Mind') and four Parsons originals. The music was fairly straight country and western, with piano, bass, drums, rhythm, lead and steel guitars. It was an honest, pleasant, but not a strongly exciting album.

Next, Parsons joined the Byrds, staying with them long enough to make *Sweetheart of the Rodeo*, the country album recorded in Nashville, which, though not a complete success, was one of that year's best records. When Parsons left the Byrds he formed the Flying Burrito Brothers.

The Burritos' first album, with roughly the same instrumentation as Parsons's two previous ones, has perhaps less surface charm than

Sweetheart, but is the best, most personal Parsons has yet done. The *Gilded Palace of Sin,* unlike *Safe at Home* and *Sweetheart of the Rodeo,* is about life in the big city, where even a pretty girl, as Parsons warns on the first track, can be a 'devil in disguise'. 'Sin City', the second track, predicts destruction for the city, 'filled with sin', where the slickers in their 'green mohair suits' advise you to 'take it home right away, you've got three years to pay'. But, the song cautions, 'Satan is waiting his turn':

> It seems like this whole town's insane
> on the 31st floor
> A gold-plated door
> Won't keep out the Lord's burning rain

The two following songs, 'Do Right Woman' and 'Dark End of the Street' by Dan Penn of Memphis, the only ones on the album which Parsons had no hand in writing, are given new depth of meaning by their juxtaposition with what preceded them. 'Do Right Woman' is especially outstanding: though obviously quite different, it is in no way inferior to the original Aretha Franklin recording. 'My Uncle', the last track on side one, does honor to the great tradition, equal to the tradition of Southern war heroism, of hillbilly draft-dodging. It is delightfully good-humored 'protest' in the best, healthiest, most direct and personal sense:

> I'm heading for the nearest foreign border
> Vancouver may be just my kind of town
> 'Cause I don't need the kind of law and order
> That tends to keep a good man underground

The second side opens with a return to a mood like that of 'Sin City', except that the emphasis is on how out of place 'this boy' feels, very much as in the old gospel song, 'This World Is Not My Home'. 'Wheels' ends with a plea to 'take this boy away'. In 'Juanita', the next song, 'an angel . . . just seventeen, with a dirty old gown and a conscience so clean' finds him abandoned and alone 'in a cold dirty room . . . with a bottle of wine and some pills off the shelf' and brings back 'the life that I once threw away'.

'Hot Burrito No. 1', which follows, is perhaps the best song Parsons has yet written, and he has written some very good ones. A rather old-fashioned rock and roll song, it might have been recorded in 1956 by the Platters, except for one line, the most effective on the album, 'I'm your toy – I'm your old boy', which no one but Parsons could sing so movingly. 'Hot Burrito No. 2', an uptempo secular love song, breaks the gospel-honkytonk taboo, which is just as strong as the black blues-in-church taboo, when Parsons sings, 'You better love me – Jesus Christ!'

The next-to-last song is the only repeat from an earlier Parsons album. 'Do You Know How It Feels To Be Lonesome' from, ironically, *Safe at Home,* is the statement of a young man who must feel at home nowhere, not in the big city or in Waycross, Georgia. 'Did you ever try to smile at some people,' he says, 'and all they ever seem to do is stare?'

'Hippie Boy', the final song, an updated version of Red Foley's 'Peace in the Valley', is recited by Chris Hillman, possibly because his accent is less countrified than Parsons's. It tells a story with a moral: 'It's the same for any hillbilly, bum, or hippie on the street . . . Never carry more than you can eat.' The album's ending somehow summons up a vision of hillbillies and hippies, like lions and lambs, together in peace and love instead of sin and violence, getting stoned together, singing oldtime favorite songs. The album closes with a fine, fractured chorus of 'Peace in the Valley', with whistles, shouts and rattling tambourines.

Perhaps Parsons, coming from the country, feels more deeply than most the strangeness and hostility of the modern world, but he speaks to and for all of us. Gram Parsons is a good old boy.

11

BLUES FOR THE RED MAN

In October 1969 the Stones, with new member Mick Taylor, came over for an American tour. I flew to Los Angeles to see them, met Gram Parsons, and as Max Shulman said, 'Bang! Bang! Bang! Bang! Four shots ripped into my groin, and I was off on one of the strangest adventures of my life.' At the end of the tour I went to England with the Stones, returning months later to Memphis, where I was arrested on drug charges. (My mistake was having a few hemp plants in my vegetable garden.) Then I went to the Ozarks, holed up in a cabin, and meditated on music and death while in the world outside the most precious heroes kept falling.

A few of the very bravest men in the tribe constitute a small group known as the 'Contraries'. As the name suggests, these men always do the opposite of what is said; i.e., they say 'no' when they mean 'yes', approach when asked to go away, and so on. In battle, they are possessed of a specal magic, a 'thunder bow', which causes them to accomplish acts of extraordinary bravery. One is called to the society of Contraries by a special vision, and thereafter he eats alone from special dishes, lives in a red lodge, and associates with ordinary people infrequently and in a distant manner.

Elman R. Service,
A Profile of Primitive Culture

He wanted to be buried under a tree beside the White River in Arkansas, where he loved to camp and fish and get high and turn bright red, but you almost have to be born there to be buried there, and Freeman was born in Memphis. 'They don't call it Bluff City for nothing,' Freeman said.

Freeman (C.F. Freeman III, 31, Musician) boasted that no one could say Freeman I, II or III had never been drunk. When his father died drunk in East Memphis, trying to see how fast his car would take Dead Man's Curve, Freeman was one month away from entering the world.

Freeman's mother was a waitress. She married again, a man named Red, a Baptist who worked for the Firestone Tire & Rubber Company. Red and Freeman found little to share.

Freeman's health was delicate. He suffered from rheumatic fever, asthma, nervous complaints, like Brian Jones, like many another gifted child. Doctors prescribed medicinal substances. Freeman discovered that he liked taking medicinal substances. He took as many medicinal substances as he could for as long as he lived.

Much of Freeman's early cultural life, the life of the spirit, centered around his neighborhood movie theater, the Normal on Highland Street. There he was a member of the Roy Rogers Fan Club and later an usher, riding to work on his moped, wearing a motorcycle jacket. His local heroes were Speed Franklin, Griff Rimmer and Donny Creel, zip-gun hoods, but his idol was Lash LaRue. Watching Lash LaRue, Freeman imagined himself turning renegade to ride the owlhoot trail, to be revealed only in the end as the hero. When Lash LaRue came to play the rodeo at the Memphis Mid-South Fair, Freeman planned to join him and go on the road. Before Freeman could apply, LaRue was arrested by the Memphis police for possession of stolen goods, namely typewriters and sewing machines.

When Freeman was an adolescent, Memphis was a dry town, run by the fundamentalist religious groups and segregationists who represented just what Freeman was interested in rebelling against. But across the river, in the awful Arkansas rice-and-cotton-field bottoms, in West Memphis, the most dismal flat truckstop town in the country, in what looked as if it might be the last night club in the world, the Plantation Inn, Freeman and every other punk alive were doing what the neon sign said, Having Fun With Morris.

Lash LaRue, 1973 (© William Eggleston)

The bouncer at the Plantation Inn was a beefy Golden Gloves boxer named Raymond Vega. At his best, wearing gloves, Vega would run out of gas in the third round. At his worst, tight and in a cummerbund, he could be knocked across the dance floor and into the tables by a slender youth in a short-sleeved blue button–down collar shirt. No one kept order at the Plantation Inn, and the clientele included killers. Dago Tiller, for example, had literally snatched a woman bald-headed. Her picture was in the newspapers.

Freeman survived one of the frequent Plantation Inn brawls by standing in the middle of the dance floor kissing a girl named Bobbie Sue until the battle was over. Bobbie Sue and Freeman both went to Messick High School, in the same neighborhood (one-family houses, small lawns) where Freeman had ridden his moped. Sometime, years before, Freeman had been given a gun and a guitar, possibly by an uncle on his father's side of the family, and at Messick he started a band, inspired by the Largoes, the band at the Plantation Inn. The Largoes were Guitar Friday, Blind Oscar on organ, two tenor saxes, a bass player and a drummer named Big Bell. The singer was called Wild Charlie or Tennessee Turner and wore heavy eye make-up and dark red nail polish.

Freeman's band included Duck Dunn, Don Nix and Steve Cropper, who would later play with practically all the people in the world who were musicians and many who were not. They had come together from two groups, both of whom had played the Messick High School assemblies. Calling themselves the Royal Spades, they began to find work at the St. Michael's and Little Flower C.Y.O. dances and at roadhouses like the Starlight Supper Club, Neal's Hideaway and Curry's Club Tropicana. Steve Cropper played rhythm guitar, wearing a harmonica on a wire rack around his neck, singing Jimmy Reed songs. This was in 1958 or 1959. At the Rebel Room in Osceola, Arkansas, the stage was separated from the customers by a screen of chicken-wire. The band discovered the reason in the middle of their second set, when the fists, bottles and chairs began to fly. Freeman was happy that night. He had a band that played no better than the Largoes in an even worse place than the Plantation Inn.

The tenor sax player in the band was Charles 'Packy' Axton, whose mother Estelle owned with her brother Jim Stewart a recording studio called Satellite Records, later to be renamed Stax, from the first two initials of their names. The availability of the studio, in an old movie-house on a black street (at first it was behind a Dairy Queen, and Packy had to sell hamburgers between takes, but never mind), led the band to try making a record and to change their name, from the marquee that was still on the building, to the Mar-Keys. They tried and failed to cut several songs, among them one called 'Last Night'. Finally 'Last Night' was recorded, but by somewhat different personnel from the original Messick band.

When Freeman finished high school he could read music well and was a more than competent player, much better than he had to be to play roadhouses. He accomplished what he had attempted in his Lash LaRue days by leaving town to go on the road with the Joe Lee Orchestra, the best legitimate band traveling out of Memphis. They sat down and played written arrangements. Freeman had left the Mar-Keys for better things. Then one night in Chicago, Freeman said, 'I heard the record and the guy who played it said, "That was the number one record in the country, 'Last Night', by the Mar-Keys." I thought, That's my band. I better go home.'

Freeman reassembled the band, and they played a few places in and out of town while waiting for the drummer, Terry Johnson, to graduate from Messick. Then they were on the road in a bus, a group of teenaged white boys with a number one rhythm and blues hit, among the first Anglos, as Sam the Sham said at the funeral, to play the chitlin circuit. Mrs. Axton, Packy's mother, and Carla Thomas, who at eighteen, black and beautiful, had recorded the studio's first hit, 'Gee Whiz', went with them, but the air in the bus soon became too thick, and the ladies went home, leaving the Mar-Keys and the chitlin circuit to fight it out among themselves. This was in 1961. Before the Rolling Stones had begun to get into trouble for playing nigger music to whites, before the Rolling Stones existed, the Mar-Keys were appearing at the Regal Theater in Chicago. Not even Elvis Presley had attempted the things the Mar-Keys got away with. Freeman jumped off the stage at the end of the show, landing on his knees, playing the guitar high over his head.

It is not certain just when Freeman started to turn red. He turned red when he got high, and he had been getting high most of his life. Turning red was not the half of it. When Freeman was in Milwaukee with the Mar-Keys, one of his girlfriends in Memphis received a call from him which began, 'Baby, you may not believe this, but I'm up in the corner of the phone booth looking down at myself.'

On their second national tour, in St. Paul, the Mar-Keys (they had a new piano player now, a Yankee named Bob Brooker whom they called Bear and did not especially like) had a fight onstage during which someone hit the Bear with a chair. That broke up the band, although groups including most or some or none of the original Mar-Keys still made appearances around the country. The originals were on various cuts on some of the albums, *Last Night, Night Before Last* and *Do the Pop-Eye*, but most of the tracks were cut by Steve Cropper, who did not go on the road, and the studio musicians who had been playing with him, from whom Booker T. and the MGs emerged. Freeman played sessions and club dates around Memphis. There was at this time a thing known as a Charlie Freeman contract, the terms of which were that the promoter hired a band called the Mar-Keys with Freeman and God knew who else. Freeman collected the grand or two the promoter was paying, and the other musicians got $10 or $50 or whatever they could get. But this was not a satisfactory state of affairs for Freeman, playing occasional gigs. It was very different from being on the road following a hit record.

Freeman missed the madness of the tour, he missed turning red and leaping off the stage each night, he missed the exhilaration. Freeman loved exhilaration, and when you are booked into an insane gig on the roof of the concession stand of a drive-in movie in a strange town, under some unfamiliar sky, and you start to play and Packy, not hearing anything, thinks the mike (one mike for seven instruments) doesn't work, and he's saying, 'Hey! This fucking mike's broke', his voice coming through loud and strong on all the little speakers hanging inside all the cars on the lot, 'Somebody fix the fucking mike', and the people begin to honk their horns in protest, so you play louder, and Packy, coming up to the mike to take a solo, steps back just far enough and falls off the roof, and – it's just fucking exhilarating, that's all.

Freeman loved the road; even being in Texas, where he always got into trouble, was better than not being on the tour. One night at LuAnn's in Fort Worth the Indian waitress Freeman had been sleeping with sat down at the bandstand in front of Freeman and raised her dress. Underneath she was wearing nothing but the pistol with which she intended to kill him, and this was her way of letting Freeman know it. He escaped as usual, but he used to say, 'People from Tennessee should stay out of Texas. Remember Davy Crockett and the Alamo.' Freeman saw the Alamo once. All over the walls, top to bottom, tourists had written, FUCK YOU.

Freeman was arrested twice in Texas, both times when he was with Jerry Lee Lewis. He had tried, when the Mar-Keys' contracts declined, to adopt a more normal way of life. He had enrolled at Memphis State University, where he made good grades, even attended meetings of the philosophy club, but it didn't last. Freeman had an offer to join Jerry Lee Lewis, the Ferriday, Louisiana, Flash, the Killer, one of the original Memphis Sun Rock and Roll Immortals. 'I might have become a pseudo-intellectual,' Freeman used to say, 'but I went on the road.'

Freeman was with the Lewis band between Fort Worth and Dallas in a place called Grand Prairie the first time they were arrested. They were coming back to their motel with 700 pills, 200 for Jerry, 500 for the band. It was Freeman's birthday, and the cops let him take along the drink in his hand on the ride downtown. They spent the night in jail, posted bond in the morning and went to Canada for their next show. They were too busy to appear in court. They might drive to Canada and then to Miami for a matinée the next afternoon.

Months later they came back to Texas, feeling sure that their trouble with the law would have been forgotten. During the last show at Panther Hall in Fort Worth the cops started coming in, and by the end of the show the band was surrounded. Freeman put down his guitar, took the Seconals out of his pocket, swallowed them, and told a girl who was standing by the stage to wait right there, he'd be back in a minute. Then he walked up to a sheriff and shook his finger in the man's face. 'Look here,' Freeman said, and the sheriff slapped the handcuffs on him.

Walter Cronkite reported the arrest on the CBS Evening News, and Freeman was pleased. He escaped again and stayed on the road, living to freeze almost to death in a blizzard between Sioux Falls and Omaha. Freeman and two of Lewis's other musicians fell asleep in the front seat of a white Fleetwood Cadillac, wrapped up together for warmth, staying there in the minus 30-degree weather from 9.30 until 8.00 the next morning, when a snowplow found them. They were a couple of days in the Omaha hospital thawing out, taking glucose in the arm, but soon Freeman was flaming red again, dancing atop the piano bench, the drummer dancing on his snare and tom-tom, Jerry Lee dancing on the piano keys, all of them wired out of their minds. At the big finish Freeman dived off the piano bench onto his knees, playing the guitar high over his head. It was like traveling with a circus.

But two years with the same circus were about all that Freeman could stand. He came back to Memphis, got married and started playing sessions at the local recording studios, cutting everything from radio and television commercials to albums with Chuck Berry, Slim Harpo and Bobby Bland. Freeman was tall and thin, and when he left the road he looked, with his black shirts, bouffant hair, lip goatee and shades, like a super-cool pimp. Living in Memphis again, he went hunting and fishing regularly for the first time since his uncles had taken him when he was a boy, and his hair fell lank and his beard grew in dark wisps. Freeman began to look Indian. He claimed his mother was part Choctaw and his father was part some other kind of Indian. Anyone who saw Freeman, blood-red, walk into a studio and throw a brace of fresh-killed stewing squirrels on the console, or saw him shoot with his shotgun a hole in the ceiling of the studio, knew he was, if not an Indian, at least a real renegade riding the owlhoot trail.

In spite of himself, Freeman rose in his profession. A recording band collected around Freeman and Tommy McClure, a bass player who'd been in Freeman's old outfit, the Roy Rogers Fan Club at the Normal Theater. An album they cut with Texas blues guitarist Albert Collins was nominated for a Grammy, and Jerry Wexler, the Atlantic Records executive and producer, hired the band to work in Miami as the house rhythm section at Criteria, one of the world's best recording studios.

Billed as the Dixie Flyers, they cut records with Sam the Sham, Ronnie Hawkins, Lulu, Petula Clark, Little Richard, Dion, Brook Benton, Aretha Franklin, Carmen McRae, Delaney and Bonnie, Taj Mahal, Sam and Dave, Jerry Jeff Walker and the Memphis Horns, the remainder of the horn section from the Mar-Keys, the band Freeman started in high school. Freeman went on, as he had all his life, taking as many dangerous drugs as he could get. A Synanon therapist who happened to meet him described Freeman as 'a Mozart of self-destruction'. He passed out on the studio carpet at times, but he would scrape himself off the floor, strap on his guitar, and Wexler, who produced many of the Dixie Flyers' Miami sessions, would stand in the control room transported: 'Listen to that Charlie Freeman,' he'd say. 'High as a kite and playing like a bird.'

He had long been the only man besides Keith Richards, the world's only bluegum white man, who played the songs of Chuck Berry, the archetypal rock and roll guitarist, worse than Berry himself. For Ronnie Hawkins and Sam the Sham he played rock and roll that becomes space jazz, taking solos that sound as if the strings are sliding off the guitar. On ballads like 'Breakfast in Bed' with Carmen McRae and 'The Thrill Is Gone' with Aretha Franklin, Freeman's playing has such grace and feeling that one note can break your heart, if your heart's in the right place.

But there was too much ecstasy in the mixture; the Dixie Flyers were too volatile, like all Freeman's bands. They blew up. Freeman moved in the rare high atmosphere where music lives and breathes and the record company gasps for air. Coming out of the studio in Miami after hours and hours of drink and dope and music, he was seen to look at the sky, look at his watch, and say, puzzled, 'Hell, man, it's eleven o'clock in the afternoon.'

The Dixie Flyers left Miami at the end of 1970. They recorded and toured in America and Europe with the singer Rita Coolidge, but she started traveling with Freeman's friend, Kris Kristofferson, and in March 1972 the Dixie Flyers disbanded.

In the last months of his life Freeman played very little. He went places, Los Angeles, Woodstock, looking for work, not asking, just hanging out, staying cool, making himself available. He was too proud, too Indian, to do more than that. Even the most jaded musicians, who had played with everyone from Perez Prado to the Rolling Stones, sat in awe of his presence. They listened to his stories, threw knives with him, tried to get as red as he did, went into comas, woke up and went back to their mundane pursuits on a more sober level, leaving Freeman, the legends' legend, high and dry.

He came back to Memphis and moved into Orange Mound, a black ghetto adjoining his old high-school neighborhood. Even in Memphis he could find no work. 'They know where I am, they can call me,' he said, when he did not have a telephone. His wife Carol went to work as a waitress, and Freeman went fishing. He went to Jack's Boat Dock on the White River so often that Jack offered him a job as a guide. When a neighbor scolded him for sitting on the porch drinking while Carol cut the grass, Freeman held up his magic fingers and said, 'These hands were never meant to touch a lawnmower.'

Finally, after the sheriff had come for the cars and Freeman had taken to sitting all day in his grandfather's old chair, shooting a pistol into the fireplace, Freeman decided to return to the bad-luck state of Texas. Tommy McClure, the bass player, was in Austin working with Marc Benno, a Texas guitarist who'd joined the Dixie Flyers when they were with Rita Coolidge, and they asked Freeman to come. He had looked for work in all the best places; now it was time to confront the worst. 'I should've had a feeling about Texas,' Carol said.

Freeman went to Austin and began playing with McClure and Benno. On his fourth night there he passed out, as he had on the three previous nights, as he did nearly every night, from taking as much as he could of whatever there was to take. Only this time, he didn't wake up. He was declared dead on arrival at Breckenridge Hospital at 2.11 p.m., January 31, 1973. The primary cause of death was listed as pulmonary edema.

Freeman died wearing his favorite jeans and red plaid flannel shirt, even his favorite red underwear. He had his arrowhead, his gold guitar pick and his grandfather's knife in his pocket. He died with his boots on. Remember the Alamo. FUCK YOU.

Like Lash LaRue in the movies, Freeman was revealed in the end to be a hero. They put him on an airplane in a crate, and at Memphis Funeral Home just before two o'clock on Saturday afternoon there were sprays of flowers, all kinds, all colors, along the walls and in great banks behind the steel-gray coffin, where Freeman, dressed in the gold-embroidered blue robe he'd worn onstage at the Albert Hall, was laid out on white satin. There were flowers from all the studios and record companies that had not been able to give Freeman any work toward the end of his life.

Charlie Freeman, *c.*1952

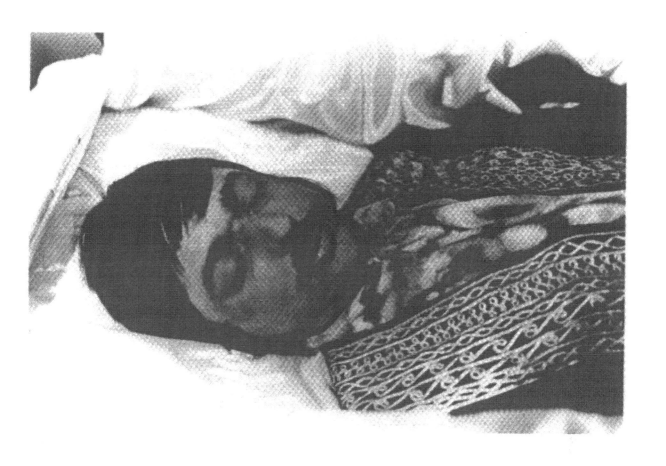

Charlie Freeman, Memphis Funeral Home, 1973 (© Randall Lyons)

The pews were filled with Freeman's relatives and friends, including musicians from all the bands he had played in and even the engineer from the Memphis studio he'd shot up. The president of the musicians' local came, but he had to leave before the service started.

A Baptist preacher who had never seen Freeman alive found the grace to praise his 'ministry in song' and closed by saying that to those who knew him, Heaven seemed closer now because Freeman was there, a thought that many of his friends must have found to be true but not comforting. Fred Ford, also known as Daddy Goodlow, one of Freeman's closest friends and one of the greatest living jazz reed players, a big black man in a black suit, looking with his long gray beard and large dark eyes like a great African minister of wisdom and death, praised Freeman for his strength and his sense of humor. 'If he were here he would say, "Be strong",' Ford said, 'and it seems like he is smiling.'

Actually, Freeman wasn't smiling. His lips, pale under the pale lip rouge, were swollen slightly inside the corners where the undertaker had stapled them together. Still you could tell that he had smiled once with satisfaction before he nodded out, Freeman's smile of victory that you saw just before his head dropped.

They took his old acoustic guitar, draped with red roses, out of the coffin, closed the lid, and carried the coffin in a long procession away from the river to the edge of town, where the land starts rolling eastward, to the graveyard where a hole had been dug for Freeman's body. The funeral party crowded around the opening of fresh yellow clay. The preacher read from his book, said that he had a wedding at three o'clock, and left. Sam the Sham, wearing his gold earring and a denim jacket, said a few words that remained to be said about Freeman. 'When Freeman was good he was the best, when he was bad he was the worst,' said Sam, who has been known to brandish a weapon in a studio himself. 'If all the people were pall-bearers who wanted to have that honor,' Sam said, 'the handles on this coffin would be a mile long.' All around the grave people were crying: Freeman's relatives, musicians, dope dealers, criminals, madmen, tears streaming down their faces. It was quite a sight.

Sam closed with a prayer, and the crowd dispersed quickly. The sun was bright, but the wind was chilling.

'I bet it's cold in that hole,' Sam said as we drove back to town.

'Freeman's not in that hole,' somebody said.

'I didn't *say* he was,' Sam said in his beautiful gypsy voice. 'I said I bet it's cold in there.'

Tomorrow Sam was leaving Memphis for Los Angeles, his current home. I took him to the place where he was staying and listened to tapes of his new songs while he packed. Sam had picked up an old valise that he'd left at the Sun recording studios since 1966, and he went through it, packing his gold records of 'Wooly Bully' and 'Little Red Riding Hood', throwing away old fan letters, motel bills, a business card from a limousine rental service. 'The limos of youth,' I said.

'They have a way of turning into rattletraps,' Sam said.

He was going across town to see a girl he'd wrapped in furs a few years before, so we said goodbye. McClure and Benno, who had driven up from Texas, came over to my place later. We drank and took things and talked about the Normal Theater and the Plantation Inn. I remembered the night at Freeman's house in Miami when McClure was carrying his right hand in a sling after having smashed it against a wall, Sam was preparing to terrorize the studio with a revolver, and I, after traveling for lifetimes with the Rolling Stones in such places as England, Alabama and Altamont, was phosphorescent blue and undergoing attacks from giant golden spiders. I drove to the studio that night with Freeman and guitarist Duane Allman, the Midnight Rider. We were talking about our beautiful bandit friend, Mike Alexander, who played bass in Duane's first band, and who, the month before Duane's fatal motorcycle wreck, would take a shotgun and blow the top of his head off in Memphis at the Alamo Plaza hotel. Now Mike, Duane and Freeman were all dead.

'Freeman wasn't no Indian. He put it off on the Indians. Freeman was just crazy,' McClure said, his mad eyes swirling into mine. It was surprising to see any of us still alive.

Early in the morning McClure and Benno left, heading back to Texas. I locked myself out of the house, broke a window, climbed in and passed out.

When I woke up I took some medicinal substances for my mind and body and started to write, listening to a record by Freeman's original favorites, Roy Rogers and the Sons of the Pioneers:

The Red Man was pressed from this part of the West,
It's unlikely he'll ever return
To the banks of Red River where seldom if ever
Their flickering campfires burn.

Home, home on the range,
Where the deer and the antelope play,
Where seldom is heard a discouraging word
And the skies are not cloudy all day.

12

ELVIS'S WOMEN

About the time Charlie Freeman died, my long friendship with Christopher came to an end. I entered a deep depression that I would not escape till I had gone crazy, had fits, married two more times and come back to (excessively) robust health. On August 16, 1977, Elvis Presley and one of my marriages died. (The marriage had lasted thirty days.)

Reviewing Priscilla Presley's book and one by Elaine Dundy called Elvis and Gladys *gave me an opportunity for a backward glance.*

My mother and Priscilla Presley used to visit the same beauty parlor in Memphis. Recently I told my mother that I was reading Priscilla's book and finding it even stranger than I expected. 'She lived in Memphis for ten years, more or less, and she still doesn't know that the east-west streets are called avenues. It's as if she were in a cocoon all that time.'

'She was in a cocoon,' my mother said. 'It was on top of her head.'

Among the photographs in *Elvis and Me* there are several from the days when Priscilla Beaulieu, the daughter of an ex-model who was married to an air force officer (Priscilla's natural father, a navy man, was killed in World War Two) was being groomed for the position of queen to the king of rock 'n' roll. One of the pictures is captioned, 'The way Elvis liked me.' In it, Priscilla's hair, dyed jet black, is piled up in a baroque bouffant mound, and her eyes peer out from behind layers of mascara and liner, looking, in the words of her father, Joseph Beaulieu, like 'two pissholes in the snow.' (Priscilla's father and my mother could have been critics.)

When Elvis met her – in Germany, where he was in the Army and where Priscilla's father was stationed – Priscilla was fourteen and in the ninth grade. Elvis, twenty-four, already a millionaire and one of the most famous men in the world, was suffering, as he would for the rest of his life, from the loss of his mother, Gladys Presley, who had died the year before. Priscilla, though different from his mother in many ways, was like her in that she was gentle, attentive and did not judge him. She was, as he told her father, someone he could talk to. After his return to the United States, Elvis persuaded her parents to let Priscilla visit and later live with him. They were together for five years, having lots of sex but no intercourse, as Priscilla tells it, before they were married. Nine months to the day after the wedding, their daughter, Lisa Marie, was born. The marriage lasted six years, they were divorced in 1973, and four years later, Elvis died.

So much has been written about the life of Elvis Presley that one day there will probably be an Elvis Presley Library, devoted to nothing else. Two recent books, Priscilla's *Elvis and Me* (Putnam) and Elaine Dundy's *Elvis and Gladys* (Macmillan), while far from being literature, are valuable additions to the Presley canon and provide revealing contrasts. Most books about Elvis, including the ones by his relatives and many best friends, accomplish little more than the unintentional character assassination of their authors. Elvis's story seems at times like a fun-house mirror. In these two books, once again, the facts do not appear so important as how they are perceived.

Priscilla's name appears once in *Elvis and Gladys*, which begins with the creation of Captain Marvel Jr. (I am not making this up), proceeds to the cohabitation of white settlers with the Indians in the 19th-century Mississippi Delta – one of Elvis's great-great-great-grandmothers was a Cherokee named Morning Dove White – and concludes with Gladys Presley's death. Priscilla's book mentions Gladys but briefly and covers the time from Elvis and Priscilla's meeting through the end of Elvis's life. If, years ago, Priscilla had been able to investigate as Elaine Dundy has the family she would become part of, her life with Elvis might have been of a different duration – longer or shorter. But even if Priscilla had been up to the task, Elvis, having too much to hide, could never have permitted it.

Elaine Dundy, an American who lives in London, is the author of three novels, a play and a biography of the late English actor Peter Finch. Her style, insofar as it exists, is execrable. Of the minds taken over by Elvis's songs, she writes, 'They also have the largest repertoire to choose from than any other popular artist. . .' Again and again she misplaces adjective phrases and commits other sins against coherence and the English language, but still her book is not unreadable. She cares about the subject, which is more than previous biographers, such as Albert Goldman, have done, and the first part of the book, at least, about Elvis's family background and early life, is well researched. The Captain Marvel Jr. business is overemphasized – many American boys identified with that cartoon character – but Dundy has a real insight into the weaknesses of Gladys Presley's makeup and enables us to see how as a young woman she could twice run away with men of little account, the second of whom would become Elvis's father. Dundy's bad writing, her bizarre preoccupation with such subjects as handwriting analysis and numerology, and her inability to understand such key figures as Sam Phillips, who laid the foundations of Elvis's career, render her book an interesting but badly flawed document.

Its villain is Elvis's manager, Colonel Tom Parker, also known as Andreas Cornelius van Kujik, of Breda, Holland. Dundy makes almost as much of Parker's origins as if she had discovered them. She demonstrates his venality by recounting his vicious practical jokes, analysing contracts he wrote, examining the plots of Elvis's films. There can be little doubt that he did what he could to keep Elvis from taking the chance of growing as a performer in any medium.

The Colonel, whom Priscilla refers to as 'Colonel', if he were named that, like a dog, is treated in *Elvis and Me* as a lovable uncle, determined to protect the interests of Elvis and his estate. In the light of the estate's having sued the Colonel, charging him with mishandling Elvis's affairs from the beginning, this is a bit hard to swallow. The closest thing to a villain in Priscilla's book, aside from Elvis himself, is a hairdresser named Larry Geller, who introduced Elvis to Eastern philosophy. This occurred during the most stagnant period of Elvis's life, when he was driven from sheer boredom to try to develop extrasensory powers, and the harmless Geller received the blame. 'The mischievous games he'd once played on movie sets had been superseded by studious pursuits. Elvis buried his head in books,' Priscilla says. The Colonel was alarmed by any evidence of thought on Elvis's part, and so, it seems, was Priscilla. Finally she told Elvis that the books 'were literally destroying us'.

' "Would it make you feel better if I just got rid of them all?" Elvis asked. I nodded.

'That night, at three in the morning Elvis and I piled a huge stack of his books and magazines into a large box and dumped them into an abandoned water well behind Graceland. We poured gasoline over the pile, lit a match and kissed the past goodbye.'

Could Eva Braun have said it better? The Elvis of *Elvis and Me* is a tender but troubled lover, a drug abuser, a liar, a philanderer, a concerned father, a violent tyrant. The book is studded with Elvis's angry reactions to Priscilla's unintended offences – expressions of opinion about music, or suggestions such as the one that Elvis should try to look more like Rickie Nelson. (In fairness to Elvis, it's hard to think of anyone who wouldn't be offended by that.) Priscilla was Elvis's playtoy, his living doll, but he could not program understanding as he could select a hair style. Priscilla's book reveals no perception of Elvis's nature or of what he might have been, only Priscilla's problems in keeping up with him, in being what he wanted without learning what he might have needed. He nearly died the day after their divorce, but there is nothing of that in *Elvis and Me*. Even a diary entry about Elvis's overcoming his reluctance to have sex with her after the birth of their child reveals all the hidden warmth of porcelain: 'I am beginning to doubt my own sexuality as a woman. My physical and emotional needs were unfulfilled.'

Whatever else Elvis Presley may have been, he was an archetypal artist, a kind of genius. For almost the entire last half of his life, he was also a terribly lonely man. Sam Phillips gave Elvis his start, and perhaps the last word on his protégé should be what Phillips said the day after Elvis's death: 'I think it's entirely possible to die of a broken heart . . . and I think that was a contributing factor.'

13

WIREGRASS

When, in 1984, my book finally emerged from its mossy cocoon ('That took longer to write than the Bible,' Keith Richards said) I left Memphis, where I'd lived twenty-five years, and returned to Georgia.

I must have fallen asleep as we drove in the shiny new black 1947 Ford sedan along the white sand road into the slash pine forest, because the first thing I remember is opening my eyes to see the red swamp water that had overflowed the ditches, covering the hub caps, drowning the engine, leaving my parents and me marooned in a sea the color of old blood. A smiling black man named Frank Porter came out in a gum truck, a big flatbed vehicle used for hauling barrels of turpentine, and towed us to a hill. In the Okefinokee territory, a hill is a place that's not under water.

I was five years old, and I had come to live in Wiregrass, where it seemed I would never be sad. Even after Frank Porter tried to stab my grandfather, I loved the swamp country. At times there I was afraid, but nothing in the woods was as frightening as what I would find in the world outside.

Each weekday morning, Wiregrass was awakened by a short, rotund man named Butler, whose yodeling yoo-hoos seemed part of the pre-dawn fog, along with the slave-code shouts the woods hands gave as they trudged from the shotgun shacks of the quarters to the stable where the mules and horses were kept, where the gum-drenched wooden wagons waited. Some days I would go out with them, riding my buckskin pony while the hands chipped faces – scraped the bark from pine trees – or dipped gum – gathered turpentine. Other times I would go alone into the woods, carrying a light lunch to be filled out with such plant foods as pine nuts and palmetto shoots. I washed my hands in the red water with the dark green leaves of po' man's soap and spent mornings watching a sundew plant devour a fly or opening pitcher plants to release the still-living insects trapped inside.

Years would pass before I understood what was happening in Wiregrass, where life went on as if Emancipation had never been proclaimed. The black workers, many of whom had been brought in from Mississippi by the owner of the turpentine company, were paid in cash and in script, a kind of play money that could be used only at the company-owned commissary. Almost all of them were in debt to the company, making them its property. Men from other turpentine camps came in the night to steal them, family, furniture and all, and my grandfather would find the rustled families and bring them back. The system was hard on everybody but me. All I knew at the time was that I loved the place I lived and the people there. Among the woods hands were men with names like Cat, Slick, Shoejohn and Dollbaby. One of the black women was called Mony because she had once said, when asked how she was, 'I don't feel good. Feels like I gots de mony,' meaning pneumonia.

Mr. MacDuffie, who ran the commissary, was a philosopher and the author of many wise sayings, such as 'One man's just as good as another one and a whole lot better.' Speaking of automobiles, Mr. Mac said, 'Brand new's the best model.' Fired numerous times for being found in the woods, where he was supposed to be checking the hands' work, sitting in the wagon wearing carpet slippers, Mr. Mac was still employed by the turpentine company in Wiregrass when he had the first of a series of strokes that killed him. I was a teenager then, no longer living at home, but the company owner's son and I brought the partially paralysed Mr. Mac a hospital bed from a nearby town. 'Aren't you going to thank these boys, Mac?' asked his wife, a fine, religious woman. 'They're just like your other friends, they've been praying for you.'

Mr. Mac, well read in the classics, especially Shakespeare and the Bible, fixed us with a baleful glare and said, 'The prayers of the wicked availeth little.'.

Ambition, first my parents' and then my own, would take me away from Wiregrass – to other towns and cities, other countries. I came to know love, hate, friendship, betrayal, mansions, jails, poverty and wealth. But at last my exile would end, and I would return to the scenes of my childhood.

This time I approached Wiregrass from the north-west, not stopping except for fuel until I could see Georgia. I was headed for the coast, but after driving through such garden spots as Sylvester, Ty Ty, Enigma and Willachoochee, I detoured south to the place where I had lived nearly forty years before. The old house was still there, and so were the trees I had climbed and fallen out of. The pay-building where Frank Porter made his almost lethal move was deserted, and all the workers were gone, their quarters long ago sold for $25 apiece. The commissary was padlocked, the stable had been torn down, and a spot that once rang with shouts was silent except for the wind sighing through the pines.

The red water still ran in the ditches, the palmetto and gallberry bushes were still there, but the humor and sorrow, the passing shadows I knew as a child, existed only in memory. I had come back alive, though, and that in itself was a miracle.

My daughter, the six-year-old starlet, Rock and Roll Ruby, was waiting for me at my parents' house on St. Simons Island, so I left Wiregrass again, knowing that the ghosts would be there whenever I wanted to visit. The important thing was that the stories remained, and now it would be my job to tell them.

14

GARDEN OF MEMORIES

In the spring of 1985 I attended the birth of the Stones book in England, Wales, Scotland, Ireland and Northern Ireland. I had fallen in love with London on my first visit to England – then, living there with an unhappy Christopher, I had longed for death – so to come back in an atmosphere of celebration, with a book released, parties, interviews and appointments, made me feel good.

Back in the US later that season, I went at the behest of Chris Wohlwend, editor of the Atlanta Weekly, *to New Orleans in search of a successful repetition. I found it, I suppose. This one called herself April – we used up most of the hot water in my hotel.*

I had forgotten how hot it gets in New Orleans. The Japanese magnolias bloom in February, and by the end of April the air is so humid that just standing in the shade makes you sweat.

In my mind, in New Orleans I am still twenty-two, playing stickball, one-handed stickball – a martini in the other hand, under a big oak's swinging Spanish moss, in the street outside a big green rambling (screen-porched downstairs and up) house where lives the lady who made the drinks, who's running delicately and like a lady but running pretty good after the ball, small hard black rubber ball dancing and spinning away from me and her second son, fifteen and almost my size, who likes me even though I am his mother's friend, and I am dizzy with pleasure in the soft New Orleans dusk.

'Do you know what your life pattern is?' she asked me one night.

'My what?'

'Your – they say your life goes in cycles, you do the same things over and –'

'I don't think so.'

We were lying upstairs in her bedroom with the lights out, alone, the next minute about to be joined by one of her four children (youngest nine, oldest seventeen, all supposed to be someplace else for the night) coming upstairs. She hid me in the attic – naked, cowering, imprisoned in the dust and dark by a beautiful woman who didn't want her child to catch us. Jack and Bobby Kennedy were alive then, Martin Luther King was an obscure Southern preacher, many things were right with the world, but I was in an impossible situation. Sitting on my heels in the attic, I had found, though I didn't realize it, my life pattern.

I had forgotten a lot of things in the twenty-odd years – half my life – that had passed since I left the Crescent City. But some things you can't forget.

I entered graduate school at Tulane University a few weeks after a bomb planted in the basement of a black Birmingham church killed four little girls. I learned at the school cafeteria that Jack Kennedy had been shot. A grad-student party I attended on Freret Street was raided by the police because it was mixed. Driving to Memphis, where my parents lived, for Christmas in 1963, I saw in south Louisiana, outside certain houses, crosses burning.

Back in New Orleans after the holidays, I heard Cassius Clay win the heavyweight championship and saw the Beatles on the Ed Sullivan show. I had left school because it distracted me from writing, or maybe because it didn't. I enjoyed living in New Orleans, but the lack of money and the bad feeling I had about the racial climate there led me back to Memphis – an ironic move. After what seemed a very long time, about three years, the stories I wrote began to find publishers. I started traveling then and for the next twenty years lived in a series of widely separated places. What with one thing and another, I did nothing more in New Orleans than pass through.

When I lived there, if you wanted to hear local music your safest bet was Preservation Hall, on St. Peter Street. Many a night I listened to

George Lewis, an immaculate man always dressed in black trousers, a black bow-tie and a starched white shirt, soulfully play the clarinet, an instrument which, with his leanness and his dark skin, he resembled. At Preservation Hall I also heard Billie and Dede Pierce, Punch Miller, and Sweet Emma the Bell Gal, because they were accessible. I knew more music existed in New Orleans – Poppa Stoppa played it every afternoon on his radio show – but I didn't know how to get to it.

In 1969, some years after I left, the Jazz and Heritage Festival was started – one weekend in Congo Square with 300 musicians playing to a crowd of half that number. Over the past fifteen years the Festival had spread like kudzu, taking over the last weekend in April through the first weekend in May; this year 3,000 musicians were appearing from racetrack to riverboat (and other places) for a combined audience of over a quarter-million. Idols of my youth, like Miles Davis, lifelong accomplices and erstwhile companions would be there, and the story would, I thought, cost me only about twice as much as I would be paid for writing it, so I decided to go.

Passing the big graveyard on the way into town, I asked the taxi-driver to remind me of its name. 'Garden of Memories,' he said, and I remembered that Gram Parsons was buried there. New Orleans: the land of dreams, Jack Teagarden and Glenn Miller called it, but the land of dreams is the country of nightmares.

On the long drive downtown, observing the franchise motels and fast-food joints that do their best to make all modern cities look like theme parks, I thought how different the landscape would have been for the few who saw it in, say, 1712, the year importing of black slaves began in Louisiana. At that time the province extended north to Canada, encompassing all or most of what are now thirteen states, from the Wisconsin to the Idaho borders. The entire 827,000 square miles contained fewer than 300 Caucasians, only 28 of them women – 'correction girls', deportees from Paris prisons whose influence, out of proportion to their number, was so unfortunate that a priest suggested sending them back to France.

Lamothe Cadillac, Governor of Louisiana from 1713 to 1716, responded by saying, 'If I send away all the loose females, there will be no women left here at all, and this would not suit the views of the King or the inclinations of the people.' As the soldiers' ranks increased, the need for white women became so great – hard to believe, I know – that more correction girls were imported. At last the Mississippi Company, regulators of commerce in the area, found non-criminal women – called *filles à la casette*, or casket girls, to indicate that they had been chosen from decent, honest families – who went under guard to New Orleans, where they soon found husbands. In his book *The French Quarter*, Herbert Asbury remarks that none of the correction girls seems to have had any children, whereas each of the casket girls must have had hundreds – the proof of 'these biological miracles' being that 'almost every native family of Louisiana is able to trace its descent in an unbroken line from one of the *filles à la casette*.'

During the eighteenth century, ownership of the state passed from the French to the Spanish and back again. In 1803, when Napoleon sold Louisiana to the United States for $15 million, New Orleans consisted mostly of the few blocks now called the French Quarter, inhabited by about 10,000 people, half of them white, 2,000 free blacks, the rest slaves. It was already becoming the city that best loved dancing and parades. The Latins, knowing with what justice they were hated, had introduced such measures as the Black Codes, which among other things forbade blacks to assemble in public. The Americans, strangers to civilization themselves, let the slaves dance.

We were approaching Rampart Street, having passed the Superdome, a building with all the lilt of a nuclear power plant. To our left, at Rampart and Orleans, was the slaves' main dancing place. Once a field sacred to the Oumas Indians, where they held their corn feasts, it came to be called Congo Square. 'No meaner name could be given to the spot,' George Washington Cable wrote. 'The negro was the most despised of human creatures and the Congo the plebeian among negroes.'

The songs of Congo Square, sung in a *mélange* of foreign tongues by a kidnapped and orphaned people, echo through history, along with the music of the churches, the masked balls, the voodoo chants, the funeral and Mardi Gras parades, and the legacies of Picayune Butler, Corn Meal, Buddy Bolden, Joe Oliver, Jelly Roll Morton, Tony Jackson, Sidney Bechet, Louis Armstrong, Johnny and Baby Dodds, Tuts Washington,

Professor Longhair, Champion Jack Dupree, Fats Domino, Dave Bartholomew, Allen Toussaint, Jesse Hill, Earl King, Chris Kenner, Little Richard, Lee Allen, Earl Palmer, Mac Rebennack, the Neville brothers, the Battiste family, the Marsalis family, Terence Blanchard, and a great many more.

Downtown, past Rampart on Canal, a street that used to be a very wide moat, or canal, and for that reason remains the world's widest business thoroughfare, I saw that giant hotels and office buildings had sprouted, and buses, not streetcars, were running. All the New Orleans streetcars had been stopped except the St. Charles, even the one called Desire. But they can't stop Desire.

I was going to cover the Festival, but my motives for returning to New Orleans were more complex. I wanted to know whether it was still the town I had loved when I was young and broke and confident.

My hotel, a sixteen-storey turquoise tower, was called the Sugar House, because it was where a cane refinery used to be, among the warehouses down by the river near the site of the 1984 World's Fair that had caused so many millions of dollars to disappear. I moved in, phoned the Festival office, because my tickets were there, and spoke to Susan Mock. Susan said that she and Anna Zimmerman had to go to a meeting at the racetrack, but they'd call me in a couple of hours, when they got back to the office, and I could come round for the tickets. 'Fine,' I said. 'And Anna says you should bring some grapefruit juice,' Susan said. 'Grapefruit juice,' I said. 'Yes,' Susan said, 'we already have the vodka.' 'You have,' I said, 'a deal.'

With a little time to kill, I walked down to the Pearl Oyster Bar, on St. Charles, to see if they could still shuck. They could; the oysters were as fat and jovial as I remembered, and the beer, in frosted mugs, was excellent. But by the time I walked back to the hotel – stopping on Canal to pick up grapefruit juice and a bottle of champagne (just in case) – I was soaking wet.

I showered, Susan called, I went to the office bearing grapefruit juice. Anna and Susan were blonde, sane, charming and relaxed. In attending more musical events than I care to remember, including 'festivals' where people were killed, I have found that the more impressed people are with the importance of what they are doing, the less likely they are to be good at it. Anna and Susan produced vodka, continued answering phones and writing press releases that I couldn't stop myself from editing, and carried on with a lovely, amused professionalism. Anna gave me my tickets, and because I was late for dinner with friends, I finished my drink, said thank you and went out into the warm New Orleans night.

At the Fair Ground's racetrack, on the two Festival weekends, from noon till seven o'clock nine stages feature continuous music. When I came into the gospel tent, the Fortier High School Gospel Choir, twenty-five young black folk in blue acetate-satin robes, led by a gray-haired piano player, were singing 'All God's Children':

> Everybody talkin' 'bout Heaven
> ain't goin' there –

At stage five, a band that played new New Orleans music, Uncle Stan and Auntie Vera, were playing old-hat new-wave riffs. Though I must say on their behalf that I like any band with a girl tenor player.

At stage four the Golden Star Hunters, a black Indian band, were playing. It's not unusual for American blacks to 'go Indian', but in New Orleans they do it in a manner more overt. There is a tradition of this, with its own language and social structure and the most wonderful costumes, the kind of things Nudie of Hollywood might have sold if the Rodeo Tailor had been a psychedelic Indian freak. Many feathers, bright colors, magnificent head-dresses. The Golden Stars performed New Orleans classics like 'Barefootin'' and songs from Wild Tchopitoulas, another tribe-band.

In the crowd I encountered a friend from Memphis, who right away altered my consciousness, making me feel brave. I recalled seeing a sign that said BBQ Alligator. The alligator is my totem animal, and though I've killed one, I had never eaten the meat. I bought beer and alligator and sat down under an oak. As Brian Jones once said about eating a goat, it was like Communion.

Soon I was off again, back to the gospel tent, where the Parish Prison Singers, twenty young men in white-trimmed burgundy robes, were deep into 'Of Thee I Sing'. 'Mine Eyes Have Seen the Glory' followed. Different singers, two or three together, shared the lead on each song.

They did some pieces I didn't know, one containing this passage:

> I've had heartaches like this before
> And disappointments by the score
> And claimed the victory at last –
> This too shall pass

They were marvelous: dope dealers, thieves, rapists, killers, singing like angels.

On my way out of the Fair Grounds I passed stage one. Young Battiste brothers, ones I'd never heard, were playing. They did 'Big Chief', the calypso song 'Matilda', 'Fever', 'Iko Iko', 'Shout', and closed with 'Lil Liza Jane'. They would be the best band in town almost anywhere except New Orleans.

I went back to the Sugar House, showered, then ventured out again, to Louis Armstrong Park's Theater of Performing Arts, across the street from Congo Square. Miles Davis and Wynton Marsalis were sharing the bill for the Festival's first evening concert. Miles was already onstage, looking like Zorro in red boots, black leather trousers, a black jacket with rhinestones, shades, and a black sombrero. Over the last thirty years I have heard Miles in many different contexts, but I never heard him sound so exuberant, so triumphant, as he did in New Orleans. In his sixtieth year, he eclipsed Marsalis, the twenty-two-year-old jazz and classics virtuoso. Miles played two two-hour sets, doing songs from sources as diverse as Cole Porter and Michael Jackson, dropping phrases from 'We Are the World' as he left the stage.

On the following day I stayed inside and wrote. That night I went out on the *President*, a riverboat, showboat, to hear the Dirty Dozen Brass Band, Allen Toussaint, and the Staples Singers. Even without music, a ride on a Mississippi riverboat is its own reward. (That is, however, the only characteristic it shares with virtue.) The DDBB play a wide variety of songs and are certainly good-humored. I may have been less than interested in their performance because the gumbo served on the boat was filled with tasty morsels, crab-legs, shrimp, okra – the New Orleans music festival may be the only one a deaf person would have good reason to attend.

Allen Toussaint, aided by his wife and other family members, performed his songs, from 'Mother-in-law' to 'Southern Nights'. Toussaint is a fine songwriter and record producer, but he seems a bit shy as a performer. Maybe he was saving something for next weekend, when he would close the Festival. I'd heard Roebuck Staples had retired, but 'Pops' was there, playing that lovely, loose-stringed, clanging guitar. His daughters Cleo and Mavis sang like the superb performers they long have been. Their material, forged in struggle, is as timely as ever: 'Respect Yourself', 'In the Ghetto' and 'Why Am I Treated So Bad?' To hear them, I thought as they played and sang, was a religious experience. This reminded me of how badly I needed to go to church.

But on Sunday, the next day, no church, back to the racetrack. Sippie Wallace, the Texas nightingale, who, now that Helen Humes and Alberta Hunter are dead, may be the last of the classic female blues singers, was working in Economy Hall, a big yellow tent in the broiling sun. Sippie, a stocky little woman in a burgundy church hat, a matching long-sleeved dress, and tennis shoes, sang 'She's Got Good Jelly' and 'You Got to Know How', referring to herself in the lyrics as 'fair brown' – and you knew it was true; what a prize she must have been as a young woman. She still had spunk, coming back after she closed the set with 'Just a Closer Walk With Thee' for an encore: 'Everybody Loves My Baby, but My Baby Don't Love Nobody but Me'. Then she blew kisses to the crowd, sat down in her wheelchair, and a young man from the festival staff rolled her away.

One unfortunate result of having nine stages is that sooner or later you'll have to choose between two or more performances you really hate to miss. On this day I missed Dave Bartholomew, who wrote the Fats Domino hits, and William Dixon, Chicago's master blues writer. Mac Rebennack – 'Dr. John' – was at stage three, and I didn't think I could afford to miss him. The original Dr. John was a big black man, the greatest voodoo priest of New Orleans, the male counterpart of Marie Laveau. In the late '60s the session guitar and piano player Mac Rebennack came out of the voodoo closet. *Gumbo*, his album of New Orleans R & B hits, solidified his persona. Now he was a local god, like Toussaint. Fathead Newman, the tenor player from Ray Charles's small group of the '50s, was with Dr. John's band. They did 'Junko Partner', 'Those Lonely Lonely Nights', 'High Blood Pressure', 'Don't You Just

Know It' and 'Tipiteana'. Mac Rebennack is a much bigger sensation in New Orleans as Dr. John than he ever was as himself.

Dr. John was followed at stage three by Roy Orbison. Wink Martindale wouldn't have Orbison as a guest on his Memphis television show, 'Dance Party', because Orbison was 'too ugly'. Orbison is no better looking now, but he has two young women singing with him who take up the slack, and he still sounds fine - 'Pretty Woman' and 'Only the Lonely' seemed to come over the PA system with Sam Phillips's unique echo from Orbison's original recordings.

The Neville Brothers were at stage one, closing the first weekend. They are the best band in any town, even New Orleans. Aaron Neville sang 'Tell It Like It Is' and in the heat and the damp, gritty humidity of the racetrack I got chill bumps.

Early Monday afternoon I expressed a story out, ate a room-service sandwich and toddled down to one of my favorite old haunts, the Napoleon House. Many years before, I had written in my notebook about 'drinking gin and tonic in the pink-tiled front room, watching the slanting sunlight catch the hair of the girls passing on the sidewalk, while the slowly turning wooden-bladed fans above kept the heavy air moving'. Twenty years had, to my delight, changed the place very little. The biggest difference was that now there were more people I knew.

On Tuesday night I went back to the Theater of Performing Arts to hear Ellis Marsalis, sire of the clan, and Sarah Vaughan. Marsalis for years accompanied Al Hirt, a man who, while not to everybody's taste, is technically a very proficient trumpet player. At the Theater Marsalis played such songs as 'Jitterbug Waltz' and 'The Man I Love', suggesting Teddy Wilson, Bill Evans, Debussy, all music. Sarah Vaughan, her tacky self, was transformed when she sang into a great musician. There is a limit to how miserable one can be while listening to songs like 'I've Got the World on a String', 'Easy Living', 'Lush Life' and 'Lucky to be Loving You'.

Wednesday afternoon I made it out to ferret in French Quarter bookshops and to pray and light candles at St. Louis Cathedral. Sitting at the Napoleon House bar I ate half a muffaletta sandwich (a good meal for $3) and discovered that Dixie beer has a new, drinkable formula. I took a bus out Magazine Street, spent a fortune on records at Leisure Landing and came back to the Sugar House, where I could sign for pack animals.

Thursday, with the week fading fast, found me at the Café du Monde as the noon chimes rang from St. Louis. I walked past the mules, the sidewalk artists, the squirrels and the pigeons, went into the softly lit, cool cathedral, said more prayers and lit more candles.

Then I went to the tailor's. In a way, that was the truest test. I had bought clothes from Terry & Juden even when I didn't live in New Orleans. They had a man who roamed the South with a tape-measure, giving customers fittings in their homes. That old gentleman, they told me, had long ago departed for the big haberdashery in the sky, where they move so much yardage of flowing white raiment. For my purposes I wanted something more mundane, like a new seersucker number. I found one on the rack, bought a bow-tie to accompany it, and left Terry & Juden with a springier step.

I strolled to the nearest streetcar stop and took the car, when it came, out St. Charles past Milan, where I used to live, to Pleasant Street, walked across to Magazine and spent another fortune at Metronome, another record store. But I had to stop and return to the hotel – back to the riverboat tonight.

Blues night on the *President*, with Gatemouth Brown, Albert King and Stevie Ray Vaughan, in that order, which is the order of diminishing returns. Gatemouth Brown, with his baby daughter, was magical, as he never fails to be. I was on the top deck when he started, surveying the river and the burgeoning south-east moon, so I may have missed a song or two. The first one I heard him do was 'Ebb Tide'. His daughter, five or six years old in her violet frock, yawned. Gates played everything from 'Foggy Mountain Breakdown' to 'Drown In My Own Tears'. The baby sang 'You Are My Sunshine'. Gates was on the road, trying his best to make a living. The baby's mother was someplace else, and it's hard to find babysitters you can trust. Gates left the stage with his daughter in his arms.

Albert King, the left-handed wizard of the Flying V, played a good heavy-handed set, but it seemed positively dainty against the exaggerated shenanigans of Stevie Ray Vaughan.

I was glad to get off the boat. I walked down Decatur Street to Fun's.

In 1964 it was called Fong and you could get red beans and rice, a big plateful, for 35 cents. Beef and Chinese vegetables, $1.65. A white-haired man named Wong used to add up the bill on an abacus. There were scratchy Chinese records beside Ray Charles's on the jukebox. Today, no jukebox, no Wong, no red beans, nobody who remembers 1964. I ate beef and Chinese vegetables and drank hot tea and it cost $8. I didn't mind the increase in price so much as the decline in character. In an effort to cheer myself up, I went to the Napoleon House and sat at the bar drinking cognac until it closed.

I wasn't the only one who needed cheering up. On Friday a man went out on an upper-storey ledge at the Hale Boggs Federal Building and threatened to jump if he didn't get a cheeseburger. Somebody gave him a cheeseburger, and he dropped out of the pages of history.

Friday afternoon Ry Cooder and his band, including Jim Dickinson, came into town. Dickinson joined me for dinner at the Sugar House, and we spent the evening, as usual, shining the light of consciousness toward the darkness at the end of the tunnel. Dickinson made his customary dire pronouncements: 'Music is over.' Meanwhile we were still rolling right along.

The next night, Saturday, Cooder played on the riverboat, preceded by Bonnie Raitt and Bobby Bland. I sat on the top deck and watched the full moon rise pale violet against the mother-of-pearl sky over the dark line of Algiers woods across the river. The *Natchez* sternwheeled past us and then the *Creole Queen*, sparkling with red and yellow lights, churning upriver.

Bonnie Raitt played and sang country blues songs by Fred McDowell and other traditional artists. Bobby Bland, with his pinky diamond, dark-blue shirt, light-gray suit, and his band that sounded almost like Basie's, was impeccable. He did 'Soul Deep', 'St. James' Infirmary Blues', and his own hits.

Cooder, with his fine band, played a powerful set, composed of songs like these: 'Smack Dab in the Middle', 'Look at Granny Run Run', 'Denomination Blues', 'If Walls Could Talk', 'How Can the Poor Man Stand Such Times and Live', 'Little Sister', 'Fool about a Cigarette', 'Feelin' Good', 'Dark End of the Street', 'The Very Thing That Makes You Rich Makes Me Poor' and 'Crazy 'Bout an Automobile'. Anna and

Susan and I were crowded with a lot of other people into a reserved-seating area looking down on the stage, and Cooder's music made us get up and dance. Anna graciously provided me with tickets to the second show, but I thought I'd better get inside before the full moon drove me stone crazy.

The next day, the last day of the Festival, I went back to the Café du Monde and sat with my coffee, looking across Jackson Square at the Cabildo – the first American apartment buildings – and the Cathedral. I remembered Jackson Square when the flag was at half-mast for President Kennedy. Things had certainly changed while I was away. Now the light and dark folk could meet in public.

At the Fair Grounds (passing through church – prayers, candles – on my way) I found the people in congress assembled. Anna and Susan were there, and I thanked them for their help. But no matter how good the help, by the time you reach the end of such an overgrown event, there will be no backstage passes for people who are working, but burnt-out hippies wearing four passes wandering in restricted-access areas, staring into the sun.

Cooder played more good songs, 'Jesus on the Mainline' outstanding, and then, as he does each year, Allen Toussaint closed the Festival. I was by now shell-shocked and could only tap my feet fondly to 'Brickyard Blues' and 'Southern Nights'. I dragged myself back into town, ate soft-shelled crab and raw oysters at the Monteleone Hotel, then walked over to the Fairmont, as they call the Roosevelt now, to sit among the gilt and red carpet listening to the bad cocktail pianist, drinking the house's famous Gin Fizz. I had three and taxied back to the Sugar House.

The morning was bright but overcast. Passing the Garden of Memories on the way to the airport I said a prayer for Gram Parsons. Gram hadn't survived his youth, but I had lived to return to a part of mine. I felt lucky.

1 5

PSALMIST OF SOUL: AL GREEN

About a year after leaving Memphis, I met an editor who hired me to write about Al Green. Heartbroken over the death of Otis Redding and preoccupied with one thing and another, I had never really heard Al Green who, it turned out, sings superbly.

I went to Memphis, checked into the Peabody, and discovered what a pleasant place my vicious old hometown could be to visit.

Al Green's office building is set well back from the road (Winchester, the four-lane that fronts the airport), so I turned at the sign and walked into the place next door. Excusing myself to the people in curlers, I went back to the one-storey brick house occupied by Al Green, Inc.

Tina, Al's pretty niece, didn't exactly welcome me but told me to sit down on the leather couch in the big reception area. 'Merry Christmas,' she said each time the phone rang. 'Israelite Productions, Al Green Music Company.' Her side of the phone dialogue was familiar music-business material: 'OK OK, he just got in, I can't do nothin' until he tell me to do something. . . Do you want me to forge his signature? . . . OK. We'll do it now. Thanks, hon.'

I sat thumbing a copy of *Ebony*, mentally rehearsing major events in Al Green's life. Born in Forrest City, Arkansas, in 1947, Green joined his father's gospel group when he was nine but was thrown out for listening to the worldly music of Jackie Wilson. After his family moved to Grand

Rapids, Michigan, Green and some high-school friends formed a pop group called the Creations. Renamed Al Green and the Soul Mates, the group recorded a single, 'Back Up Train'. In 1969 Green was working small clubs – the 'chitlin circuit' – when he met Willie Mitchell, the Memphis trumpet player and producer of hit rhythm and blues records, in Midland, Texas.

At Mitchell's invitation, Green came to Memphis. In 1970 Green and Mitchell made their first album, *Green Is Blues*, for Memphian Joe Cuoghi's Hi label. The next year they cut their first gold record, 'Tired of Being Alone', the beginning of a series of hits that would include 'Let's Stay Together' and 'I'm Still in Love with You' – seven top-ten records in three years.

In October of 1974, with things going well for Green, a woman who'd asked him to marry her and been refused walked in on him in the bath and poured boiling grits (Memphis napalm) down his back. Green was hospitalized, but the woman had gone on to lock herself in a bedroom, write a suicide note and, with a pistol belonging to Green, kill herself. Green said that he had been through a religious conversion the year before, but after the grits and bullets episode he entered a period of deep spiritual study that continued even though, as Green admits, he tried for three years to deny his religious experience. In 1976 Green became a minister but encountered so much opposition from professional clergy that he bought his own church, the Full Gospel Tabernacle in Memphis. The next year, he began recording some gospel songs and producing his own records.

In 1979, during a concert in Cincinnati, Green fell from the stage, hit a steel instrument case, and spent the next fifteen days in the hospital. 'I was moving towards God, but I wasn't moving fast enough,' Green said later. 'The fall was God's way of saying I had to hurry up.'

The Lord Will Make a Way, Green's first all-gospel album, was released in 1980 and won the Grammy for best gospel performance. In 1982 Green appeared on Broadway with Patti LaBelle in the acclaimed gospel musical *Your Arm's Too Short to Box with God*. His album, *He Is the Light*, was Green's first gospel work produced by Willie Mitchell. Some people say the album is Green's best since he and Mitchell parted.

Tina had kept on answering the phone, throwing pink message-slips on the red carpet. There was a little mound of them when, wearing a purple velvet jacket, the Reverend Mr. Green came in. We shook hands and went back to his office, where I took a seat in a leather chair beside his desk. 'We'll only be ten or fifteen minutes,' he had said to Tina. 'After all,' he added to me, waving a hand at the gold records that ringed the room, 'the handwriting is on the wall.'

'Do you remember that song?'

'What song?'

'"Handwriting on the Wall", by the Trumpeteers.'

'*Yeah.*'

'They did "Old Blind Barnabas". Remember that?'

'*Sure.*'

'Those were the first records I heard as a kid in south Georgia, records by groups like them and the Statesmen Quartet and the LeFevre Trio. What was the first music that you responded to as a child?'

'Soul Stirrers.'

'With Sam Cooke.'

'And Rebert Harris when he was with the group. Fantastic.'

'When you met Willie Mitchell, he said, "In a year and a half you can be a star", and you said, "I don't have that long." Why did you say that?'

'At the time, I didn't feel like I wanted to take that kind of time, seemed like to me that was a long time to take. I thought it had taken too long already.'

'Did you know Joe Cuoghi?'

'Papa Joe. Joe Cuoghi loaned me my first fifteen hundred dollars. Died seventy or seventy-one. Beautiful cat. He was a believer. You gotta be a believer. It's impossible to please God or anybody else without faith. Cuoghi had faith in me. I said, "Joe, I want to, uh, sing some songs," and I was kind of shy or something, so he called Willie Mitchell and asked Willie about this kid named Al Green. So Willie says, "Yeah, he's gonna be all right." Joe says, "You think he's gonna be able to cut the mustard?" and Willie says, "I think he'll be able to cut the mustard all right." Joe says, "He also wanted about fifteen hundred dollars to get some lead sheets and some contracts and do some copying or something" – and also to pay his rent, by the way – and Willie says, "Aw, give it to him, give it to him, he gone be fine." And Joe gave me that fifteen hundred dollars, and I never asked him for any since. Paid him back, too.'

'There are some fine people in the Memphis music business, you know, like Sam Phillips, Furry Lewis, Rev. Herbert Brewster.'

'Rev. Brewster, shee, seems like he's been goin' forever.'

'Elvis used to go to Rev. Brewster's church and hear Queen C. Anderson sing his songs, like "Move On Up a Little Higher" and "As an Eagle Stirreth in its Nest".'

'This cat is *bad*. I'm lookin' forward to going to see him. I wanted to go see him in '85, but he was ill.'

'He's great. I've been lucky to know some of the people I've known in the music business. I spent the last week of Otis Redding's life with him. Watched him write and record "Dock of the Bay". Said goodbye to him on Friday, and Sunday night he was dead. Broke my heart.'

'So many tragedies. So many great talents run into so many tragedies. So many obstacles. And such great talents. But when they are alive other people don't realize how great their talents are. All the honor and glory and magnificence comes after you're . . . deceased. It's a shame, that we've had so many prophets here – and when I say prophets, I mean prophets in music, prophets that play the organ, prophets that play stringed instruments. Prophets in words, prophets in deeds, prophets in many, many ways. Only to be neglected.'

'Memphis is the home of the neglected artist.'

'You know something? You are absolutely right. There are so many neglected people here – but you stay here and you stay here, and after a while, the thing that makes you so different and so gifted tends to wash away. Little by little, it begins to wear away into the common denominator, and people forget, and cause *you* to forget. Now if the person were to pass, oh, yeah, let's pull out all the old albums, where before that, never. The recognition of man is very shallow. Beware when men speak well of you, my brother.

'It's so unfortunate, though. If a prophet could be taken – like Jimi Hendrix, so fabulous – I said a *prophet*, now. I hear the songs he played. That's fine, I hear what he's saying. I can just about perceive the influence. I can hear the songs Elvis sings, and I can just about perceive the influence, knowing his cook, and knowing the people around him very well, I can perceive that. And I still say, a fabulous prophet. Hendrix, Presley, Otis Redding, Sam Cooke – *what things happen to such people*. I knew Jackie Wilson, and as wild as Jackie was, I'm surprised it didn't happen twenty-five years earlier. But I myself was told to come away from that side of it.

'I met a man, a painter, from Enid, Tennessee, named DeWitt Jordan. Brilliant. I bought two of his paintings. He don't even know he's a prophet, but he's a prophet. The next week, he's fooling around with some girl, drinking, in Enid, right? And gets himself shot. And killed. And he never finishes my painting, called "The Harvest" – he painted the mules, the cotton, the workers, the wagon, but he never got to draw the scales, I thought that was significant – and got snuffed away in a night. In a flicker of time, drunk, arguing with some guy about some girl that's irrelevant, all of them drunk, washing themselves away in their troubles, you know? Once you're so talented, and people don't recognize it, you get a bit frustrated.'

'Life's hard enough when you *can* pay the rent.'

'I thought it was great when Sinatra, at his seventieth birthday party, said, "I thank my creator, my maker, for keeping me here so long." I thought that was very, very important, coming from such a kingpin as Sinatra.'

'When you wake up in the morning, do you think about God or Mammon?'

'If you're called, you work to be chosen. Because many are called. So we're working now on our probation. Trying to be pleasing to God. Not boastful. Some people think I'm boastful when I drive a Rolls-Royce. But I bought my Rolls-Royce car when I was singin' the blues. And I figure, if I want to drive my car, I'll drive it. I want to live in peace, I want to write my songs, I want to minister to the needs of the people, and that's about it. Now, when I get up in the morning, whether I think of God or Mammon, I think the basic question boils down to: Do I feel comfortable in singing rhythm and blues now, intermingled with gospel music? To answer that question – I feel basically like David, I suppose, that I am called, I am chosen. I couldn't be honestly called and not be honestly serious. I hear the sound of the money – jinglejinglejinglejingle – I see the prosperity, I see the beauty, the glamor, the

Grammies, the tinglejingle and the I-love-you tadadadadada. But it's hard – I mean, you can sing, "I love you baby", but when you're used to singing, "Jesus Jesus Jesus" or "Lord Lord Lord" and meaning it – it's hard to turn around and sing "Baby baby baby, you've left me and I'm about to lose my mind". It's trivial. It doesn't mean anything.'

'I remember your saying in an interview that it was one thing to sing a song by Al Green, but "Amazing Grace" is serious business.'

'We were doing "Amazing Grace" on this last tour. And there were people in the audience not only crying, taking a handkerchief and dabbing it to their eyes, but there were people beginning to – rejoice. And – not be ashamed about it. To throw up both hands in the I Surrender position. And say Thank you. Thank you. Thank you. Now when you start getting a person in tears, then you know it's difficult to put your hand to the plow looking back. Pillar of salt, maybe.

'But there are different elevations. I'm working on my priesthood now. It's a lot of study, a lot of work. I'm glad about – several things. I'm so glad not to be one of these musicians that have been so overcome in the mind by life's ups and down as to be high and drunk on all sorts of pills and amphetamines. I'm happy about that. Because so many of my brothers and sisters have become so nauseated by the press of life until – "Gimme a Scotch and water. And another. And another. And –". I'm glad that my life is basic – three kids – my kids are six, five and four, I've been married seven, eight years now – I really can't complain. I tried to complain the other day, and I got stopped.'

'It didn't work.'

'No, it didn't work. I got stopped right smack in my tracks.'

'What did you try to complain about?'

'Everything. I really did. I woke up one morning and wanted to complain. I went to my study and wrote all the bad that had ever happened to me that I could remember. Then I thought, "Now I'm gonna flip the page, I'm gonna write another page on the good things." I wound up making a sermon titled "Count Up the Cost". What the Devil has done, compared to what God has done, can't be measured. It's not even to be mentioned. Sure, there have been some bad things, if you're about anything, you gonna have that. But I went to my wife and I said, "You know what? The cotton-pickin' good things outweigh the cotton-pickin' bad things." And I went out and apologized to my raccoon.'

'You did what?'

'Well, I had shot at my raccoon, because he keeps goin' in my incinerator, and he have cans all over my yard. He digs in there, and my wife puts biscuits and things in there – I kind of think she's putting them there on purpose, 'cause she knows he's been living out there three years. So I went out there with my pistol and went bang bang bang and he went drdrdrdr toward a tree, and he finally made it. And my pet bull, Ralph – he weights two thousand pounds, a *big* bull, black Angus and Brahma, with a big hump on his back – and all the animals were looking at me, they are so sensitive, they were looking at me like, "What are you doing? Do you actually want to hurt the little raccoon?" I have two horses, and they were looking *very* sad. The cows, the horses, the bull, they looked at me like, Thumbs down for Al. I said, "Will you guys just clear out of here?" Because I felt real bad, real corny about shootin' at the poor raccoon. So I called my horse, and he went the other way. I really got the cold shoulder from everybody. So I called out in the woods, I said, "Hey raccoon! You can come back over here now!" And I heard him making a noise, coming back to his favorite tree. I said, "Are you people – excuse me, are you *animals* satisfied now?" '

'To change the subject, tell me how you feel about Willie Mitchell.'

'He's like "Pop" Mitchell, he's like an older brother. Willie Mitchell is plain, not so sophisticated, not high and mighty. He has a Rolls-Royce too, but he lets his wife drive that, he drives a '54 Chevy. You'd never catch Willie Mitchell driving a Rolls-Royce. It's not his thing. I didn't work with Willie Mitchell for nine years because we sat down together and Willie said, "Al, I don't know nothin' about gospel. I don't know how to cut it. I never cut gospel before." I said, "But Willie, I've got to cut gospel." He said, "Well, I don't know what to tell you. But I just don't know how to deal with it." Then when we were cutting this last album, we did "He Is the Light". I'm not bragging, because I didn't write the song – Willie and Julius Bradley wrote the song – but I sang that song, and Willie said, "Now. Now I understand what you are all about. Now I know what you're singin' about." You need to talk with him. Good man. Sweetest man in the business.'

As I was leaving his office, Al said, 'What was that other song by the Trumpeteers? "Yes, I'm goin' to walk –"'

We finished the chorus together: ' "On that milky white way, O Lord, some of these days".'

A few days later, I attended Sunday morning services at the Full Gospel Tabernacle. The church is not old and grand, but it was pleasant, eight-sided like a Navajo hogan, and it was filled with good spirit. In the course of his remarks that morning, Green made some interesting autobiographical references: 'When you sing a song like "He Cares" or "His Eye is on the Sparrow", that speaks to your heart. Now I came here, an ex-blues singer – and I don't know what God needs with me. He could do very well without me. There are enough preachers in the city of Memphis alone to preach to the United States. Memphis is full of preachers, and full of little churches, there are churches everywhere. And good churches and good preachers. But – "The hand of the Lord was upon me, and I couldn't help myself". And carried me out into the midst of the church world. And set me down in the middle of the church world. And I've never seen such hatred – I've seen hatred out in the pop world, but boy, you haven't seen no hatred till you get in the church. When I was out doin' rhythm and blues, doin' my thing, nobody said nothing. You go to church, whoo.'

The burden of the sermon was the question, 'Can these bones live?' The answer was that they can live, our bones, through the resurrection of Christ. 'You got that? All right. So, you got it, I don't have to preach no mo'.' At that point a woman with a clear, cutting, alto voice, seated in a pew to my right began singing: 'I can do all things through Christ, who strengthens me'. I thought she was just a parishioner who had gotten into the spirit, but after one chorus she stood up, leaving three lovely little girls, and finished the song standing by the pulpit, singing with the minister. She was Shirley Green, the minister's wife, and the little girls were their daughters.

The service ended after the Reverend Mr. Green sang 'Nearer My God to Thee'. The last track on the latest album, it is about as fine a performance as he has ever recorded.

'Thanks for coming,' he told me when the service was over. 'I hope this gave you something more.'

'You gave me a lot already,' I said. 'But this morning you gave me more.'

A few days before, after leaving the office, I had stopped by the little studio, a converted movie theater, where Willie Mitchell was working. In that studio he had cut many great records, among them Ann Peebles's 'I Can't Stand the Rain', Al Green's early hits, and the scorching blues songs of Lynn White. Mitchell, a tall, thin, dapper man, said, 'I come to the studio every morning. I might stay till ten, I might stay till three o'clock in the morning. It's my life, I'm not gonna do anything else. Cutting the Al Green album was mo' fun than I've had in I don't know when. I never laughed so much, laughed at the mistakes – but when it was over, and I put the tape on, it really was a good feeling. Because he can sing. There's no doubt about he can sing.'

16

THAT'S WHY THEY CALL IT THE BLUES: STAX IN ATLANTA

When the twentieth anniversary of Otis Redding and Martin Luther King's death arrived, the memorial concert took place not in Memphis but in Atlanta. Covering the event gave me the chance to renew my acquaintance with the angelic Carla Thomas.

At the redbrick Police Athletic League gymnasium on Hill Street in Atlanta, on the mild, rainy Saturday afternoon before Easter, as I waited I noted that the rehearsal was a typical Memphis music event in that it was happening someplace besides Memphis and was starting late. Bobby Walker, one of three partners whose Aquarius Productions was presenting the Stax Reunion concert the next night at the Civic Center, had told me the day before of 'the need for a celebration to honor both Martin Luther King, who was from Atlanta, and Otis Redding, who was from Macon, Georgia, 87 miles south of Atlanta'. The day after Easter would mark the twentieth anniversary of King's assassination. Redding had been dead twenty years the previous December. Walker had said the rehearsal would be in the afternoon at the PAL, by whom Aquarius Partner Sandra Essex is employed. Now it was four o'clock, and there was no one at the PAL but me and some cops in blue sorting baseball uniforms and some kids in sweats shooting pool. The kids reminded me of the Bar-Kays, the upcoming second-generation Stax house band that died with Otis Redding.

What became Stax records began in 1958 with a one-track tape recorder owned by a white brother and sister, Jim Stewart and Estelle Axton, and located in Brunswick, Tennessee, behind the Satellite Dairy, a take-out ice-cream parlor. Estelle was a grammar-school teacher and Jim was a bank teller and a country fiddle player. They had little knowledge of what they were getting into, but they had incredible luck. For one example, Estelle's son Packy rehearsed on weekends at the Dairy with the Royal Spades, a rhythm and blues band of white Messick High School students that would develop into the Mar-Keys, the Stax house band. For another, in 1960 they found an empty movie theater that rented for $100 a month – the Capitol at 926 East McLemore – in a black South Memphis neighborhood. And Rufus Thomas brought the first hit to Stax. Thomas, who had started out on Beale Street at the age of six playing a frog in a show at the Grand Theater, had been a Rabbit's Foot Minstrel, MC at the Midnight Rambles, half the dance team of Rufus and Bones, a local radio announcer, and the first person to have a hit on the Sun label. 'Cause I Love You', a regional sensation sung by Rufus and his teenaged daughter, Carla, was followed by the first national hit on Stax – 'Gee Whiz' – a solo by Carla, who had written it when she was about fifteen. 'Last Night', the Mar-Keys' instrumental; 'You Don't Miss Your Water', by Memphis band singer William Bell; 'Green Onion', by Booker T. and the MGs, the Mar-Keys' rhythm section; Rufus's 'The Dog' and 'Walkin' the Dog', the latter covered by the Rolling Stones complete with whistles by Brian Jones, kept Stax in the pop spotlight.

In October of 1962 Stax released its first Otis Redding record, made in half an hour at the end of a Johnny Jenkins session. At WLAC radio station in Nashville, announcer John Richbourg, who had wound up with part of the publishing rights to the record, played 'These Arms of Mine' night after night for months, until it became a hit. Other hits followed for Otis, among them 'I've Been Loving You Too Long', 'Try A Little Tenderness' and 'Satisfaction' (one of Keith Richards's proudest days). Blues singers Johnny Taylor and Albert King, the Staples Singers gospel group, rhythm and blues singer Eddie Floyd, even local Memphis groups like Ollie and the Nightingales and the Mad Lads had at least small hits on Stax. Atlantic Records, Stax's distributor, brought Wilson

Pickett and the duo Sam Moore and Dave Prater to the label. In 1967 a Stax Revue toured Europe, and at Monterey Pop, as *Esquire* observed, 'the most tumultuous reception of the Festival' went to Otis Redding and the Mar-Keys.

There was the feeling in the air that summer – the summer of Monterey, of Sergeant Pepper, of LSD – that people were coming together, red and yellow, black and white, in peace and love.

In December Otis Redding would record 'Dock of the Bay'. None of us knew what was coming.

In the wake of Martin Luther King's death, the climate for an integrated business in a black neighborhood changed, even on East McLemore Avenue. The front door at Stax, which had always been left open – Carl Cunningham, the Bar-Kays' drummer, had come in one day with his shoeshine kit and stayed to become a musician – was locked. Then one day it was locked for good. Today Stax is a crumbling shell. It was as if Stax had such good luck in the beginning that when at the end the bad luck came it was annihilating.

It was nearly five o'clock at the PAL gym when the guitarist Leroyal Hadley and several other musicians from the Joe Tex band came in, followed by Eddie Floyd. I had never met Floyd before. He had come to Stax from Washington in 1965 with Al Bell, Jim Stewart's partner at the time Stax went bankrupt, still a controversial figure in the record company's history.

'The first time I went to Stax', he told me, 'was for a Carla Thomas session, the song was "Comfort Me". I had started talkin' about writing in 1965. I wrote "Stop – Look What You're Doin' to Me", then "634-5789" for Wilson Pickett, then "Knock on Wood" I really wrote for Otis, I wanted to submit it for him to sing, and they heard it and put it out, just the demo. Well, there wasn't no demo, we just did the song. One take. It was rainin' the night we wrote it – you know that part in there, "Seems like thunder – lightnin'" – it was a rainstorm goin' on. That song has been recorded now sixty or sixty-one times. The last time I was at Stax was about one hour before the federal marshals said, "We closin' this joint." I was at the studio, and by the time I got home and called back, a federal marshal answered and said "Stax is closed."

'I'd like to still be there recording, because of the studio, the people, the atmosphere. Everybody was together, I'd sing background on a Johnny Taylor song, we were real helpful to each other. Toward the end the company brought in a lot of new people, but they weren't the right people because they drained the company.

'Why are they having this show in Atlanta and not Memphis, you'd have to ask the people in Memphis. You ask me can I see it happening again, William Bell has a label now and we have some new records out. Me, William, and Luther Ingram, we gone try to make it happen here in Atlanta, Georgia.'

While we had been talking, the band had been setting up and Rufus 'Snow White–Bear Cat–The Dog' Thomas, the World's Oldest Teenager, had come in, wearing a blue-and-white warm-up outfit and a red bill-cap from Shelby State, the Memphis college starting a cultural scholarship fund named after him. He laid a clutch of manila folders on the wooden bleachers, picked up a stray basketball, dribbled out to the free-throw line and made a few shots as Eddie Floyd began rehearsing with the band, doing his current release, 'My Baby Loves the Soaps', which includes a long list: 'General Hospital – yeah! The Young and the Restless – all right!' and so on.

Losing interest in basketball, Rufus Thomas drifted over and sat on a guitar amp, drinking from a quart carton of sweet milk and glaring at Floyd, who was waving his right hand in arcs, directing the horns as they played 'Dock of the Bay'.

William Bell and Luther Ingram had come in, Bell springlike in white cotton warm-ups, Ingram dressed in jeans, leather jacket, army-reserve camouflage cap, mirror shades, on his arm a thin yellow woman in red high-heels. Bell said the concert was like 'a family reunion'. Having it take place in Atlanta 'is ironic – I was born and grew up in Memphis – but Atlanta is my home now, I've lived here fifteen years. I think as far as music is concerned, Atlanta will be the next city. Memphis is tied to Atlanta because of the death of Martin Luther King and because some of us, like Isaac Hayes and me, live here now. I think Atlanta is tops. There's a good attitude here.'

Eddie Floyd finished rehearsing and some of the musicians began to look over Thomas's charts.

'What instrument is this for?' one asked.

'I have no idea,' an older one said. 'I know those are music notes, I remember seein' that in school.'

As Thomas passed out the sheets he spun around, making gestures behind his back, finger symbols representing fines for miscues and bad notes. 'You know about that,' he said. 'Joe Tex did that to you.'

Some of the musicians laughed. About half of them were veterans of Joe Tex's and other bands, but none of them had played at Stax, and the other half looked too young to have been with any organization that didn't also have a football team.

Carla Thomas swept in wearing a blue denim skirt with zippered maxi midi and mini tiers and a wide-brimmed blue straw chapeau, a perfect honeychile. When Otis Redding was the King, Carla Thomas was the Queen. If her work lacked the complexity of Aretha Franklin's, so did her life, and this, one suspects, has been her good fortune. Since the death of Stax she has not released any records, though she still performs and was at that moment waiting for the chance to rehearse. She stood by as the tension mounted while her father, starting with 'Walkin' the Dog', fought the odds of being among musicians far different from the Mar-Keys and Booker T. and the MGs.

Ronnie Hawkins has said that in his youth he would advise east-bound Arkansas musicians to 'go straight to Nashville, don't even slow down in Memphis, they got garbage collectors there that'll blow you off the stage'. Memphis has so many good musicians – and such is the public's indifference to them – that even the best are often unemployed. Great players come from everywhere, but the products of studios like Sun, Stax, Hi, Goldwax, Sonic, American, Onyx, Fre-Tone, Royal and Ardent demonstrate that the level of blues playing in Memphis is the highest. An old black Memphis musician stood one night in an alley beside a young white guitarist, pointed to the stars, and said, 'You don't plays de notes – you plays de molecules.' Certain rhythm patterns, certain accents and syncopations, become second nature to a Memphis player as he acquires a stylistic shorthand that in the end becomes a musical language, one that is a bit opaque even to a New Orleans player. Rufus Thomas's act is in essence comedy, and no comedian is more aware than The Dog, a.k.a. The Frog, that old tap-dancer, of the need for perfect timing. Over and over he questioned horn players' readings: 'Wait on me – *Now*, the time to go up – if you gone squeak, don't make it.' He grimaced, listening. Between this venerable minstrel, who would say to his radio audience, 'This is chocolate lightnin',' and the young musicians, communication was imperfect. 'I can't teach you the blues,' he said at last, exasperated. 'You got to *know* them.'

Luther Ingram rehearsed after Thomas, but instead of giving the band sheet music, he played each song on a small cassette-player while sitting slumped and uncommunicative behind his mirror shades. The music was simpler than Thomas's had been, and the band learned their parts quickly. William Bell rehearsed next, with a band from Macon called Danger Zone that included the kids I had seen shooting pool. Behind Bell's warm baritone they sounded strong and precise. By the time Bell had finished, it was too late to get the other band together again, so Carla Thomas, taking the charts written at the PAL by her younger brother Marvell, went with her younger sister Vaneese to Smyrna, an Atlanta suburb, where some friends had laid on a soul-food feast.

I kept asking everyone I talked to why the concert was taking place in Atlanta rather than Memphis, partly because I knew that earlier this year the Memphis Mayor's office had released a press statement announcing a concert much like the Atlanta one, to honor Martin Luther King and show how far Memphis had come since his death. It sounded like a good idea to David Less, entertainment director of the Peabody Hotels, who called to offer his help and was told that all participants would be expected to contribute their services. 'But wasn't Martin Luther King in Memphis to help garbage workers get paid?' Less asked. 'You intend to honor his memory by not paying musicians?'

Carla, with cynicism born of a lifetime begun in a Memphis housing project, attributed the Memphis concert plan to a desire on the Mayor's part to recoup some of the face he had lost by resisting the January Martin Luther King holiday for municipal employees. Marvell Thomas told me that when a Memphis Symphony musician called him on behalf of the Mayor's office about the concert, he'd advised the man to drop the matter, and the idea did go away. Of Memphis civic leaders, Marvell said, 'Those people think so small. They can't accept that the only value Memphis has in the international community derives from its black music. They want to ignore it.'

The next day, standing in a corridor backstage at the Atlanta Civic Center, Isaac Hayes, also speaking of Memphis civic leaders, said, 'Those assholes. That's why I left Memphis. They're supposed to be statesmen and leaders and they so ignorant. There's still bigotry. It's disgusting and frustrating. They wanted to do a concert to show how far Memphis has come, and not pay anybody. That shows exactly how far.'

We talked about friends in Memphis, and I mentioned my favorite Isaac Hayes album, the first one. 'Oh God, I was drunk. We were all drunk,' Hayes said. His new album, the second for CBS, was just finished, and he was thinking of touring this summer. 'Tonight will be my first live show in this country in ten years,' he said, giving a rueful downward glance at the extra 40 pounds over stage weight he had collected. He had gone from a poor Memphis neighborhood and a job cleaning the floor in a slaughterhouse to being a writer of classic hits like 'Soul Man' and 'Hold on, I'm Comin'' and a star of stage, screen and television. But in his dark shades, red-leather fez, red, black and yellow print slacks and red T-shirt, he was nervous. 'I'm sweating this rehearsal. I was spozed to do a sound check at three o'clock. Damn, Carla, come on.'

Carla Thomas, who had emerged from a white limousine in an apricot silk jumpsuit and matching wide-brimmed straw, looking devastating but preoccupied, was onstage working with the band, her manner as painstaking as her father's had been. 'Don't forget,' she told the horn players, 'you got to get right back in there. After the solo I don't go back, I go to "sigh with the feelin'", back to the beginning and the vamp.' Because the musicians were different from the old Stax band, every moment of rehearsal was valuable.

Rain sprinkled and threatened all Easter afternoon. Backstage, singers, musicians, photographers, bodyguards, various kinds of managers and promoters, all mingled. I had time to make the acquaintance of Sam Coplin, from Dallas, Texas, sitting just inside the back door of the Civic Center on a metal folding chair. Coplin, who looked to be maybe fifty, was dressed in polyester velour athletic drag, with light brown hair and plastic-rimmed glasses. He said he'd done personal appearance contracts for such people as Muhammed Ali, George Foreman, Joe Frazier, Rod

McKuen (what a fighter), Charlie Rich, Joe Tex, Dionne Warwick and Henry Mancini, and told me he was having the concern recorded (on a 24-track mobile unit parked just outside) 'to see how many of these people still have it, see if we can do some more of these shows'. Also backstage was the silk-suited Thomas 'Shotgun' Morgan of Rentz, Georgia's Shotgun Productions. Shotgun was featured in the *National Enquirer* last November for having saved the life of a man whose car had crashed through a bridge and down an embankment on the Atlanta Highway. Shotgun showed me the story. 'It's holp me a heap,' he said, and promised to send me tickets for a show he's promoting in Macon.

At 7.30 – twilight – Eddie Floyd opened the Stax Reunion show. The Civic Center, a blond brick building two years old at the time of Martin Luther King's death, held on this occasion a bit less than its capacity of about 3,000, most of whom appeared not young and not white. A six by eight-foot picture of Otis Redding hung from the stage's rear curtain. Eddie Floyd was always an effective performer, and he is leaner and better-looking now than when he was at Stax. The audience remembered 'Never Found a Girl', 'Knock on Wood' and 'Dock of the Bay', and seemed to like the new soap-opera song.

Floyd was followed by Rufus Thomas, who was seventy-two that day, and came onstage in a red jacket, red knee-length shorts, a red cape, and pink suede high-laced boots. It was not quite like playing Switzerland, but the minstrel tradition and the Atlanta Easter crowd seemed distant. Still, 'Walkin' the Dog', 'The Funky Chicken' and 'The Push and Pull' got them going. Rufus Thomas can, as Mama Rose Newborn says Gatemouth Moore used to do at Memphis's Brown Derby, 'sing the blues till the hair stand up on your head', but one got the feeling that the Atlanta audience hadn't had the hair stand up on their heads in a long time.

Next Carla Thomas, radiant in a white dress and drop earrings, did 'Lovey Dovey', 'Baby, Let Me Be Good to You', Donny Hathaway's 'Someday We'll All Be Free', 'B-A-B-Y' and 'Gee Whiz', the last of which has been in her repertoire for almost thirty years and still has the power to raise goose bumps. From Carla, who is much given to good works in Memphis for causes like literacy, there emanates a genuine glow of goodness, and something – possibly clean living – has enabled her to maintain an *ingénue* quality. Atlanta adored her. The next day I found this line in my notebook: Is there any place besides Memphis where singers like Carla Thomas and Anne Peebles go unrecorded?

The first half of the show was closed by the new Sam and the old Dave. The original Sam and Dave had not performed together in years. These two did 'Hold On, I'm Comin'', 'When Something Is Wrong With My Baby', 'Soul Man', 'I Thank You', and for the first time that night, I thought of a performance from twenty years earlier – the real Sam and Dave (not that they were ever as real as, say, Isaac Hayes and David Porter) at that WDIA Goodwill Revue in 1967, all in white, with their band strung out in a line across the stage, all dancing. The comparison with the dirge-like performance in Atlanta was cruel, making even more ironic Dave Prater's death six days later in a car wreck.

After the intermission, spent reviewing the astonishing outfits in the lobby, I went in to see William Bell and Danger Zone onstage and in command. I had never seen Bell, Stax's pipe-smoking intellectual, perform, and seeing him, relaxed and open in a blue jumpsuit, doing 'Everybody Loves a Winner', 'Every Day Will Be Like a Holiday' and 'You Don't Miss Your Water', I found myself wondering how, even without Otis Redding and the Bar-Kays, a studio with as much talent as Stax could also have the executive ability to destroy itself. William Bell and Carla Thomas were the best acts I saw all night.

Almost as good, though, was Luther Ingram, who came onstage next, still wearing dark glasses, now with a black velvet suit. Ingram hides behind the glasses and an offhand manner, but onstage he is most accessible, a performer of deep feeling and unexpected humor, with a voice not so different from Al Green's – less acrobatic but no less convincing. He opened wisely with 'Stand By Me', building to 'If Loving You Is Wrong'.

While Ingram was still on I went backstage to congratulate William Bell and Rufus and Carla Thomas, and walked into a controversy over Sam Coplin's taping, which nobody had noticed until the show was well under way. Some of the tapes, cassettes and quarter-inch, had been confiscated from the truck in the midst of threats from the musicians not to go on and from the musicians' union to stop the show. By the time I got back to my seat Johnny Taylor was on. He looked good, in a black sequined jacket, but he was hoarse. Still he stayed on forever, doing an impressive and eventually numbing series of hits – 'Who's Making Love', 'Disco Lady' and a thousand more.

The technique of staying onstage until there is no audience for the performer following you probably antedates the minstrel days, and all Memphis performers know it. Isaac Hayes's set was late and anticlimactic. It began with a fanfare from behind a closed curtain, long synthesizer chords becoming a boogaloo rhythm pattern, curtain up, the whole thing developing into the Doors' 'Light My Fire' and, after a bit, 'Never Can Say Goodbye'. Then as Hayes, dressed in a black-tie outfit, sat at the baby grand and performed a touching number called 'Windows of the World', people who had to get up early in the morning began to walk out. Isaac Hayes's talent is not in question, but that night the audience had no energy left to give him. His set closed with 'Shaft', from his Oscar-winning film score.

After the show it turned out that all the unauthorized tapes were accounted for except the 24-track master. Most of the performers went to an Atlanta club where there was supposed to be food, a banquet table for the Stax family. The air there turned out to be bad, the lights aggressive, the banquet grim. The performers were herded into the foyer and photographed for the club's celebrity-photo wall. Carla was waiting for the limo to come back from taking Johnny Taylor to his hotel when closing time came and she found herself standing on the club's steps. She had come from benighted Memphis to progressive Atlanta, where she had worried, she had worked, she had done good. At the club she had been used and insulted, and at the concert, in her view, perhaps robbed. She was exhausted and she wanted to sit down. This music is about redemption. A friend, putting an arm around the magnificent shoulders of Carla Thomas, said, 'Don't worry, baby. That's why they call it the blues.'

17

THE BURDEN OF THE BLUES: ZZ TOP

In 1988, having heard that Phineas Newborn, Jr., the greatest musician I have ever known, was doing poorly, I scouted around for a story that would take me to Memphis. It turned out to be ZZ Top and a visit to Clarksdale, Mississippi, home of the Blues Museum, a town that has done itself much economic good by recognizing its musical heritage. Memphis could gleam like a moonlit pearl in the world's regard if its politicians would honor Jimmie Lunceford and George Coleman.

The first time ZZ Top left Texas was to play at the 1971 Memphis Blues Festival. 'We showed up the afternoon of the show,' Billy Gibbons recalled, 'and we wound up staying in the Linden Lodge there on Linden and Second, all huddled up in one room. Ham says, "Let's take a walk, Beale Street's just a block up," and I said OK. So here we were cuttin' down the sidewalk, he's talkin' – *foom* – a big dirt clod flies past. He says, "Whoa, wait a minute." There was this black guy and this woman screamin' at each other, throwin' dirt clods at one another. Ham kinda laughed, he said, "Only in Memphis. Beale Street. I'm glad to see not too much has changed." That night we're standin' in the wings waiting to go on, and Ham taps me on the shoulder, and he says, "Man, are you seein' what I'm seein'?" The guy throwin' the dirt clods was onstage. It was Johnny Woods and his wife, and they were gettin' along famously.'
  I was at the Festival that night, and as I told Gibbons, I would regret having left without hearing this unknown band, ZZ Top, had I not gone

with Furry Lewis to an East Memphis society party where we were thrown out. We ended up early the next morning drunk in a friend's kitchen. 'I want to pick "When I Lay My Burden Down",' Furry announced. 'My guitar's in the car – please bring me my burden.'

'That says it. Bring it on,' Gibbons said. 'Walter Baldwin, my old Houston buddy who had moved to Tennessee, was responsible for taking ZZ Top's first album over to Steadman Mathews, a producer of the blues show, and that was our first out-of-state gig. After that show I made friends with the Memphis faction of vintage guitar-freaks. A Memphis guitarist backstage said, "I see you're into the old shit, you got that old Fender amp and that old Gibson guitar. We locals need to meet you cats." And that's what started the Memphis connection.'

That year acts from the Memphis Blues Festival, including Furry and ZZ, went a day or so later to New Orleans.

'We were playin',' Gibbons said, 'and I noticed Dusty had this rather gleeful look – or maybe *worried* – 'cause Furry Lewis was marching – he was just doing a stagger-step toward Dusty, waving a white handkerchief, comin' from the wings, right out onstage. Here's these young white guys, y'know, gone do a *show* – Dusty says, "Man, what next?" '

ZZ Top had, that day in New Orleans, one album on the London label, produced for about $12,000. Nearly twenty years later they were one of the most popular acts in the world and had sold more blues records than anyone ever. How did they go wrong?

Billy's father, Fred Gibbons, a transplanted New Yorker whose talents at keyboards and arranging made him the top Houston society bandleader and brought him work with film studios in Hollywood and big bands in Las Vegas, gave Billy a Gibson Melody Maker guitar and a Fender Champ amplifier for Christmas in 1963, thirty-three days after Jack Kennedy'd been killed in Dallas. Billy had become fourteen on December 12. Unlike most blues players, from B.B. King on, who perfected their craft in the face of their families' insistence that they stop that racket and get a job, Billy had a father who encouraged him not to do something else but to do what he wanted better. Fred Gibbons knew, because he did it, that a musician could make a good living. The Gibbons family lived in Tanglewood, which has been called 'the second nicest neighborhood in Houston'. One thing they had no shortage of during the '50s and '60s was maids, black women who would come in to cook and clean. The maid at Billy's house was called Big Stella to distinguish her from her daughter, Little Stella, who took Billy and his younger sister Pam to see Little Richard.

'Everybody learned it from the yard man,' Jim Dickinson said, speaking of his Southern white musical colleagues, and it is true that many of the great ones, including Jimmie Rodgers, Hank Williams and Sam Phillips, have named specific laboring-class black men who taught and inspired them. Gibbons may be the first lucky enough to have learned from the maid's daughter. 'Little Stella was always buying the records and that's what we were listening to,' he was quoted as saying in Deborah Faust's book *Bad & Worldwide*. 'All the Little Richard stuff, Larry Williams's "Short Fat Fanny", Jimmy Reed, T-Bone Walker, B.B. King, the usual line-up of R&B stars.'

The boogie disease dropped Billy like a shot. A germ within him seems to have been awakened. A classmate at Houston's Lee High School – Don Lampton, who went on to play rhythm guitar in Fever Tree – said, 'I don't know too many people that at fourteen can fall down on their knees in front of a bunch of other kids and do James Brown's "Please Please Please" and pull it off.'

High school found Billy in a band called the Coachmen, after a Houston teen club, the Coachman Inn. They changed their name to the Moving Sidewalks when they recorded '99th Floor', a song Billy had written in his eleventh-grade math class. The record became a regional hit, and when the Sidewalks graduated they were playing regular club gigs in Texas and Louisiana. They opened for the Doors in Houston and played in Dallas, Houston and San Antonio on a show that starred Jimi Hendrix. Eric Clapton heard the band rehearsing at the Catacombs, a basement club in Houston, walked onstage and shook Gibbons's hand. None of these events brought overnight success.

In time the Sidewalks became ZZ Top, changing personnel early on to settle into a trio format with Gibbons and two hardcore blues players, bassist Dusty Hill and drummer Frank Beard, Dallas high-school dropouts who'd played with Dusty's brother Rocky in a band called

American Blues. They also acquired what may have been a vital ingredient: their Svengali, Bill Ham.

Ham, who could double for Kenny Rogers, had had a single on Randy Wood's Dot Records, had done promotion work for the label, knew Pat Boone in Dallas, had worked with Huey Meaux. Gibbons said, 'We had crossed paths when Ham was in Houston, traveling with John Mayall. Mayall had come to town, he was doin' a swing through the cities, doin' a little one-man promo tour, the Blues Breakers were startin' to happen – Mayall requested a jam session in Houston and we volunteered to fill the bill. After it was over we went back and and made acquaintance with Ham, who was showin' Mayall around the city, acquaintin' him with what was happenin', and a few months later we approached Ham to accept a role in a management position. Here was a guy that had his priorities in the same place we did – a man that loved them blues – and it's been like that ever since. He writes with us, he'll get right down there and scratch with us.'

Ham has been cited by the press for 'erratic behavior'. So have others. Atlantic Records producer Ahmet Ertegun called Leonard Chess to say that he'd phoned an Atlanta disc jockey and threatened the lives of his family if he didn't play more Chess Records. Then Ertegun asked Chess, 'So what are you doing for Atlantic in Chicago?' Billy Sherrill has told about the time when Sam Phillips, after six months' absence, came into a studio Billy was running for Phillips in Nashville. 'There were all sorts of recording accounts overdue, one company owed us $20,000. I was scared to death of what he'd say. When he started out he pointed to the Coke machine. "People been takin' them Coke bottles," he said. "Every time one of them bottles walks out of here it's two cent *gone*." I could quote stronger examples – arriving at Sam Phillips's Madison Avenue studio in time to see a background singer, whom Jim Dickinson must have failed to inform of his intention to record live ammunition on the last track, attain full flight – my point being that erratic behavior among record producers is, shall we say, not unheard of.

Ham had done a study of Colonel Parker, that erratic Dutchman, and it is easy to see the Colonel's method in much of Ham's madness. Bill Ham has over the years severely limited access to ZZ Top, and having ZZ appear onstage with livestock is reminiscent of Parker's master-stroke, the parade down the Las Vegas Strip by the Elvis Presley Midget Fan Club. But Ham, unlike the Colonel, cared about the music.

ZZ Top's first winter was 1969, the time of Vietnam, Manson and Altamont, the season of the witch, when Dusty dropped and broke the wine he and Frank had bought with their last few coins. Two years later they were playing the Memphis Blues Show with acts none of whom made a living from music. It was not until 1974, when they came to Ardent Studios in Memphis, that the record-business lightning struck. Terry Manning, an engineer at Ardent since the '60s, who had worked with Led Zeppelin and made one of the better Furry Lewis recordings, done on location at Fourth and Beale with Furry in bed, engineered and mixed *Très Hombres*, and for the first time the band started receiving serious royalties. (Would that Manning had bestowed such riches on Furry.) Old Ardent hands say that for the first three years Ham would, for instance, tell Manning to turn up the guitar on a cassette tape, and Manning would twist a few controls. The important thing is, Ham and ZZ Top knew what they wanted to hear.

ZZ Top were playing three hundred nights a year, a regular blues player's schedule, but with a difference. According to the musicologist Deborah Faust:

On June 9, 1974, they broke Elvis's record at the Nashville State Fairgrounds. On September 23, 1974, they broke the Rolling Stones' record at the Long Beach Arena in California. On July 3, 1975, they outdrew Leon Russell in his Tulsa hometown, at the State Fairgrounds. On July 26, 1975, they broke Led Zeppelin's record at New Orleans' City Park Stadium.

Their next album, *Fandango!* – one side recorded live at the Warehouse in New Orleans, the other recorded the same way, it would appear, at Ardent – contained the classic, 'Tush', and Top graduated to another music-business weight class. They supported their 1976 album *Tejas* with a world tour that included, live and onstage, a buffalo, a Texas longhorn, a wolf, five buzzards and a nest of snakes that died of the vibes. No act had ever carried such a load – about 75 tons of equipment, not counting livestock – and after that tour, ZZ Top did not work for three years.

This Texas boogie band enjoyed a vogue during 1975 and 1976, when its concerts broke attendance records set by the Beatles, among others. But on record, ZZ Top was never more than a poor man's Lynyrd Skynrd – some rural feeling but mostly just numbing guitar drive. Rock 'n' roll can be mindless fun, but it never deserved to be this empty headed.

Dave Marsh, *Rolling Stone Record Guide*

Few artists realize, when they pick up their crayons or their ukuleles, that when they grow up and go public they will be considered fair targets for personal insults. *De Guello* – a Mexican expression meaning 'no quarter' – it was what Davy Crockett and Jim Bowie heard, waiting inside the Alamo – 'was a turning point for me', Gibbons said. 'That was the first release following that three-year disappearing act, and so much had changed on the music scene. Disco had come and gone, that scene in England had just wiped out everything as we knew it and left it with a really different stroke, and there was such a feeling going on at the time, I don't know if words could describe it, all I knew was I wanted a piece of it. Because it was really – music was getting fun again, and that's what came out of it. I shared that with my partners, and I knew that it was true when we got together and discussed it, not having seen each other for a year. They each felt it too.

'Old Lester Bangs, while he was alive, gave me a high compliment. He played the album for some of his younger pals, didn't tell them it was ZZ Top, and they liked it. That blindfold test says it. You can tell people, "Dig this, it's the new so-and-so", and if they happen to be happening at the moment, everybody says, "Oh, yeah, it's great." But that was a high compliment.'

The albums that followed, *El Loco, Eliminator* and *Afterburner* – the last two multi-platinum megahits, *Afterburner*'s appeal supercharged by the clever videos of Randy Newman's cousin Tim – have given ZZ Top the power to bestow boons, and that is how we happened to meet. 'Last summer, as time would have it,' Gibbons recalled, 'we were permitted to drive to Clarksdale to pay a visit to Sid Graves at the Delta Blues Museum – and that particular afternoon he advised us that he was heading to Stovall Plantation, twelve miles up the road, to inspect the cabin of Muddy Waters, because the highway department had requested it be dismantled for safety reasons. It'd been recently hit by a tornado, and the Stovall family were quite concerned over the interest suddenly given the cabin. We did indeed drive up there, and while we were there I was handed a log out of a stack of discarded roof timber that had caved in, and it was on the way back to Memphis the thought popped up to turn the log into a guitar. The Pyramid guitar company in Memphis accepted the commission to take this battered piece of cypress – which really held no promise for much of anything at that point – and transform it into this rather appropriate symbol.' ZZ Top then donated the guitar, white enamel with a representation of the Mississippi river down the neck – one of two Pyramids made from the piece of cabin wood – to the Museum, with civic ceremonies featuring Clarksdale's Mayor, Sheriff, Chief of Police, and ZZ Top, before an audience including two battle-strength platoons of journalists imported from MTV, big-city papers, music rags.

The event's purpose was to launch the Blues Museum's $1 million fund drive and to honor the memory of Waters, who had played a number of Texas dates on ZZ's world tour.

'When we came down to do some home dates we were just wondering what flavorful addition we could include to really embrace the feeling that we were trying to give back to our home state,' Gibbons said. 'The blues being such a big part not only of our music but of everybody's music in Texas, Muddy Waters seemed to be a logical choice. The band was tiptop. He was doing some of his best playing. It was really a very moving experience.'

At the Clarksdale ceremony Gibbons said, 'We've been fans of what goes on here in the Delta for a long long time and it's with great respect we would like to make this official by presenting the guitar that was constructed out of Muddy Waters's house, as a focus of the spirit of the American art form we've known as the blues.'

Recording artists as profitable to their label as ZZ Top inevitably receive promotional assistance sufficient to make physically uncomfortable and to waste the time of anyone trying to carry on a profession, such as journalism, around them. While the troops waited outside the Carnegie

Public Library in the Delta heat for ZZ Top to appear at any moment, I had time to photograph polyester-clothing shops, a hardware store with a sign outside saying 'Music Lessons', and a blonde library assistant with whom I had fallen in love, but I never got to see the museum. Then as fate would have it, the film was lost in the mail, and the tapes of my interview with ZZ Top, later that afternoon in the library (of all places), turned out blank. My first question to the band had been, 'Do you guys have anything for pain?'

But I'm glad I went to Clarksdale. I had never seen a Southern community with the sense to increase its stature by recognizing its true nature. And later on, remembering Sam Phillips's story of how he campaigned to buy uniforms for his high-school band, the civic scene seemed to make more sense.

Later, Gibbons and I talked on the phone. Our conversation opened with a bit of gossip, to which he contributed the story of Muscle Schoals' bass player Eddie Hinton 'sitting on a park bench holding his belongings – on his last dime, and they ushered him into one of these rescue missions where they passed the hat, made enough money to do a session, and cut an album on Eddie Hinton from donation money, and put it out on this rescue mission record label. I thought that was the finest thing I'd heard lately,' and I offered up the fact that Domingo Samudio – Sam the Sham, who did 'Wooly Bully' – is preaching on the street in Memphis.

These days Gibbons divides his time between Houston, Memphis, and the rest of the world. I suspect that one reason he likes Memphis, besides hearing Rufus Thomas on the radio, is that he gets to hang out with the likes of Albert King, whom he had just left when we talked. 'I gave him this guitar – his birthday was last month, and I have this guitar layin' around, and I took it over, he said, "Strike me an E on the piano." My next note was the proper, schoolbook way of tuning a guitar. He said, "Man, that's all I need. I take it my own way from here."'

Guitarists like King and Gibbons worked for years to get sounds now obtainable by any teenager with enough money to buy a Rockman amp, and I asked Gibbons how he felt about that.

'The Rockman,' he said, 'was the missing bridge between those with and those without. And we are talking about Tone with a capital T.

I think it has gone unheralded as just that. I think that with today's global marketing measures it's very easy to pigeonhole this thing and call it another fuzzbox. But you get the gamut using it, from serious jazzers to sixteen-year-old USA in the bedroom, just pluggin' in for the first time. It delivers – mammoth – on your doorstep: Tone.'

'But that was something you got without the Rockman.'

'Brother, I tell you, where was he when I needed him, right – but it's funny, that bridge – let's just call it what it is – those with and those without – it is a convenience, but the real test is not to rely on it and run the risk of becoming homogeneous. There's one saving grace, and I know you can connect with this. I'm a contrarian to the saying, "You can have too much of a good thing." I don't think you can.'

Far from connecting, I was getting a bit lost. 'So,' I asked, 'do you use a Rockman?'

'*Yeah* – in fact, I don't know how the manufacturer feels about it, but I may be one of the few guys that leapfrogs 'em, y'know, plugs one into the next one which goes into the next one, and so on and so forth. And you really can get way out.'

I had only recently learned of the existence of the Fairlight, 'the Ferrari', Gibbons told me, 'of modern computer musical instruments, the one instrument that contains enough sophistication to step beyond being shackled to it. This sucker is deep. I always figured if ZZ Top gets involved with synthesizers, or shall we say electronic music, I want to get my hands on the one that sound like garbage cans. This thing is so damn deep that we can't get past it sounding like garbage.' (I mentioned this to Jim Dickinson, whom Gibbons seems to regard as a shaman, and he said, 'Billy's being modest. He may be naive about some of the things he's doing with the Fairlight, but his application is far from naive.')

'What pisses me off,' Gibbons said, 'is I waited and waited and all the time – see, it's like anything else, in order to learn the big stuff you had to've started with the simple stuff. But that made too much damn sense. So we're playin' catch-up.'

I asked Gibbons what he thought of the tendency for young players to play as fast as possible. 'There is, of course, room for all of it,' he said, 'and what's encouraging is to finally run out of space – you know, you get so many notes between the lines on sheet music, and there's no more paper to write on, so where do you go, you have to go to Tone – it may be the next frontier – because after the technical expertise code, shall we say, is cracked, the really impressive moments cease to be such. Let me see if I can unravel what I'm thinking. Guy walks in, plays a bunch of rapid passages. Two years later, thirty people have done it. Another year later, everybody does it, and it's like – ah, no big deal. Then you get a guy that does it with tone or taste or a little quirk. Give me one note or a hundred, as long as you dredge up emotions.'

At this point I went off into a tirade about Whitesnake, whom I had seen in Jacksonville, Florida, 'where,' as the lead singer said, 'all the women have big tits'. After confessing to Gibbons that for the next week I had shouted, 'Tipper Gore is right!' I observed that touring with the Stones had never been like that. With the Stones, Gibbons said, 'we're talking at least some semblance of restraint. Taste and Tone. Frank and Dusty, my partners, concur with this one hundred per cent. That is one of the reasons we've stayed together for twenty years. At the bottom of all of it you've got a deep love of music and a robust sense of respect.'

'But ZZ Top appeals to at least part of the same audience as some heavy-metal bands – how come?'

'I used to wonder, and an engineer came up to me – real analytical – and he said, "You guys play eighth-note chugs slightly behind the beat. I listen to you guys do ballads, and they sound a hundred times heavier than if you played it right on top of the beat." That's it. It's the weight. There was a time, keep in mind, the term heavy metal was derogatory.'

'Isn't it still? I intended it to be derogatory,' I said, and after reminiscing for a moment about early heavy metal – 'Remember that guy in Blue Cheer used to play with cut-off broomsticks for drumsticks?' Gibbons said – we got back to talking about the blues.

'That day in Clarksdale, our true intent was not to do anything more than a little illumination on what the museum stands for. There are many of these cats – as long as the originators are still around – the interpreters better fold their arms and be smilin', because they're very lucky. So many art forms die, and then it's a matter of guesswork and nobody can ever be sure if it's right.'

'What do ZZ Top and Muddy Waters have in common?' I asked then (because a Yankee editor had told me to, and I loves to serve).

'Three chords,' Gibbons said, giving the question the proper amount of shrift. 'To expound on that would be an injustice – to get too far beyond the scope of the original three chords. I have suddenly realized how much of an influence the Rolling Stones have been. On my music, on everybody's. I always kept in the back of my mind what they had done as a whole, but you get so used to hearing, "influenced by the Rolling Stones," it's like, you don't miss your water. Elvis left us, our kind-of groundbreaking guide to what to do after forty – and now I'm sayin', "Goddam, please, Rollin' Stones, don't mess up, somebody gotta keep on, man." Keith Richards made a real apropos statement. He said, "As long as I can just introduce some new twist to those same three chords, we'll stay in business." He pointed out that Muddy Waters, Mississippi Fred McDowell, all these cats were doin' it till the day they died, and havin' a great time.'

18

KEITH RICHARDS AT FORTY-FIVE

When, after the Rolling Stones left Atlantic Records for Columbia, Mick Jagger refused to tour with the group, Keith Richards recorded a solo album and went on the road with a band called the X-Pensive Winos. I dropped by to pay my respects.

> The fiddlers or guirots are reckoned rich, and their wives have more crystal, blue stones, and beads about them than the king's wives . . . and it is remarkable that after all this fondness of the people for music, and yet the musician is held in great contempt and is denied their common right of burial, instead of which the corpse is set upright in a hollow tree and left there to rot. The reason they give for this treatment is that the cantators have a familiar converse with their Devil, Ho-Ré.
>
> *Green's Collection of Voyages*, London, 1745

The first time I saw the Rolling Stones, they were on television: five funny-looking boys on *Shindig*, one of the rock and roll shows that sprang up like mushrooms (and faded just as fast) in the wake of the Beatles' 1964 invasion. I had seen the Beatles, but I thought Chuck Berry did his songs better. The Stones, though, got my attention because they had brought along Howlin' Wolf. Whoever these guys are, I thought, if they with the Wolf, they somebody. (Sam Phillips was pleased to discover Elvis Presley, but when he first recorded Howlin' Wolf, he said to himself, 'This is where the soul of man never dies.')

When I was working for the Tennessee Department of Public Welfare. I would come out of a house that reeked with the urine-stench of poverty, turn on the radio, hear the Supremes' bouncy cheer, and turn it off. But the Stones I could listen to no matter where I'd been or what I'd had to smell.

So in the autumn of 1968, that year of assassinations, riots, and undeclared war, I went to England to meet the Rolling Stones. Three flights up in an old building at 46A Maddox Street in London, they had an office whose floorboards creaked. Their secretary, an American girl named Jo Bergman, had read Henry James. Their publicist, Les Perrin, had also worked for Louis Armstrong and Frank Sinatra. Bergman and Perrin, in other words, possessed frames of reference – the kind of thing you still need to understand Keith Richards and what in time he would become.

Keith and I spent an afternoon in the flat of art dealer and heroin addict Robert Fraser, talking, mostly about blues. I'd heard more blues than he had; I had been to college and read more books, but there was something about him that astonished me. We had, all of our generation, fallen in love with the singing cowboys in westerns; in our boyhood games we had all – including Keith – pretended to be Roy Rogers, but Keith, it seemed, wasn't pretending. That day I was wearing a razor cut, a tailor-made tweed jacket, flannel trousers, and brown loafers. Keith wore leather trousers and his hair might have been cut with a tomahawk. He had become a renegade version of Red Ryder's Indian sidekick, Little Beaver: 'You betchum, motherfucker'. The image would acquire enhancements, but the little English schoolboy in his blue jacket and beanie had been replaced. Keith's intensity of focus and his obvious rejection of middle-class values almost made me speechless. He was heavy lidded and remote until the end of the afternoon, when he played a Robert Johnson record.

'Me and the Devil was walkin' side by side,' Johnson sang.

'That's like the song on the new album,' I said lamely. ' "Sympathy for the Devil".'

'Yeah,' Keith said. 'All of us pursued by the same *daemon*.'

One pleasant evening, a few minutes after seven o'clock, I came out of the house where Mick Jagger and Anita Pallenberg, the north-Italian model and actress who had left Brian Jones for Keith, were filming *Performance*, and there was Keith in the Bentley.

'Waiting for Mick?' I asked, all ignorance.

'Waitin' for Anita.'

'I have an idea,' I said, and told him about the magazine cover I'd dreamed up for the story I was writing. These were the days when the news magazines were full of rock and roll and war. (*Time*'s cover story dated April 15, 1966, proclaimed 'London, the Swinging City' and shared space with news of the increasing intensity of US bombing attacks on North Vietnam.) It was my tasteful scheme to procure a helicopter from a nearby US Air Force base and photograph the Rolling Stones in American uniforms with severed Vietnamese heads. Charlie Watts was to be the pilot in olive tank-top and bill cap; Bill Wyman, in a vest of grenades, would stand in the chopper's cargo door; and Mick, Keith and Brian, armed with various weaponry, were to pose behind a line of dark-haired decapitees. I figured the photo would provoke outrage.

'Get it together and we'll do it,' Keith said.

The cover never happened, but not because Keith wasn't willing. My point in telling this story is not political – just that Keith didn't take a long time to make decisions. 'Politics', he has said, 'are what we were trying to get away from in the first place.' He participated in Bob Geldof's Live Aid concert because Bob Dylan had asked him to do it. 'The rehearsals were great,' Keith said, 'and I loved the idea of it, but you're not going to solve the problems of the world with a few rock concerts, a satellite deal, and a knighthood to the guy who gets it together. It's like trying to put a Band-Aid on a rash.'

Back in America in the summer of 1969, I was on to other things when the phone rang twelve times one night and I answered it to hear Jo Bergman tell me that Brian Jones had drowned in his swimming pool. Three days later, the Stones performed in Hyde Park before a crowd estimated at half a million. By October they were in Los Angeles to rehearse for their first American tour. I joined them two or three days after they arrived.

By the midway point of the tour, with the shows selling out and the Beatles rumored to be breaking up, the Stones were perhaps a bit less scared than they had been. They sent the Beatles telegrams inviting them to close two shows the Stones had scheduled in London after the tour. No Beatles replied. The Stones were succeeding on their own terms, playing rock and roll but also playing the songs of old black men too poor to put glass in their windows.

'The world isn't perfect,' an advertising executive in a white shirt and a red necktie told Keith on an airplane. Keith said, 'No, the world *is* perfect.' We were on our way to San Francisco and Altamont, where the Hell's Angels killed a young black man in front of the stage during the Stones' performance of 'Under My Thumb'. Horrid publicity ensued – some of it using such Stones rhymes as 'satanic-messianic' to imply that they'd had the killing staged. We had, with the best intentions, recreated Vietnam at Altamont, and it seemed an entire generation retired into seclusion to contemplate its destiny. I went back to England with the Stones.

One afternoon the next summer, Keith and I were sitting on an oriental carpet in the side yard of Redlands, his thatch-roofed country house near Dover, while 50 yards away, outside the high board fence and moat that bordered the keep, two men with chain saws trimmed a tree. Anita Pallenberg, now the mother of Keith's baby son, leaned out of an upstairs window: 'Keith, Marlon can't take his nap; make them stop.'

We walked over and stood under the tree for about five minutes while the chain-saws went *arngg*! until the men deigned to notice us and turned off the saws.

'Hey, man,' Keith said to the one who was lowest in the branches, 'my kid's tryin' to sleep, and you're keepin' him awake 'cause those saws're so loud. And I know somethin' about loud, 'cause I'm in the loud business.'

'Right, mate,' the man said, turning the chain-saw back on. 'We'll be done in a few minutes.' *Arngg*!

We walked back, and there was Anita again: 'Keith . . .'

Keith Richards, the personification of rock and roll, who could control the heartbeats of thousands in concert and speak his mind to judges and Hell's Angels (at Altamont, he'd been the only one to say of an individual Angel, 'That one *there* – stop *him!*'), had, in the real world, no effect whatever on his common-law wife and two guys with chain saws. That weekend at Redlands, a heroin junkie passed out in the bathroom, and Anita refused to come downstairs, leaving the ham on the rotisserie to blacken.

The Stones' next American tour, in 1972, an ugly scene full of amyl nitrate, Quaaludes, tequila sunrises, cocaine, heroin, Truman Capote, Princess Lee Radziwill, and too many *pistoleros*, left me with more material than I could ever use. At its end, I weighed about 100 pounds. I went off to the Ozarks, and by the time the Stones came to Memphis in 1975, I no longer had the heart to go across town and see them. Keith left the day after and was arrested driving recklessly across Arkansas in a rented Chevrolet and spent eight and a half hours in the Fordyce (population 5,175) jail. If he'd been in a Cadillac, the police would have had more respect. The incident was a comic foreshadowing of his unfunny arrest for heroin possession in Toronto in 1977. The next time the Stones came to Memphis, Keith got on the phone and told me to come to the hotel. (Time is an elastic medium to junkies, and we had managed to stay in touch, sending each other tapes, drug dealers, guitar makers, Indian traders.) We were both, to provide a frame of reference, emerging from a decade of addiction.

I didn't see Keith again until January 1986, at the First Annual Rock and Roll Hall of Fame Banquet, where he inducted Chuck Berry. By now almost everything around the Stones had changed. Only Charlie Watts's marriage had lasted. Mick Jagger had recently finished a solo album.

When I had first met them, Keith and Mick were like twin brothers, nearly the same height and weight, with a unique ability to communicate. In their songwriting sessions, Keith would play guitar and sing sounds. Mick, listening, would translate Keith's sounds into words. Each wrote a song on his own now and then, but that was their usual way of working, and there seemed to be complete trust between them.

By the time the next Stones album, *Dirty Work*, appeared in March 1986, relations between Keith and Mick were at an all-time low. Jagger refused to tour with the Stones in support of their album, choosing instead to perform on his own with a rented band. Keith, hurt and angry, settled down at last to making his own solo album. 'Having to make a record without the Stones was a failure in itself for me,' he said. 'It meant I couldn't keep my band together. But when you start making it, you realize how much room there is to grow.'

When I heard Keith's album had reached the final mix, I arranged to meet him at a soundstage in Los Angeles where he would be shooting the video for the first single release, 'Take It So Hard'. I found him in a greenroom with his Rebel Yell and a new band. Two things were clear at once: the band he'd put together, the X-Pensive Winos, was a real band (they finished each other's sentences like Donald Duck's nephews, Huey, Dewey and Louie); and Keith was more relaxed and flying lower than I'd ever seen him. It cost us, in the old days, about a hundred times more to get through an evening. But the psychodrama among Keith and the Winos was about on a *Dobie Gillis* level, which made relaxing easy. 'What do ya get when ya cross a pit bull and a redneck?' Wino Ivan Neville asked the room, then answered: 'An all-white neighborhood.'

Ivan, son of the classic New Orleans singer Aaron Neville, on keyboard; Waddy Wachtel, LA session guitarist for Linda Ronstadt and Emmy Lou Harris; Charlie Drayton on drums; Steve Jordan on bass — the Winos, who got their name when Keith found three of them hiding in a studio with a bottle of Dom Perignon, played the entire song every time the video people changed camera angles, even though the video would accompany the song's single-release version. The set was built around a charred car, with a backdrop of postnuclear rubble. The band played on a little raised wooden platform painted black. Stage-hands kept putting dust and ashes on the cymbals *pour l'effet*.

During a break, Keith and I took to discussing our deterioration. When I first knew him, Keith had what I'd described as 'rotting fangs'. Now he had fine white choppers.

'But hit me in the mouth,' he said, 'and it's like those *Nightmare on Elm Street* movies – Freddy's back.'

He was wearing green suede boots, corduroy jeans, and a sleeveless T-shirt that revealed what he referred to as 'bruises' – deep, irregular grooves in his deltoid muscles.

'From *what?*' I asked, tactful as ever, and Keith mimed shooting up in the shoulder. I'd seen many drug-related disfigurations but never anything quite like those scars. Instead of injecting his veins with heroin, Keith, having plenty, had just shot it into his muscles, necrotizing great furrows in the tissue.

'I thought. They're just bruises; they'll go away in a week – and I still got 'em.

'I always felt I had a safe margin,' he continued. 'That's a matter of knowing yourself, maybe just on a physical level. I come from very tough stock, and things that would kill other people don't kill me. To me the only criteria in life are knowing yourself and your capabilities, and the idea that anybody should take on what I do or did as a form of recreation or emulation is horrific.'

Patti Hansen, the American model Keith married five years ago, arrived from Disneyland with their little girls, Theodora and Alexandra. Patti does few modeling assignments nowadays, spending her time with Keith and the girls at their residences in Manhattan, Jamaica and England. 'When I met Patti, I was reliving a rock and roll childhood,' he told me. 'I could have gone back. Easy. It could have gone either way for me, life or death.'

I baby-sat the girls, who slept, worn out by the Magic Kingdom, while Patti stayed on the soundstage to hear Keith play. 'I haven't heard him live since he was finishing *Dirty Work*,' she said. 'And there was a lot of anger then.'

At three in the morning, when the taping ended, the crew gave Keith and the band a standing ovation.

The next afternoon, Keith and I spent a couple of hours talking in the living-room of his suite at the Mondrian on Sunset Boulevard. We spoke first about family and friends, living and dead, and then about how our survival had been aided by our having children.

'Your kid gives back to you that bit of love you gave your own parents, the bit of life you don't remember,' he said. 'It's vital knowledge, like a missing piece in a jigsaw puzzle.'

When Keith and the Winos went on the road, I joined them for the first show, at the Fox Theater in Atlanta. One at a time the Winos entered, looking a trifle jittery. Keith and Steve Jordan were in a corner, teaching the lyrics of 'Make No Mistake' to Sarah Dash, who would be singing them in a few minutes. She was writing, with a ballpoint pen, on the palm of her hand.

On earlier tours, Keith had played Huck Finn to Mick Jagger's Tom Sawyer. Mick had taken care of business (literally), and Keith took care of the rest. Simply put, Mick had been the head, Keith the heart, of the Rolling Stones. The defection of his oldest friend had left Keith with much to prove. A New York editor had told me that his publication was giving *Talk Is Cheap* a bad review because they wanted the Stones to get back together. There was talk of radio stations refusing the album airplay for the same reason. Keith, on his own, was forced to compete with himself and to take care of all the more mundane aspects of the tour. But the basic question was whether he and the Winos could reach the people who came to the shows.

When the band took the stage at the Fox, the audience stood up and never sat down. I'd never seen audiences on their feet for entire Rolling Stones shows. It was the same story for twenty-four days in eleven cities. *Rolling Stone* magazine said that Keith looked like a 'vampiric aristocrat' whose singing was as raw and natural and appealing as his playing – which amounted to 'definitive, essential rock and roll' and left little doubt about 'who constituted the backbone of what was once called the Greatest Rock and Roll Band in the World.'

The tour's last show was at the Brendan Byrne Arena in Meadowlands, New Jersey. At 8.30 in a room backstage, a TV set was showing 'Benson' with the sound off; a Christmas tree's lights were flashing. Keith was sitting on a couch, with a guitar and a couple of sheets of tablet paper, studying the lyrics of Little Walter's 'Crazy Mixed-Up World', with its opening line, 'I'm a crazy mixed-up kid.' It was the eve of his forty-fifth birthday. A large black man wearing a Blueberry Hill bill-cap, white shirt, burgundy pullover, light-blue slacks, and brown tassel loafers snoozed in a chair at Keith's side.

'This is Johnnie Johnson,' Keith said.

The pianist on the classic Chuck Berry sessions opened his eyes and took my handshake between his warm, peaceful hands, which seemed the size of catcher's mitts.

'I wanted to play with this man,' Johnson said, nodding in Keith's direction. 'I can play rock and roll with this man.'

'In 1969,' I said to Johnson, 'I was in New York, on tour with the Rolling Stones, and we were talking about this great pianist Johnnie Johnson. I've listened to you all my life – I'm so glad you could be here.'

'Yeah,' Johnnie said. 'I like gigs like this. It break the monotony.'

At 9.15 the lights went down and the show started. Once again, as they had for the entire tour, the Winos played to a standing audience. People responded perhaps not so much to what Keith has survived as to his being a real (as opposed to political) conservative, a true traditionalist – with Johnnie Johnson on this night as he'd been with Howlin' Wolf the first time I saw him. Toward the end of the show, the crowd sang 'Happy Birthday'. There were teenagers among them as well as people in their forties. The concert had a bravura quality. Keith's singing, spotty in Atlanta, had improved – at least he was singing into the mike more often, and Sarah Dash's vocal technique made up for whatever Keith's lacked. 'To wish you a merry Christmas and a happy New Year,' Keith said during the encore, starting 'Run Run Rudolph'. Johnnie Johnson, now in a white double-breasted jacket and matching yachting cap, played the way the original Stones' pianist, Ian Stewart, used to play back at the Crawdaddy Club on the Thames, like a boogie king.

After the show, there was a birthday party for Keith, attended by five hundred of his closest friends. People stood by the backstage entrance, now barred to those without All Access badges, then were led down a corridor to an elevator, where they rose in batches to a big room with tables and chairs and platters of shrimp and finger sandwiches. Paranoia, a staple of the New York rock 'community', led some people to think they'd been shunted aside, the pink shrimps actually red herring, the real party going on elsewhere. But then Keith, Patti, the little girls, Anita Pallenberg, and a number of other people came in, as if wandering into a scene from a Fellini movie. Virgin Records presented Keith with a gold record of his album, and he cut a birthday cake done in a gold-record motif.

'I have something rather private to ask you,' Anita told me. She was thin again, wearing a leopardskin pillbox hat. 'Do you have my Brian Jones scrapbooks?'

Later, I found myself sitting next to Patti in a smaller room across the corridor from the party, talking to the four-and-a-half-year-old Miss Theodora, who'd seen her father work that night for the first time.

'Did you enjoy the show?' I asked her.

'I wanna be a black girl,' she said.

I asked her again, just to be sure, and she said it again.

1 9

FASCINATING CHANGES

This piece was written before Phineas Newborn, Jr., died, but it ran in the Village Voice *as one more obituary. I don't like it, as a poet once said, but I guess things happen that way.*

As Charlie Freeman's body was being lowered into the grave, under that cold gray sky, I stepped closer to Fred Ford, the large, white-bearded black man who had spoken at the Memphis Funeral Home.

'This is not the time,' I said, 'but I think Atlantic would like to do the Phineas Newborn album Charlie wanted to produce, sort of as a memorial.'

'Give me a number where I can call you.'

I took a card from my notebook and jotted my number on the back.

That was Saturday, February 3, 1973. Monday, Fred called. 'Do you know what you gave me?'

'I'm not sure,' I said.

'You wrote your number on the back of a ticket that said "Club Handy Benefit Dance for Bill Harvey – to Buy Him a Leg." I went on the road with Bill Harvey and the Harlem to Havana Revue when I was fifteen years old. I'll keep that the rest of my life.'

It must have been sometime that night I said to Fred, 'I can't believe I'm sittin' next to the man who barked like a dog at the end of Big Mama Thornton's "Hound Dog."'

'Yeah,' Fred said, his large, dark eyes looking into the smoky neon depths of the cinderblock Fabulous Club Gemini. 'I was gonna meow like a cat, but it was too hip for 'em.'

I knew almost nothing about Phineas Newborn except that he was a jazz pianist whose records I'd seen reviewed in *Down Beat* in the '50s. He'd had some problems, been under lock and key in New York and California in the late '50s and the '60s, and now he was back in Memphis, living at his mother's house on Alston Avenue, south of Crump Boulevard.

At the Gemini, Phineas played with a junkie drummer and a kid bass player. Sometimes the drummer nodded, and the bass player didn't listen, but Phineas was phenomenal.

I have known only one other person like Phineas Newborn, a Japanese karate master who lived for a time in Memphis, where he had a girlfriend. One night he and a young student were at his girlfriend's house when her old boyfriend happened by. '*You* know,' the karate master said to the student, smoothly changing the subject from whatever it had been, 'I can hit you – kill person behind you.' He gave his chest a modest touch. 'I can do.' Phineas Newborn is just like that. We will return to this point. In fact, we will not depart from it.

Phineas Newborn, I would learn, was to some people a living symbol of African–American genius, the ultimate product of a tradition whose roots are mysterious and deep. His family life and American music were one and the same, with a cast including Elvis Presley, B.B. King, Count Basie, Benny Goodman, Charles Mingus. His style resembled that of Secretariat, or the young Muhammad Ali. He could think of things to do that no one else had ever done, and then he would do them. He had, another Memphis pianist once observed, 'a boogie-woogie left hand, a bebop right hand, and this . . . third hand'. But it was not simply unsurpassed technique that made his work so affecting: his music derived power from its own emotional range – the outer-space comedy of 'Salt Peanuts', the nostalgic humor of 'Memphis Blues', the rhapsodic sadness of 'The Midnight Sun Will Never Set', the majesty of 'The Lord's Prayer'.

The day after hearing Phineas at the Gemini, I phoned Atlantic Vice-President Jerry Wexler to tell him that Phineas was playing better, if possible, than ever. That afternoon Wexler went to a Newport Jazz Festival promotion party at the Rainbow Grill, where he told the guests that 'people these days talk about Atlantic and rock and roll, but it's really a jazz label – and I want to report that Phineas Newborn is cookin' in Memphis.' People stood and cheered. 'Wein wants to book him,' Wexler told me that night, 'and so does D'Lugoff, who says he'd like to manage him.' When I told Fred Ford, he said, 'Have mercy.'

The next time I saw Phineas – Junior, 'Gates', Little Red, 'a five-foot-four, 140-pound genius' who could, as Fred Ford says, 'reduce a 3,000-pound piano to smolderin' ashes' – he and Fred were coming in the back door of Memphis's Ardent Studio, Phineas in a snap-brim, Fred in a Russian fur cap, both wearing dark overcoats. Both ready for the 52nd Street of their boyhood dreams. In the control room the engineer, seeing Phineas approach the Yamaha grand, without knowing who he was, rolled the tape. Phineas began playing 'Memphis Blues', stepped on the damper-pedal, and sat down. In that order. 'Who *is* that?' the engineer asked.

Phineas and Fred stayed in the studio for over an hour, with Fred, whose own sax had he said been indisposed since September, fighting a cold and unfamiliar baritone while Phineas coaxed cascades of advanced harmonics from the facile Yamaha. When they stopped for a break, Phineas paused in the door of the control room to light a Pall Mall. 'Thanks,' Fred said, accepting a cigarette and a light. 'You sho do play some fascinatin' changes.'

Phineas plays with such total ease that mere mortals, watching him, are mesmerized into thinking they can do it too, and leap on the set. Years ago at jam sessions at Andrew 'Sunbeam' Mitchell's Club Paradise on East Georgia Avenue, Phineas would baffle leapers by changing the key a half-step each chorus. 'Horn players would play a few notes, jam the mouthpiece tighter, try again,' Fred said, laughing like Uncle Remus talking about Brer Rabbit.

The reply to the New York offers was that for the moment Junior would stay in Memphis. I was elected spokesman, and here are the notes of the message I sent to Atlantic:

I talked to Fred. He and Phineas appreciate everyone's interest and are working hard on their two-album set. I think we may get some of that to listen to soon. On the live gigs, as far as money is concerned, I understand Phineas couldn't consider leaving town for less than $2,500 for a five-day week. He's doing fine, he's not destitute, and he's not eager to up and go to New York. He was up before, the hot jazz star, and it had bad results for him – nervous breakdown – so Fred is being very protective, which is understandable, but they are recording and working hard.

This was, though I didn't know it then, too much like asking for a rain check. On September 23, 1973, I wrote Wexler again:

Enclosed you will find something that I have never sent you, namely, a demo tape. The tape is of Phineas Newborn Jr., playing impromptu solo piano, and he has no peers. No one, not Art Tatum, not even Blind Tom, compares with him for unpredictability, inevitability, ingenuity, power and range of imagination. Yet it is never far from ragtime and the blues, the roots of his music.

Blind Tom, Thomas Greene Bethune, a Georgia slave born in 1850, is supposed to have known 5,000 pieces of music and been able to listen to a brass band, a grind organ, a whistled tune, and then repeat the music on the piano, even if he heard them all at once. I kept preaching to the converted because lots of people had enjoyed the way Charlie Freeman played, and he died out of work like Dewey Phillips. Watching Memphis's most brilliant products die out of work had made me fervent.

I knew, too, that Wexler had doubts about Phineas's mental state, because he kept asking, 'Can he take care of business?' I gave glowing reports of Phineas's playing and said nothing about other aspects of his behavior, such as his close association with the psychiatric ward at Veterans' Hospital and his reaction to women – I do not think the word aggressive is too strong.

January 9, 1974. Today is Wednesday. Saturday night about eight o'clock Phineas was admitted to John Gaston Hospital with multiple cuts, bruises, broken bones. He had been living in a halfway house on Vinton, near the red-light district. Earlier Saturday night a blonde girl, hair in a ponytail, wearing slacks, came to see him there. 'Phineas,' she said, 'I want you to come with me, there's somebody I want you to meet.' He was in bed, but he got dressed and went out with her. A short while later he came back, just barely alive.

When I got hold of Fred he volunteered nothing, let me tell him what I'd heard, let me ask questions: 'These people any particular color?' 'The opposite.' 'What kind of people would do that?' 'Animals,' Fred said.

That night Fred and I drove around Memphis with my rifle in the car as we'd done once before when one of us was being measured for a frame by a mutual acquaintance. I soon realized that Fred had been fishing: he knew no more about who had done Phineas harm than I did, and Phineas wasn't going to tell. Nesuhi Ertegun heard what had happened to Phineas – in those days Atlantic was Wexler and Nesuhi and Ahmet Ertegun – and sent a check for $2,500.

January 16, 1974. Just back from Alston Avenue, a street of small single-family dwellings where, in the white frame house at no. 588, I met Phineas's mother, a little red woman in a green dress and a red sweater, a short orange pencil stuck in her graying, slightly processed hair. The front room was crowded, pictures of Phineas and his father and brother Calvin on the piano. She moved the footstool, covered with clean laundry, so I could sit down, and she sat on the piano bench. I gave her the check. She looked at it and said she didn't know whether her son would accept it. I told her how I came to have it, and she told me about when he was in Europe playing and his agent and his wife were in Florida laying out in the sun. 'Phineas came back and told the agent, "Don't book me no more" – but the agent wanted to send him on these long hikes, and his wife starts after him, "You don't want to work," and his agent is mad because he wants money, and he's sweet on his wife. Then Phineas goes to Europe the second time and comes home to find every stick of furniture in the place gone except the piano.

'So he has been used and misused, and he's very wary of people – sometimes he don't even trust me, won't even take a chance on me, and I scratched and went to the cotton fields and paid up to $5 a lesson so he could take lessons, because I was his first fan. Because I took such pleasure in his playing. He'd play, and he'd ask me, "How does that sound, Mama?" and I'd say, "It sounds good, son, play it again," and he'd bap it again.

'But for the last few years he has been emotionally disturbed. When I came in the hospital the other day and saw the shape he was in, all beat-up, I had to hold back my tears. I turned aside and told myself, This is no place to cry, and held his cigarette. My hand was trembling, but I held it for him. I told the woman administrator down there that I wanted to move him to the Veterans' Hospital – she said, "Aren't you satisfied with the care he's getting here?" And I said yes. I looked her right in the eye – I can look them right in the eye – and said I am very grateful for what you've done. But first of all, my son went to the Army. He has earned the care of the VA hospital. And second, no matter how long he has to stay there, he can stay and get treatment and it won't cost anything – and a nurse standing there said, "That's reason enough." So I called the Ford Funeral Home and told them not to send a hearse or a long funeral car but to move Phineas, and they did, and I went down to pay them – called their names, been knowing them, Congressman Ford and all of them, all their lives – and they said, "Oh, no, we can't let you pay, this is a gift to Phineas." I said, "God bless all you thugs."

'So I will get what he needs – I remember when he was little, he asked me, "Mama, will you buy me a bicycle?" and I didn't know where we would find the money, but I got him one. When he sees me looking like this he won't say a word, but I go out there all spruced up, he'll say, "You look good, Mama – you look like you used to when Daddy was alive." He is emotionally disturbed. But I know he can play the piano. He knows all the tunes, he don't need no music. On his worst day, he can play piano. Not everybody knows how he is. But I do. I know him. And I love him. And I will see that he gets what he needs, and sometimes things more than he needs, just because he wants them. Because once upon a time, he was my good child. And he is still my good child. I sat beside his bed and told him, Put your hand in Mama's. Play C - D - E - F - G in Mama's hand. He played the notes against the palm of my hand, and I said, You'll be all right, son. You going to play again.'

In the early decades of the twentieth century, James Newborn, a slender, dark-skinned black man, owned a farm near Jackson, Tennessee. But he preferred preaching, wood carving and photography, leaving the fields to his fifteen sons, the fruit of his first marriage. According to the unpublished autobiography of his grandson, Calvin Newborn, James had another family with the woman who became his second wife: 'Papa had a natural instinct for polygamy.'

Although he saw no value in education, nine of James Newborn's sons went to high school, one becoming a Los Angeles chiropractor, another graduating from Tennessee State College and serving as bandmaster at Memphis's Geter High School for over thirty years. Phineas, the oldest, wanted to play drums. But his father, who considered secular music the work of the Devil, would neither buy any nor let him earn the money to buy some. Resenting this and his father's treatment of his mother, Phineas left home to live with an aunt in Jackson. One day he was trimming a hedge when who should stroll past but the russet-hued, glowing Rosie Lee Murphy. Her father, Willie Murphy, who farmed in nearby Whiteville, Tennessee, was called Son Twenty because his mother, nicknamed Twenty, had been her parents' twentieth child.

Rose was going to nursing school, living in a dormitory. She and Phineas courted, married, and moved to Memphis. The Depression was just beginning. Phineas and Rose lived in one room in Orange Mound, a black neighborhood near the State Normal Teachers' College, where Phineas went every day on his bicycle to work as a cook's helper. He was also playing drums at night with local musicians. At the end of 1931 Rose went back to Whiteville to have her first baby.

'Phineas brought a radio from Memphis,' Mama Rose remembers. 'As long as that hillbilly music like "She'll be Comin' Round the Mountain" played, Junior listened and bucked his eyes. But when Bessie Smith . . . started out singin' them slow blues, he'd let out a howl.' There was family speculation that the baby was marked for music. Or, to put it another way, that Phineas's wicked pursuit of the Devil's music had put the baby under a curse.

But Phineas, determined, missed no chances to hear and play music. 'When them bands would come uptown,' Mama Rose said, 'we'd catch that streetcar. Wasn't but seven cents each. We'd go and take that baby to that show.' Count Basie called the Newborn infant Bright Eyes because his eyes would light up when the music began.

Calvin, the second and final child of Phineas and Rose, came fifteen months after Junior. The family moved nearer to downtown Memphis and Beale Street, where Phineas played for the Midnight Rambles at the Palace Theater with bands like the Chickasaw Syncopators, led by Memphian Jimmie Lunceford, who asked Phineas to go on the road with him. It was a real opportunity, but Phineas let it go. His dream was to have a family band with his sons.

Unable to read music himself, Senior bought a piano and, when Junior started school, had him take lessons from Miss Georgia Woodruff, his first-grade teacher. After initial complaints – 'Mama, it's hard.' 'If it wasn't hard, I wouldn't have to be paying for it.' – Junior played for the love of it. 'I listened to Fats Waller and Art Tatum . . . and they encouraged me. My father was the one who let me know about the association of the pianoforte with orchestrating and general musical composition. The idea influenced me so much I developed quite a fondness for the piano.' During years of study – the first twelve volumes of exercises – Junior had to repeat one lesson.

'I told him,' Mama Rose said, ' "Look, we are poor people, and I can't afford to pay twice for this same page." ' Mama Rose never had to tell him again. 'He loved it. And the girls would drive up on they bikes, and he'd be paddlin' on that piano, and they would come on in, and I'd go in the kitchen, come back, Calvin have one them gals' head layin' in his lap, but Junior still be playin' the piano. He loved music, and he loved the piano. But Calvin was – cowboys, and shine shoes, and go to the cotton field. Went to the cotton field one time pickin' with the neighborhood girls, came back, and he was tellin' Junior, "Yeah, man, Ellis May and Ruthie Jean and all of us was out there, man, we had a lot of fun, you ought to go with us tomorrow." Junior told him – just kept playin' – "I'll take your word for it." '

Calvin started studying piano in turn, but 'Babe', Mama Rose says of Calvin, was 'kinda slow. He's kinda bad. Want to do everything but practice.'

Calvin and Junior, intrepid adventurers, inspired by the aura (ADULTS ONLY) of the Midnight Rambles, at the end of an afternoon's playing in a park near home, wandered away down the railroad tracks to Beale Street, where they ate hot dogs, listened to a jug

Calvin Newborn (date and photographer unknown)

band and a blind blues singer, watched the movies at the Palace, hid under their seats till the Rambles commenced, and were rewarded with jokes, jazz, dancing girls. 'I knew then,' Calvin writes, 'I wanted to be in show business.'

Though that evening ended with frightened boys confronting worried, irate parents, Senior soon had his sons back at the Palace. He came home from a tour with the Lionel Hampton Orchestra bringing their latest hit, 'Hey! Ba-ba-re-bop!' and the story of Hamp's teaching it to his parrot. Junior and Calvin played the song at the Monday night amateur contest, where the master of ceremonies was Rufus Thomas. They won first prize, performing as a piano duet, with Calvin also singing and dancing.

Calvin, following his father's advice and his own inclination, 'budded as a dynamic showman, while Junior became a budding piano virtuoso. After being embarrassed by Junior, I lost interest in the piano and reverted to guitar. Dad asked Riley B.B. King to take me to Nathan's pawn shop on Beale, and I purchased a guitar for five dollars.'

Already able to read classical piano music, Calvin sought lessons from a white guitarist, who refused to teach him, saying he would drive white students away. Tommy Dunlap, a friend of Senior's, began giving Calvin lessons. The first song he learned was 'Steel Guitar Rag'.

Meanwhile Junior was gaining a local reputation, performing 'Rustle of Spring' at the LaRose Elementary graduation exercises and 'The Lord's Prayer' at the Mount Vernon Baptist Church. He already knew by heart things like 'Rhapsody in Blue'.

The boys had not been long in high school the night Lionel Hampton – who named Junior 'Gates' – came back to town. They met Hamp's pianist, Oscar Dennard, a young genius from St. Petersburg and the only man, woman or child in anyone's memory who ever cut Junior. At the grand piano in the lobby of Sunbeam Mitchell's hotel, the traveling musician's home away from home, the two boy-sized beboppers battled for over a quarter of an hour with their left hands alone. Oscar started the set with nursery rhymes – he had a way of applying Bach's three-part inventions to 'Three Blind Mice'. Calvin: 'After meeting him Junior woodshedded all day and went out jamming every night for quite some time.'

Junior was studying now with Professor W.T. McDaniel, bandmaster at both Manassas and Booker T. Washington high schools, and playing with both school bands, the Rhythm Bombers and the Bookerteasers. He learned bassoon, French horn, trumpet, alto and baritone horns, tuba, drums, glockenspiel, saxophones, and other reed instruments. Calvin mastered trombone, baritone horn, piccolo and flute. Between them they took on the entire range of western musical instruments. 'He and Calvin can play any instrument,' Mama Rose said. 'Calvin, or Junior, could play anything but the harp. And they went out and took some harp lessons.'

Memphis musicians still talk about the afternoons in the '40s when a black boy, standing just tall enough to reach the piano keys, came into O.K. Houck's Union Avenue music store, where no one knew him, and played to perfection the sheet music, all of it, stacks each day. When the bandleader Phineas Newborn came in, the store's music teachers would tell him about the prodigy, but he said that his group was satisfied with their piano player. Then one day Newborn came in and the boy looked up, still playing, to say, 'Hello, Daddy.'

Junior said that he joined his father playing with Tuff Green and the Rocketeers when he was fifteen, but Calvin insists that he started playing with them and Junior when he knew only the 'Steel Guitar Rag' – or about three years after Junior started studying piano – so Junior must have been quite a bit younger than fifteen. Another local legend holds that Junior played piano on B.B. King's first sessions when he was so young he needed special permission to join the musicians' union, and since the recordings were made in late 1949, Junior would then have been seventeen.

The initial B.B. King session, produced in a quonset hut by Sam Phillips for Modern and RPM owners Saul, Les and Jules Bihari, employed Senior and Junior, Tuff Green and Ben Branch, the tenor player, who would enter history as one of the men talking with Martin Luther King when King was shot. Senior didn't play on B.B.'s second session, but Calvin joined Junior, Branch, Green, Willie Mitchell, Hank Crawford and the drummer Ted Curry. Ike Turner played piano when Junior didn't. B.B.'s next recording unit would include George Coleman – that's Coleman's propulsive alto on 'Woke Up This Mornin''.

Memphis swarmed with giants in those days.

Senior played with heroes like Gatemouth Moore, who, according to Mama Rose, 'used to sing the blues at the Brown Derby till the hair stand up on your head', and the formidable tenor saxophonist Leonard 'Doughbelly' Campbell, who died returning to Memphis from Texas in a car wreck that killed two other musicians but only broke Senior's arm. Calvin says the broken arm made Senior's feet stronger. He went back with Lionel Hampton for a while after that, and when he left Hamp hired two drummers.

Junior had spent his sixteenth summer on the road with the Saunders King Orchestra and would travel with the Ruth Brown-Willis 'Gator Tail' Jackson group, while Calvin, who played piccolo with the Bookerteasers and baritone horn with the Letter Carrier's Band, toured with Roy Milton. The boys' out-of-town excursions were unfortunate necessities to Senior, who had grown more determined as years passed to have a family band. The chance had come in 1948, when Senior's band started a residency at Morris Berger's Plantation Inn in West Memphis, Arkansas. There were eight instruments – Senior, Junior, Calvin, Honeymoon Garner on organ, Kenneth Banks on bass, two tenors, and trombone. The trombone player, a freshman at Booker T. Washington named Wanda, also sang. Soon she and Calvin were playing trombone duets. Movie stars like Pat O'Brien and John Carradine, big-time broads like Eva Gabor, musicians like Tommy and Jimmy Dorsey, crossed the Mississippi to see and hear the Phineas Newborn Family Showband. Calvin: 'That was where we really grew musically, the Plantation Inn.' Calvin remembers playing every night from 9.00 to 4.00, but Mama Rose says the schedule wasn't quite that demanding.

After a year or two, the Newborn band moved to the Flamingo Room, formerly the Hotel Men's Improvement Club, upstairs at Hernando and Beale, where a really dedicated (or perhaps deaf) thief robbed the cash register one night while everyone else was transported by Junior's playing. The band took a sabbatical from the Flamingo to travel with Ike Turner and Jackie Brenston, whose 'Rocket 88' was on the record charts. Also on the show were the Four Ames, who became the Four Tops, Moke and Poke, and Redd Foxx and Slappy White. Playing the Regal in Chicago, the Apollo in New York, the Howard in

Washington, the Palladium in Los Angeles, they traveled in an old Greyhound bus that nearly went over a cliff in Arizona when the brakes failed. Stranded in New Orleans, they played at the Dew Drop Inn for room and board until their booking agency sent them return fare to Memphis and the Flamingo. For the next couple of years they mostly stayed put except for summer residencies at resorts in Hot Springs, Arkansas, and Idlewild, Michigan. The Michigan engagement led to successful club gigs in Cleveland and Detroit. Senior's dream must have seemed within his grasp.

Calvin, married by now to trombonist Wanda, had become such a showman that Flamingo owner Clifford Miller booked guitar battles. 'You'd have guitar players to come in and battle me,' Calvin has said, 'like Pee Wee Crayton and Gatemouth Brown, and I was battlin' out there, tearin' they behind up, 'cause I was dancin', playin', puttin' on a show, slidin' across the flo' . . .'

One night, probably in late 1952, a teenaged white boy 'came in there, didn't have on any shoes, barefooted, and asked me if he could play my guitar. I didn't want to let him, I don't usually – I didn't know him from Adam. I'd never seen him before. In fact, he was the only white somebody in the club. He made sure he won that one. He sang "You Ain't Nothin' but a Hound Dog" and shook his hair – see, at the time I had my hair processed, and I'd shake it down in my face – he tore the house up. And tore the strings off my guitar so I couldn't follow him.' The boy turned out to have a name even more rare than Phineas Newborn – Elvis Presley. He became friends with the Newborn family, and Mama Rose has recollections of going off to church with Senior, leaving Junior and Calvin with a fresh-cooked ham in the kitchen, and coming home to find that Elvis had been there and left only the hambone. Elvis often remembered the Newborns with Christmas cards and presents, and on the day he died, Junior, touring Japan, dedicated that evening's concert to his memory.

After graduating from Booker T. Washington in 1951, Junior entered Tennessee State Agricultural and Industrial College, a black school in Nashville. The head of the music department recommended that he transfer to Juilliard, where he could concentrate on music, but Senior refused to let Junior go. This may have been the single most destructive event in the life of Phineas Newborn, Jr. (*There*'s a thesis: the Southern father, Abraham/the Southern son, the sacrifice. Or as Furry Lewis used to say, the Only Forgotten Son.) Resentful, Junior left school after the second year, returning to Memphis, spending a year at Lemoyne before receiving an army draft call.

Stationed at Fort McPherson, Georgia, Junior played French horn and tenor saxophone in the Third Army Headquarters Band. (He also wrote arrangements for a show in which, among other things, a man juggled wheels with his feet while Junior played 'Wagon Wheels'.) Back in 1952, Count Basie, playing in Memphis, had heard the grown-up Bright Eyes, and when the Basie band played Savannah, Junior renewed acquaintances with the Count. By now Junior's style – based on the music of pianists like Art Tatum, Fats Waller, Nat Cole and Bud Powell, instrumentalists like Charlie Parker and Lucky Thompson, as well as Memphis keyboard legends like Struction and Dishrag, with his group the Four Cup Towels – was fully developed. He played, at least as fast as any pianist ever heard, block-chord solos and unison runs with both hands and both feet, showing complete mastery of keyboard and pedal techniques. Basie, Junior recalled was, 'fascinated'.

Released from the Army in June 1955, Junior, still in uniform, came to the music store his father had opened on Beale Street, and chanced to meet a large gentleman Mama Rose introduced as 'Mr. Howling Wolf', whom Calvin had been teaching to read music. The Phineas Newborn Family Showband were reunited, but not for long. Later that year, John Hammond, the music critic and record producer, came to Memphis with Basie and his band when they played the Hippodrome on Beale Street, and met Junior. In 1956 Basie set up a telephone conference call with Junior, Hammond, Willard Alexander the agent, Morris Levy the promoter and Benny Goodman. 'They decided it was best for me to record and then proceed to start playing outside of New York,' Junior said. 'I worked Philadelphia, Newark, and several other places, and finally opened at Basin Street.' Junior played opposite Clifford Brown and Max Roach. *Esquire* devoted a full page to a review comparing his performances to the débuts of Louis Armstrong in 1924 and Bix Beiderbecke in 1925.

All of which represented to Phineas Senior the death of the dream that had given purpose to his whole life, because he went along only as a spectator. Playing with Junior, Calvin, and their Memphis schoolmate George Joyner (who later became Jamil Nasser) was not Senior but Kenny Clarke, whom many regard as the original modern jazz drummer. December found the Newborns back in Memphis, where W.C. Handy – blind and too weak to play at his annual pilgrimage to the Blues Bowl black high-school charity football game – passed the trumpet to Junior, who played accompanied by five marching bands.

Signed for five years to the Alexander agency, Junior, with the quartet, played top clubs on both coasts and in Canada, including twelve weeks of the first year at Birdland opposite some of the strongest players in jazz. Senior's pride in his sons could not take away the pain of not playing with them. When the quartet appeared at the Newport Jazz Festival, master of ceremonies Father Norman O'Connor asked Senior, in the audience, to stand. 'I knew that Dad wanted to be there onstage playing with us,' Calvin says, 'I could feel his sadness.'

Having opened at Carnegie Hall, the agency's 'Birdland Show of 1957', which involved among others Basie's band, Sarah Vaughan, Billy Eckstine, Lester Young, Stan Getz and Chet Baker, Phineas's quartet played Symphony Hall in Philadelpia, then headed north. 'After performing in Montreal,' Calvin writes, 'I got backstage and noticed Bud Powell butting his head against the wall.'

The late '50s was a strange time for jazz and for America. President Dwight Eisenhower's favorite musical organization was Fred Waring's Pennsylvanians. His favorite writer was Zane Grey. Henry Miller, D.H. Lawrence, William Burroughs, Jean Genet, J.P. Donleavy, Vladimir Nabokov and pubic hair were obscene. Charlie Parker and Art Tatum died, then Lester Young and Billie Holiday, who was arrested in her hospital bed. Miles Davis received what the *Amsterdam News* termed 'a Georgia head-whipping' for standing outside the Greenwich Village night club where he was working. Art Pepper drew 2 to 20 in California for his third drug bust. Young, Holiday, Gene Ammons, Dexter Gordon, Stan Getz and Chet Baker, among others, also did time for drug offenses. Bud Powell, in mental institutions five times from 1945–55, was not alone with his problems.

Phineas Newborn, Jnr. (date and photographer unknown)

The Birdland 1957 tour ended without Calvin, who received a draft notice, but Phineas carried on, with Little Rock guitarist Les Spann struggling to master Calvin's parts. Eventually Calvin was given an honorable discharge and returned to society as unadaptable to army discipline. Meanwhile Phineas, with Charles Mingus, had duetted in clubs and recorded the soundtrack to a movie, John Cassavetes's *Shadows*.

Phineas's first album, on Atlantic, with Calvin, Oscar Pettiford and Kenny Clarke, was followed by a series on RCA Victor, United Artists and Roulette, no fewer than nine albums from the period 1956–60, featuring him in settings from large string orchestras to left-hand only. (One night at the end of the '50s, Phineas honored Oscar Dennard by letting him finish the set at the Red Rooster on 136th Street in Harlem. Not long after that, Dennard toured with the New York Jazz Quartet in Europe, Russia and Africa. In Egypt he contracted typhus and died in a matter of days.) It would be laughable, were human life and loss not involved, to read some of Phineas's early notices. *Young Men From Memphis* with Junior, Calvin, Frank Strozier, George Coleman, Louis Smith, Booker Little, George Joyner and Charles Crosby, received three stars – 'good' – in *Down Beat*. Three stars were hard to get. Martin Williams gave Billie Holiday's *Lady in Satin* two and a half, calling the album 'a mistake'. Williams deplored the lack of 'logic' in Junior's playing, as if rejecting the Fauves because of inaccurate color. Junior, possessor of a dry, mordant wit, while playing elucidates the history of jazz piano as he makes ironic comments on it. The New York critics, ignorant of Junior's work with the likes of B. B. King and Jackie Brenston – and ill-equipped, even had they known, to perceive value in such 'rhythm and blues' performers – came to the consensus that no one with that much technique could have any soul.

John Mehegan, pianist, teacher, and *Herald Tribune* columnist, observed in *Down Beat* that:

Phineas has recently astounded the jazz world with what appears to be a technical virtuosity found only in the top echelon of classical pianists. However, there are little or no dynamics or shading in his playing ... he seems to know little of the orchestrative qualities of the keyboard in relation to chords and sonorities . . . Phineas is not in any sense of the word a funky player. . . To be blunt, Newborn exhibits a highly nervous lateral emotion that is never relieved and becomes an incessant mannerism that would seem an ideal sound tract for a *Tom and Jerry* cartoon. A heavy moss of classicism clings to his playing which prevents any real jazz feeling from emerging.

The absurdity of a white piano teacher from New York telling Phineas Newborn about real jazz feeling is delicious. Reviews from such people could do harm even when they were good. Phineas's RCA Victor album with strings, *While My Lady Sleeps*, worthy of comparison with the Charlie Parker and Clifford Brown sets with strings, received this compliment from *Down Beat*: 'As a pop-mood music package, this is worthwhile listening.' I was fifteen years old when I read that, and it didn't send me out into the streets looking for the album. Other pianists redressed the balance somewhat – Oscar Peterson called Junior the best of the pianists younger than himself (thereby eluding comparison); Ray Bryant, in a *Down Beat* blindfold test, said of Phineas, 'His technique is fabulous; he can get over the piano as good as or better than anybody in the business today.' Teddy Wilson said, 'He has a fabulous technique, and it will be interesting to see what direction he goes in the next few years because he certainly has the equipment at the keyboard.' But then Junior would release a record, like *Fabulous Phineas*, with its definitive 'Cherokee', and *Down Beat* would offer two and a half stars – better than fair, less than good. Even Leonard Feather's accolade – 'the greatest living jazz pianist' – is devalued by the knowledge that he said the same thing about Bernard Peiffer and later wrote that he might also have said it of Oscar Peterson after an outstanding performance.

While playing at the Cafe Bohemia in Greenwich Village, Junior re-encountered Dorothy Stewart, a girl he'd known at Booker T. Washington, who was now living in New York. They soon married and had two daughters, but didn't stay together. Calvin describes seeing the marriage end with 'two men forcing Junior into a parked car' as Phineas, having a breakdown, was being taken to Bellevue for observation. On release he drank himself into Kingspark State Hospital, from whence he returned to Memphis, and the two brothers, once so close, would not see each other for nearly ten years.

Calvin began working with Lionel Hampton, then joined Earl Hines. His wife, who had become a narcotics addict, had convulsions and died in her sleep, and Calvin began using heroin himself. By this time Junior was in California, working Los Angeles clubs and starting a series of albums with such musicians as Frank Butler, Paul Chambers, Louis Hayes, Leroy Vinnegar, Roy Haynes, Ray Brown, Elvin Jones, Sam Jones, Philly Joe Jones, Teddy Edwards, Howard McGhee, and Shelly Manne. His divorce had become final, and he found another woman with whom he lived and had a son.

One day in 1965, Calvin, still in Manhattan, dividing his time between playing and stealing to score heroin and cocaine, received a surprise visit from his father, now the drummer with Hall A. Miller's Animal Circus. Phineas Senior neither drank, smoked, cursed, nor chased women. His only vice and greatest pleasure was playing drums. But his heart was failing, he told Calvin, doctors had said he had to quit. Calvin the next day played in the circus band, where he learned that Senior had 'a spectacular act making the elephants dance to his drumbeats.' Later that year Senior, unable to stop himself, sat in with Junior in Los Angeles, walked off the stage, and dropped dead.

Junior's problems continued:

CLINICAL RECORD

NEWBORN, Phenias [*sic*]

VAC Brentwood Hospital, Los Angeles, California

1-18-68

History of Present Illnesses

Prior to the present commitment this patient was discharged in July of 1967 from unit 3 L.A. County General Hospital at which time he was to seek outpatient treatment. After a period of 3 weeks he discontinued taking his medication and ceased contact with his private physician and he reportedly resumed drinking about October 2, 1967. It was at this time that he began to show recurrent symptoms of mental illness when he was described as making bizarre movements with his hands exhibiting extreme suspiciousness and remaining mute most of the time. He had expressed the belief that he and Jesus Christ were related in a direct fashion and said he was married only once: to his mother. There was only one child: himself. The pattern of his illness pertains to his work as a Jazz Musician. When work is irregular or non-existent and he is at loose ends he gets to drinking rather heavily and his behavior develops into hostility to authority and apparently his mental symptoms exacerbate. His history of mental illness dates back however to 1958 in New York where he was committed from Belview [sic] Hospital. He in no way recognizes he is or has been mentally ill.

This 36-year-old committed Negro veteran entered Brentwood VA Hospital in a withdrawn, hostile suspicious state and continued in this general state for most of his hospitalization. He spends a great deal of the time withdrawn but playing the piano with obvious skill and appropriateness musically. He was confined to house-keeping detail in an effort to get him doing something besides going into his piano playing constantly. Last month he went on passes to his home and on evening passes to meetings of Recovery Incorporated. He has begun to socialize a bit more and appeared to be stabilizing. All he needs is an altercation with his common law wife and he is thrown back into inappropriate laughter and withdrawal and hostility. He plans on signing a contract for a piano bar performance in the local area, was put on trial visit status as of 1-12-68 to return for follow-up in two weeks.

J.L.S., M.D.

12-2-68
Hospital Summary

This 37 [sic] year old nonservice connected patient, musician by profession, has spent close to eight years in the hospital. On his admission and a large part of his hospitalization, his illness was manifested by either delusions, paranoid thoughts or else withdrawal behavior, escaped from reality in playing the piano.

Dr. F.P.

12-16-69

The patient was readmitted on 4-24-69

ADDENDUM: Patient has now again recovered from his episode and will go to live with his mother in Memphis, Tenn. Patient was given a Regular discharge effective 3-17-71.

A.P.S., M.D.

'His wife called me one time – said, "Mama Rose, I cooked him a steak, made him a salad, then he goes in the bedroom, sees clothes on the bed, says, "Move these clothes." She told him, "Come in here and help me with these dishes." Junior lays low, don't say nothin', and she calls him again. He says, "I'm a piano player, not a dishwasher."

'I told her, "Listen. *I* cook him steaks. *I* make him salads. *I* wash the dishes."

' "But they say the way to a man's heart is through his stomach."

'I said, "They mussa been talkin' about a white man, honey. The way to a Newborn's heart is by shakin' them sheets. I told her, "Get in there and shake them sheets." '

CLINICAL RECORD

NEWBORN, Phineas, Jr.

VAH, Memphis, TN 38104

10-11-72

Nature and Duration of Complaints

(Include circumstances of admission)

Bizarre behavior for the last several weeks.

History

This 41-year-old separated black man from Memphis, Tenn., was admitted to Ward 2-C, Psychiatric Service, VAH, Memphis, Tenn., on 9-23-72. His mother swore a lunacy warrant for his admittance to the hospital. Mr. Newborn is a musician and he has never come home very early at night but lately Mrs. Newborn, patient's mother, said the patient stayed all night on the streets near their house talking to himself and staring into space. People in the neighborhood literally got scared of him, so Mrs. Newborn said she didn't have any alternative but to bring charges against him. Mrs. Newborn, patient's mother, further stated that Phineas was a full-term normal baby. At school he was average student, never failed. After high school he enrolled in Memphis State University [sic] to study music. He spent 2 years at college and got carried away with his music and quit college. While he was in school Phineas was always a shy loner, and he was kind of slow in getting acquainted with the girls. He said he admires the girls but he preferred to be alone. From 1952 to 1955 he was in the Army stationed at Ft. Jackson, S.C. [sic] His rank was PFC. Apparently he did not have any problems while in the service.

He played the piano at different night spots in Memphis. He made pretty good money but he drank a lot. Apparently always his only best friend was his mother. Mrs. Newborn does not know whether he has been taking any drugs. Lately Phineas would not sleep at all, and he would not eat. He would stay up almost all night. The patient was married twice. His first wife was born in Memphis and they grew up in the same neighborhood. His agent books him in New York for concerts. His first wife read his name in the newspaper and decided to go to see him. Several months later they were married. Patient's mother said she never agreed with this marriage because her daughter-in-law was several years older than her son, and she had an 11-year-old child from a previous marriage. His wife left him because of his mental illness. They lived together several years and have 2 daughters. She left him and took all the furniture in the house, left only the piano. Mr. Newborn then left for California. He met another girl and they were going together for 3 years. A little boy was born before they got married. This marriage also did not work. Patient's mother said that Mrs. Newborn was very selfish and sadistic. She would keep him locked up all the time in a mental institution. He was in VAH, Brentwood, Los Angeles, Cal., several times.

J.H., M.D.

As the dates indicate, I met Junior when he was an inpatient – the hospital must have let him out to play the Gemini.

Admission Date   Discharge Date
6-12-73   8-14-73
Summary

This 41-year-old black male was admitted to Ward 2C of the Psychiatric Service of Memphis VAH on 6-12-73 because he had struck his mother. He has had no recent female relationships. On 6-14-73 the patient was transferred to Ward 1C to be involved in the behavior modification program. He was initially angry at his mother for putting him in the hospital and at the hospital program for insisting that he be involved and perform. He was always silent in groups and rarely talked about himself. The only time he was happy or productive was when he was playing the piano, and he seemed to use this to feel good about himself and to gain the approval of others without the necessity for closer involvement. It was arranged that he board at the Halfway House for psychiatric patients and in addition attend the Day Treatment Center program for one-half day during the week days. He was going to be encouraged to work on his piano. His mother agreed to furnish whatever money was necessary to make it possible for him to start in the program. He was therefore given a discharge 8-14-73. He is considered mentally competent and able to work. His prognosis is poor.

J.H., M.D.

The Halfway House is the one where Junior was living when he was assaulted.

Admission Date   Discharge Date
1-7-74   1-17-74
Summary

This patient was referred from John Gaston Hospital. Apparently he was attacked and beaten on the day of admission. The patient was unwilling or unable to give a past history or circumstances under which he was injured. The patient remembers absolutely nothing about his injury, what happened, or where. He was noted to have injuries of both hands, arms and had forearm casts on both arms. He was diagnosed as having a trimalar (cheekbone) fracture and when it was discovered he was a veteran he was referred to the VA Hospital. Examination revealed the nose to have crepitation on the lateral side of the dorsum of the right nose. A definite fracture could be palpated, however, the bones were in good alignment. Several lower incisor teeth have been either evulsed or extracted. There were also some teeth missing on the maxillary alveolare. The patient was admitted and after proper laboratory work he was taken to surgery where on 1-17-74 his trimalar fracture was reduced with a #22 urethral sound introduced through a skin incision over the lateral brow and into the intratemporal fossa. The fracture was elevated and an audible pop was heard. It was felt that this fracture was stable at this time. However, the next morning it was noted that this fracture was down again. The patient was then taken to surgery where open reduction and interosseous wires were placed at the zygomaticotemporal, zygomaticofrontal and zygomatico-athmoidal sutures. In view of the patient's psychiatric ailments his postoperative period was complicated somewhat. The patient removed his protective dressing over his face and pulled the packing out of his maxillary sinus. However, it was felt that all had been done for him and that due to his poor cooperation we could not get an excellent repair of this fracture. The patient was discharged OPT NSC to return in one week.

M.G., M.D.

On the evening of the day he was discharged, Phineas went to Ardent Studio with Fred Ford and recorded the triple-speed left-hand *tour de force* 'Out of This World' that would appear on his 1975 *Solo Piano* album. Hearing the performance while looking at the X-ray photograph of Phineas's broken hand is enough to make you think that Little Red, like Jerry Lee Lewis, is a bit more than human.

One rainy afternoon in October, I think, of 1974, Mark Myerson, Jr., an Atlantic representative from New York, had visited the little house on Alston. Phineas was still in bed – it was about three o'clock – and Mama Rose, greeting Mark, a well-mannered young man whose father engineered classic Duke Ellington and Frank Sinatra sessions, returned the check from Atlantic for $2,500 that I had given her. Mark took it without understanding but with perfect grace, listening to Mama Rose and nodding, discreetly putting the check away.

Into the front room, with its dilapidated piano, overstuffed furniture, many framed photographs, and bric-à-brac – a little china-colored angel playing tenor saxophone – came Junior, wearing a red shawl-collar dressing-gown, smoking as always, looking at the floor. After introductions, Junior was asked to play.

'Play Mama's favorite,' Mama Rose said. 'Play "Please Send Me Someone to Love".'

'If you want to hear that, you play it,' Junior said. 'I'll play something I wrote.' Whereupon he sat at the piano, with its forty-four dead keys, played his Coplandesque composition 'Shelly's Suite', named for his older daughter, and a number of other songs while it rained hard, torrents of notes and weather, and we listened. As Piano Red used to observe, 'When the music spirits hits you, it hits you hard.'

At length Atlantic issued another, larger, check to Phineas in payment for the album *Solo Piano* – not the double album Fred Ford had envisioned, but the twenty-years-overdue solo album – which received a Grammy nomination and many excellent reviews. Some good things resulted, but for the most part life went on as it had in Memphis. I was living in a house with a vintage snooker table, and at times Fred and Phineas would come over and Fred and I would shoot snooker while we listened to records and Junior ambled around restless because I had no piano.

I was still, six years after the events had transpired, writing about the Rolling Stones at the end of the '60s. By now so overcome with shame at my inability to finish the book that I could no longer face the Stones, I stayed at home on July 4, 1975, when they played Memphis. With me were an old friend named Susan and her young son Daniel, who were visiting for a few days. Memphis was hot and humid, and as if things weren't crazy enough, a plague of bb-sized beetles attacked the three prize plum trees in my back yard. I stood in the heat picking them out of the bark with the point of a knife. Daniel helped me for a while, which I appreciated, but then even the good-hearted ten-year-old decided it was a fool's errand and left me to my futile task. The trees would die overnight.

Into this less-than-idyllic scene descended my friend and sometime Rolling Stones pianist Jim Dickinson and his wife. Dickinson wanted me to come along and see the Stones, but he wouldn't say so, and I wanted to see them, but couldn't bring myself. Soon Fred and Phineas showed up, Junior at once taking a shine to the striking auburn-haired Susan, who, having been married to a drummer, had already had more conversations than she'd wanted with over-friendly musicians. She went into the kitchen, followed by Phineas, followed by me. Busy at the counter, Susan ignored Phineas, and he exited into the back yard where the Nazi bugs were gassing the plums.

Leaving the Dickinsons downstairs with Fred, who was saying, 'I have seen the time I could call six and have it come up, tell the dice what to do,' Susan and I went up to my office, sat on the couch and passed the time until we heard footsteps on the carpeted stairs. I looked around the door-jamb to see who was coming up and spied Fred on the landing. 'Where Junior?'

Insufferable Yankee editors have explained to me how offensive it is to quote Southerners speaking as we speak. Fred said Where Junior not because he didn't know it's correct to say Where is Junior but because he knew I knew there wasn't time to say Where the fuck is Junior?

'I don't know, he went out in the back yard, is he not there?'

Fred was waving goodbye before I got the line out. I went downstairs, looked out back, saw no one, strolled through the living-room past the Dickinsons, Jim looking now like a man on a hopeless mission, on to the front porch, and scanned the neighborhood. Junior was standing on a porch a few doors down, reading a newspaper, while in the front yard a young, shirtless, white boy, maybe a year or two older than Daniel, looking rather perplexed, clipped a boxwood hedge. He had watched a small red man amble down the sidewalk, turn in at his house, go up on the porch, and start reading his family's newspaper. The boy's

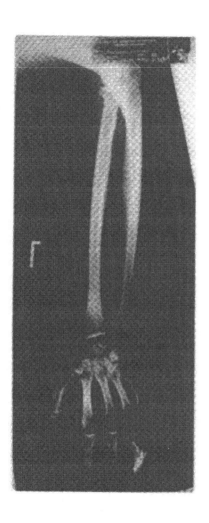

X-ray, Phineas Newborn, Jnr.,
Memphis, 1974

Phineas Newborn, Jnr.
performs for Sarah Vaughan and others
(date and photographer unknown)

perplexity did not decrease when he saw Fred Ford, the Chocolate Santa Claus, striding toward him. Fred stopped at the walkway and said, 'Little brother?' Phineas kept reading. 'Time to go.' Boy still clipping. Junior, silent, folds paper, drops it where he found it, again passes boy – clip, clip, clip, eyes rolling – and together Ford and Junior walk to where Fred's borrowed four-door sedan is parked at the curb. Fred unlocks the front door, steps back for Junior – who reaches in, unlocks the *back* door, opens it, gets in, sits back as if to say, 'Home, Jeems' – as Fred, shaking his head, slams the front door, goes to the driver's side, gets in, starts the engine, and pulls away, with Junior's posture in back seat asking – axing – the musical question, Who is the world's greatest classical-jazz piano player?

Later that month at a Club Paradise concert, the Mayor's office honored Junior with a citation 'for outstanding and meritorious service' and Mama Rose with a key to the city. The concert reunited Junior with Calvin, who had been living in Los Angeles, detoxing on methadone and playing with Hank Crawford, by now a distinguished Ray Charles Orchestra alumnus. Any doubts in Calvin's mind about his ability to hold his own with, or against, his brother should have been removed by the time they finished 'Cherokee', the last song of the evening. Phineas's playing is affected by, depends on, the nature of the occasion, the stature of the musicians accompanying him, the quality of the audience's intelligence and understanding. On this night his home community expressed pride in the Newborn family, and Junior and Calvin showed why it should be proud. That the concert was not recorded is a disaster and shows how proud of the Newborns the Memphis community really was.

In the next year, Phineas played in San Francisco and did occasional club gigs and concerts. *Solo Piano* was having a good effect, and in 1977 this unfortunate man, considered by VA physicians unable to live an unsupervised life, toured Japan all by himself. A Pablo album, *Look Out! Phineas Is Back!* with Ray Brown and Jimmy Smith, was released that year. In 1978, *Centerpiece*, a remarkable album featuring Calvin 'Newborne' and Hank Crawford, came out, and Junior finally returned to New York, where he played the Village Gate. Robert

Palmer's *New York Times* review said, 'he is back, healthy and playing superbly'.

In July 1979 Phineas returned after twenty years to Europe. We went not because we were needed but because Irvin Salky, a Memphis lawyer who had booked the engagements and was prevented by illness from going with Junior, paid our expenses, so Fred Ford and I went along. Phineas first played at the Montreux Jazz Festival; the opening concert, billed as the Piano Summit, featured him alone, playing duets with Jay McShann, Hank Jones and John Lewis, and in a double-Bosendorfer trio with Herbie Hancock and Chick Corea. At the end of the last set, Hancock and Corea were reduced to beating on the wood of their Bosie because Little David the Giant Killer, the Albert Einstein of the piano, had the keys sewed up. The next night Junior played an impromptu but memorable jam session with Ray Brown and Dannie Richmond.

Phineas's last concert of that European visit was at a jazz festival in Juan les Pins. Backstage, Count Basie's guitarist Freddie Green, seeing Junior, said, 'Where is Calvin? He's the greatest guitar player in America.' We stayed on to relax for a few days in the south of France, and Junior enjoyed being among the many beautiful naked people. He dressed up in his tux every morning so the girls would ask who he was. Fred began to call him 'The Count'. I'd go down to Fred's room and he'd say, 'You seen Drac?'

Months later I heard that Atlantic's attempts to release the Piano Summit had been stymied by representatives of some of the pianists who'd played with Junior. If this is true, it's understandable, because none of their careers would be enhanced by the evidence of how completely they were outplayed. 'Hank Jones is the only one who even put up a fight,' Fred said. 'And Phineas just let John Lewis off easy 'cause John such a nice guy.'

But each triumph left Phineas sitting on the couch in his mother's living-room. At some point in the early '80s, I called Phineas, said, 'How are you?' and was told, 'I'm just vegetating.'

Over the next decade, Phineas played a week or so each year in New York City, mostly at Sweet Basil in Greenwich Village. He played at festivals in the United States and Canada in the last couple of years, but his opportunities to work were not many and not close together.

In April 1988, in order to check up on Phineas for this story, I went back to Memphis. As I walked up on the porch of the little house on Alston, Phineas opened the door. I said Hello to Mama Rose and to Calvin, who for over a year had been alcohol- and drug-free, attending Lemoyne College, and writing his book.

Phineas and I hugged each other when I came in, but he seemed a bit restless. I sat on the piano bench, Mama Rose and Calvin on chairs, and Junior asked if I wanted a beer. It was two o'clock, early for me to take a drink, but I said sure. He brought a tallboy for me, one for himself, and sat on the couch. I started talking about Memphis in the 1940s, when Big Phineas, Al Jackson Sr. and Tuff Green had bands. They had been before my time, and I asked how many players they included.

'They had four-five horns on the front line,' Calvin began.

'Don't tell nobody you wrote it,' Junior said. '*I* know you wrote it – like these folks at the Church of God, all apeshit coons –'

'Tuff and Al had about ten pieces,' Calvin continued.

'In those days it was gettin' back to Germany, testin' some mo' of that shit,' Phineas went on. 'Just like they told you Jesus was Jehovah was a lep-er, you know.'

'They played big-band arrangements,' Calvin said. '– Had that Count Basie sound.'

Junior barked with the medical reports' inappropriate laughter, that made everyone who heard it ask, Is it mocking? Is it hostile? Why is this man laughing?

'When,' I said, 'did the record store open?' and Junior, as if in answer, began singing 'Silent Night'.

'Was the store open before Junior went in the Army?' Calvin asked his mother.

'Yeah it was open,' Junior said. 'I went there in my *old soldier* suit –'

'What year was you in the Army, Mister Soldier?' Mama Rose asked.

'I didn't ever get out of the Army. Got my dog-tags on me right now,' Junior said, reaching inside his collar. He was dressed for the stage as always in a dark blue suit and striped foulard. 'United States 52372651,' he read.

'How old were you when you started playin' with your daddy's group?' I asked, pressing on.

'Oh, 'bout fifteen,' Junior said, but he must have been younger. 'I was that age when I built that other rockin' chair back there –'

'Little rockin' chair,' Calvin laughed.

'You wasn't but a year old when your daddy built that,' Mama Rose said.

'I liked to burn up this one,' Junior said, talking about the couch, 'tryin' to get me some pussy while I was smokin' a goddam cigar –'

'Shut up!' Mama Rose said. 'Anybody can act silly.'

'What sort of material did the Memphis bands play?' I asked.

'Blues every time,' Junior said.

'No they didn't play no blues every time,' Mama Rose said. 'They played all types of music. Whatever them bands was playin' in New York City and upstate New York, that's what Tuff and Phineas and Al Jackson and them would play.'

'They had a lot of good arrangements,' Calvin said. 'They played a lot of jazz then, now it's considered jazz, but back then it was just good music. They had good arrangers in the hands like Onzie Horne and Slim Waters.'

'They were readin' musicians,' Mama Rose said. 'They weren't just out there slappin' their hips and carryin' on, they'd read that music. When the bands would come in town from other places, they'd meet down at Sunbeam's and they would jam together, you know.'

'They used to rehearse right here,' Calvin said. 'In fact I remember the first time they asked Junior to play piano. Then they asked me to play guitar. I played "Steel Guitar Rag". I didn't know but one song.'

Junior, on his way to the kitchen for another Bud, reached past me to play the opening bars one-handed. Calvin and I talked about the brothers' early playing experiences, with Junior interjecting to ask me for a cigarette and to recall that he had 'played a 4-H Club Convention and didn't get but fifty cents. Fifty cents.'

Mama Rose was answering a question about her brother-in-law David Newborn, the music teacher, when Phineas asked, 'Did David kill Goliath? I'm curious about what the church people have been talkin' about, you know –'

'Shut up when I'm talkin'!' Mama Rose told him.

It is just this sort of ironic repartee – what Phineas calls Off-Broadway humor – that has earned him such poor marks from the VA physicians, perhaps the one group less capable of understanding him than the jazz critics.

'Tell me 'bout when you met W.C. Handy,' I said, trying to keep the conversation going.

'Oh, I never met W.C. Handy,' Phineas said.

'Yes he did,' Mama Rose said.

'I happen to be Christ myself, and Christopher was his maiden name – '

'Shut up, boy,' Mama Rose said. 'He met Handy, he met all of them, 'cause we carried him with us, and he grew up and he'd follow 'em, his daddy would take him, he met all the musicians –'

'I ain't never grew up, I ain't nothin' but a nigger you know –'

'Dizzy Gillespie, Count Basie, Lionel Hampton, Roy Milton, all of them seen him. So, yeah, he met Handy, don't pay him no 'tention, that's his Bud –'

'Bud didn't do it to me. That pussy poisoned my ass, why I like bootys Bud my God-dam self,' Phineas said.

'What's the most important aspect of being a writer?' student Calvin asked.

I gave a long speech to say persistence, during which I mentioned that when I started I'd thought that I might fail but that I could at least die trying. Phineas laughed then, not the bark but a good solid laugh.

Calvin and I went on talking, about writing and our lives, while Junior went out for cigarettes. Both of us had come near to death, courted it, many times.

'You was lookin' at it the wrong way,' Mama Rose said. 'That's the weakness of your faith and all.'

That was true but it had nothing to do with Phineas, who has never had a moment's lack of faith. He has been hurt by the faithlessness of others, but his faith is steadfast. 'Had to pay my wife a hundred and fifty dollars a month child support for *years*,' he said when he was back on the couch.

I mentioned an award that Lemoyne music teacher and killer saxophonist Herman Green had given to Mama Rose, and she said, 'I'll tell you somebody else who made me feel good – B.B. King.' She told about going with her niece to hear King at the Paradise and get King's autograph for her sister.

'I asked the security, "I want to see Mr. Riley King."

' "Well, he's resting. Who should I tell him?"

' "Mrs. Phineas Newborn Senior."

'B.B. hopped up, he said "Let her in!"

'I go on in, he signs my sister's autograph and all, he says, "We go way back." Says, "You 'member when you was there at my house, and they took the draperies off the wall?"

'I said, "You know I 'member, child." He had bought some draperies from L. D. Price department store, and he wasn't payin' on them and the man came and took the draperies down from the window, and we sittin' there.

'He said – "I wanted to give up."

'He was on the radio. [sings] ."B.B. King, the Beale Street Blues Boy." And Martha, his wife, she workin' at the laundry. And she would tell him – listenin' to other folk – he need a job. And B.B. tellin' the old man and me, "Yeah, Martha's disgusted, man." Phineas said, "It's money in it – if you can ever get to it."

'B.B. told me that night at the Paradise, "Mama, I wish she'da had the sense like you."

'I said, "Don't look like I have much. But I'm rich, boy." 'Cause, see, I loved the same thing. We'd go, when they was dancin', and I'd dance and dance and enjoy that music. And sometimes we wouldn't have a cryin' quarter when we got through. But I enjoyed the music. But this woman listened at 'em, "B.B. need a job."

'B.B. told me, "The last time I saw Big Phineas – you know, the old man passed in California – he said, "His feet was swollen, and Mama I gave him a hundred dollars. 'Cause I can't forget – I'd have give up."

'One time I told the old man, "You Newborns, you just scared of money and money's scared of you." He said, "Well, I see you ain't left me." I said, "No, well, I told that preacher, For better or for worse, but I got to admit a lot of the time it's been worse" – He said, "But you still here."

'He was a good person. We were talkin', my mother and I, and I said, "Mama, that Bible says, Cast yo' bread on the water. In many days it will return", and I said, "and Rosie Newborn say it'll have butter and jelly on it."

'The old man cast his bread on the water, and people have been good to his sons, and good to me. I reap the benefit.

'Calvin was a good showman,' Mama Rose went on, 'but Junior never tried to sing or shake or nothin'. But he can play a piano. And what's amazin' to me, I don't care what condition he's in, I have seen him in a shape that I had a warrant and had him picked up, carried him to the hospital. And after they found out that he was Phineas – now the old doctor didn't know, but some young intern came in, and Junior sittin' there lookin' right ugly, walkin', drinkin' water every two minutes –'

' "Suppose they tell you you Jesus Christ and take you to the Church of God in Christ – " Junior said.' The COGIC is a big black denomination headquartered in Memphis.

'And he picked up this chart, this young doctor. He said, "Are you Phineas Newborn Junior?" '

'Junior: "Yeah." He touched Dr. Brook – "Oh, this man is a genius, this man is this, blah blah, he can play a piano –" '

'Junior raised up, touched him, said, "Look – don't tell that doctor that, he never will let me out, you know a genius is not but one step from a crazy man," and sat back down.'

'If a rabbit got an asshole, what it cost a bear to get some pussy?' Phineas said, went to his room, climbed in with his clothes on, pulled the covers over his head, and crashed.

I stayed a while longer, reminiscing with Calvin and Mama Rose – about the days when Aretha Franklin, 'only so high', would walk past on the way to her father's New Salem Missionary Baptist Church – until Calvin had to get ready to play at a Beale Street night club. It was Mama Rose's birthday.

I drove up Crump Boulevard past Elvis Presley and remembered seeing Phineas a dozen years ago standing on that corner, rumpled, unshaven, but radiating power, like Clark Kent after a bad kryptonite binge. I thought of seeing him five years ago at a piano bar on Beale Street, drinking Scotch in silent fury while a white girl played and sang 'San Francisco'. I remembered a passage in George Lee's *Beale Street* about the cornet player Sam Thomas, the street's original band-leader, and later I looked it up again. 'He was the first of a great line of musicians that sprang up on Beale Street,' Lee wrote, 'and his early activities did

opposite: Calvin Newborn, Flamingo Club, ca. 1952, photo by George Hardin

much to lay the foundation upon which was built up one of the world's greatest music centers. In view of this contribution, of his great ability, and of the fact that thousands of dollars were made by others on music that he arranged and composed, it seems an unusually cruel blow of fate that he finally died, broken and disheartened, in the Shelby County Insane Asylum.'

Reading about Thomas put me in mind of a procession of vanished Memphis music characters – among them the original Bar-Kays, Jimmie Lunceford, Gus Cannon, Will Shade, Bill Harvey, Nathan Beauregard, Fred McDowell, Sleepy John Estes, W.C. Handy, Buster Bailey, Memphis Minnie, Leonard Campbell, Tuff Green, Al Jackson Senior and Junior, Frank Floyd, Howlin' Wolf, Memphis Piano Red, Charlie Freeman, Furry Lewis, Elvis Presley, Bill Justis, Dewey Phillips, Tommy Cogbill, Booker Little, Sonny Criss. I thought of Lucky Thompson, sleeping on the beach on St. Simons Island and on a park bench in Savannah, and of King Oliver, dying in Savannah, writing to his sister, 'The Lord is sure good to me here without an overcoat.'

'I cried, Lord have mercy, what evil have I done?' Furry used to sing, 'Look like the blood in my body done got too low to run.'

I wondered what evil Furry had done, or gentle Lucky, or stoic Joe Oliver. According to Junior's medical reports, he hallucinated, drank to excess, thought he was Christ – but while I saw him depressed, detached and ironic, I never in fifteen years knew him to hallucinate. He drank too much at times, but only from boredom, and as for his occasional *comédie noire* insistence that he was Christ, it seemed to me very Christlike. Phineas had no doubt that the Kingdom of God was within him – it flowed from his fingertips. Phineas, like the Fool in *Lear*, sent back shibboleths to believers in a manner that shook their faith – the one about having one child, himself, with his mother was classic textbook stuff: the Id talks back. Betrayed, neglected, Phineas struck back with ironic humor. What a wicked man.

Another year passed, and a friend called to say that Phineas had a couple of tumors. Soon after, he was dead.

Before we went to Europe in 1979, I'd asked Phineas what he considered the most important thing for a young musician to keep in mind.

'Stay young at heart. That's the right idea as far as I'm concerned. Play young at heart. Play the way you feel. A thing of value outlasts a thing that has no value. Attempt to produce things of value as you go along. If it's worthless, it won't last; if it has value, it generally does – an eternity, almost, in minds and hearts.'

20

THE GODFATHER'S BLUES

Toward the end of 1988, a radio reporter from Augusta, Georgia, called with news of James Brown. I'd seen Brown's wife's allegations that he had beaten and shot at her, but I knew nothing more about his predicament. 'He's going to prison,' the radio man told me.

'Bullshit,' I said. 'They won't put James Brown in jail.'

On December 15, 1988, James Brown was sentenced to six and a half years in a South Carolina prison, but not for beating his wife. By the time I managed to talk with him, he had served two years and was set to get out a few months later. 'I don't even want to get into it,' he said. 'These people railroaded me and put me into this thing, it wasn't never about no drugs. Police made a mistake and couldn't cover it up. Because they shot the truck up. I'm sittin' there talkin' to another policeman. Them people took advantage of me. I done fought this mother for two years. Two years later, I'm not gone fight it. If it'd helped me then, I'da did it. I did two years because I wouldn't plead guilty. I could've pleaded guilty and walked out in ninety days. That's the deal they made me. I wouldn't take it. I made one mistake. You can't beat the police – right or wrong. I made my statement. I'm happy with what I did.

'Two years later, y'all want me to be a hero. I'm gonna say it like it is. I have nothin' to say about the system. I told BET that yesterday. I have nothing to say about blacks and whites. I have nothing to say about nothing. I did two years for nothing, I did it from integrity, nobody come forward. All those organizations and groups, and I love you very much, thank you for wantin' to do it, but I got too much manhood about me to sit up and cry about it now, 'cause somebody want to use it for a steppin' stone.'

Asked about his friend, Jacqueline Daughtry, Brown said only, 'She's a good girl.' But there was more to the story.

To hear James Brown at his best, you have to catch him in court. Hearing only his concerts and records, you miss the really soulful reaches of his voice. In the midst of his captors and tormentors, his voice becomes a wind tunnel of scars, raspier than Miles Davis's most muted solo, each suspiration of breath telling volumes of abuse borne by the black man in stoic silence.

The last time I saw him in court, on March 21, 1989, when he was called from prison to have outstanding charges dealt with, Brown didn't do much testifying. He sat on one side of the large, well lit, South Carolina courtroom, his facial planes composed into an expression of resigned suffering, while the mother of Woodrow C. Laird, the prisoner ahead of Brown on the docket, told the judge what Woodrow had said when he left home: ' "I'm goin' to get me some boots." Just as wild-lookin' as he could be,' she said. 'Wild as a goat.'

Laird, a graying white man who had previously been an inmate of the South Carolina state hospital and pleaded guilty to trafficking in marijuana, had led a chase through several counties in which a police car was destroyed. James Brown, convicted of a similar offense, though he'd caused no damage to anyone's property, had been sentenced to six and a half years. Brown's face revealed nothing as he heard the judge give Woodrow Laird – who, unlike Brown, had never quelled any riots or won any humanitarian awards and knew no presidents personally – four months in jail and five years' probation.

Just before the court went into session, Brown, dressed in a suit of small gray checks, a gray necktie and a burgundy shirt, had slipped a left-thumb-and-index-finger OK gesture to his wife, who came in wearing a silver-gray dress and sat near the front of the spectator's gallery. Nearby were William Glenn, Brown's first cousin and oldest associate, and Danny Ray, his announcer for decades.

When the time came, Brown's attorney, Bill Weeks, a tall, clean-cut young white man, an ex-basketball player, told the judge, 'Your Honor, Mr. Brown's hat is in his hand.'

Brown had no additional time added to his sentence, even though he had tested positive for PCP and marijuana. '*Please* stay off drugs,' said the judge, a man from the same area of South Carolina, near Barnwell, that Brown comes from. 'Put your troubles behind you – you can do a lot of good.'

At his Augusta sentencing, two months earlier, Brown had talked about wanting to be a model, 'not only for children but for the country as a whole'. He had worn a red shirt that day, too. What kind of lawyer lets his client go to court in a red shirt, I wondered. Albert H. 'Buddy' Dallas, of Thomson, Georgia, Brown's primary lawyer, seemed weak-chinned and shifty-eyed, but I restrained myself from forming an opinion of him based on his looks. He was pleasant, accommodating – we walked around the Augusta courthouse together, he took me to the jail door where Brown's mother and other family members were waiting to speak to him. Then it turned out that Brown would not be allowed to talk with the press. The next day I called Dallas at his office to tell him that I had a lot of respect for his client and that I'd like to write about him, but I'd rather not write anything than do him harm. Later I began to think that was the worst thing I could have said to Buddy Dallas.

That morning in Augusta, Adrienne Brown, James's wife, was sentenced for drug and traffic violations. She received twelve months' probation and a $600 fine. Her lawyer said that 'Mrs. Brown apologizes to the community for any embarrassment.' Brown himself didn't exactly apologize, but he said he 'didn't want Augusta to be embarrassed'. Of his legal situation, he said, 'I don't feel good about it.'

One day several years before, outside Augusta's Richmond County Jail, hearing the cries and noises from within, Brown told journalist Gerri Hirshey, 'You're hearing rage and frustration, and those are things I left behind.'

The question is, in Augusta, Georgia, how far behind the past can be left. Just off Broad Street, across from the liquor store, stands a stone column, known locally as the Slave Pole. Men and women about to be sold were tied to it, so the story goes, and anyone who knocks it down will die.

Leaving the Augusta court, I met Isaac Ford, a black, muscular, young man lately fired from his job as an officer of the Augusta Police Department. Before it was over, he had provided me with lists of Augusta horrors, things only a cop could have seen or known about. The things everybody knew about were bad enough.

Later I met two other ex-APD employees. Between them and Ford I heard accounts of events in the APD central station ranging from pistol-barrel-sucking to homicide. Isaac Ford was a brave man who knew a lot about the Augusta law. One of the few men who might know more, James Brown, was forbidden by prison officials to speak with the press, even though the press – Tokyo phoning at 4.00 a.m. South Carolina time – kept trying.

In his autobiography, *The Godfather of Soul*, James Brown says of his initial prison sentence (8 to 16 years for breaking into cars when he was fifteen) 'It reminded me of the days out in the woods when my daddy was gone . . .' Abandoned by his mother at four, alone in an unpainted shack without plumbing or electricity, Brown learned, before he could read or write or had a thought of singing and dancing in public, to do time.

Until well after the first half of the twentieth century, the forests of South Carolina and Georgia were filled with wealth for white men who could coerce blacks into wading water and dodging rattlesnakes and moccasins to scar and collect the resins bled from great pines, some of which had grown a foot a year for a hundred years. The blacks, paid in cash and script to the owners' commissaries, almost never avoided becoming indebted and were obliged to stay and work. Before James Brown was six, his father took him out of the woods, across the Savannah River to Augusta, which is not the same as freedom.

The site of Augusta is perhaps the most delightful and eligible of any in Georgia for a city [William Bartram wrote in 1776]. An extensive level plain on the banks of a fine navigable river . . . Augusta

. . . I do not hesitate to pronounce as my opinion, will very soon become the metropolis of Georgia.

Augusta, Georgia's second oldest city and its capital from 1786 through 1795, is today the state's second largest metropolitan area, known best as the home of the Masters golf tournament or the Savannah River bomb plant, the country's single facility producing only tritium and plutonium for nuclear weapons. The site of the first black Baptist church, Augusta has the South's oldest newspaper in continuous circulation, the *Chronicle and Herald*. Woodrow Wilson and Ty Cobb lived there. George Washington and the Marquis de Lafayette found Augusta a pleasant place to visit. On the other hand, the lower portion of the city is bordered by Erskine Caldwell's 'Tobacco Road'. In 1935, the *Chronicle* investigated, discovered people living in the conditions Caldwell described, and recommended that the problem of such human scum's existence be solved by the judicious employment of isolation and sterilization. This is not unrelated to the problem of James Brown.

The Masters tournament had existed only four years, and the Atomic Energy Commission's Savannah River Project was not yet even a gleam in the eye of a mad scientist when, late in 1938, James Brown came to live with his aunt Handsome 'Honey' Washington in her whorehouse at 944 Twiggs Avenue, where he saw, as he wrote later, 'everything'. Also living there was William Glenn, Washington's grandson, one year older than Brown. Both boys were Juniors; Glenn was called Big Junior, Brown Little Junior. 'We were as close as brothers,' Brown has recalled, 'wore each other's clothes, shined shoes together, and sometimes slept in the same bed.'

Augusta, which Brown refers to in his book as 'sin city', was then and is now divided like Gaul into three parts: the upper-class whites in the big houses on the hill looked down, literally and figuratively, on the Harrisburg district, home of the poorer whites, and the Negro territory, called the Terry. The reality of black existence at this time, when Georgia vied with Mississippi for the national lynching championship, was that in any attempt to be something besides a subservient menial worker, one could hardly avoid breaking the law, and even that didn't make life easy. In spite of their relatives' diligent pursuit of prostitution, gambling and bootlegging, Big and Little Junior searched the railroad tracks for coal to heat the house and shined shoes for rent money while dodging the police, who insisted that Augusta boot-blacks be licensed. Still it was not until James had started school and been sent home for 'insufficient clothes' that he began stealing to buy some decent garments and got into more serious trouble. The police caught him and another boy taking a battery out of a car and kept them in Augusta's Richmond County Jail overnight. When James returned home, William, who was about to join his mother in New York City, told him, 'You got to get away from Augusta.' But James Brown chose to stay, and so it happened that by the time he had reached sixteen, the minimum age for a driver's licence, he was in prison with a sentence set to last as long as he had then lived.

Brown has described his childhood as replete with torture – undeserved whippings from his father, whom he calls 'dangerous'; beatings from his uncle; being electrocuted by three white men with an electric compressor while digging a water-filled ditch. He has said that the warden of the Juvenile Training Institute in Rome, Georgia, raised him. (The warden struck him only once, with an open hand, which by comparison must have seemed like a caress.)

Locked in his father's cabin in the pines, James had played a 10-cent harmonica; as an older boy in Augusta he had played organ and piano, sung gospel songs, performed for his classmates at school and on local amateur shows; at twelve he'd formed a singing group called the Cremona Trio, and in prison he sang with a gospel quartet. Still, his first love was sports; his heroes were Augustans Ty Cobb and Beau Jack; he boxed and pitched baseball left-handed, and when, after serving three years and a day, he was paroled, it was so he could pitch for the baseball team in Toccoa, Georgia, where he had spent his last year. 'That's when I learned there's no such thing as law,' he said. Being given a harsh sentence that was rescinded when the baseball team was faced with a crucial game embittered Brown, but what had perhaps a more profound effect on him was his exile from Augusta. The Richmond County Solicitor agreed to Brown's parole only on the condition that he stay away from the town where his family lived. 'Years later, when I was living in one of the best neighborhoods in Augusta,' Brown states in his autobiography, 'I met Solicitor Haines's son and told him, "Your father sent me away and didn't want me to come back, but I want you to know I don't hold it against him."' Then he adds: 'I *think* the boy was embarrassed.'

Much of what Augusta resents about Brown is contained in that quote: he presumed to return, to live in a white neighborhood, to behave as if he, and not the empowered local whites, were 'quality'. The Old South doesn't like uppity, and Augusta is, or believes itself to be, the Old South.

The journey back to Augusta was not short. A young pianist in Toccoa named Bobby Byrd gave Brown a place to stay (in the Byrd family's small house with Byrd's grandmother, mother, sister and four other family members) and an address to give the parole board. He worked first at a car dealer's and then, after wrecking a customer's vehicle – 'one way or another', Brown's book records prophetically, 'my troubles always seemed to involve a car' – at a plastics factory.

Brown carried on boxing (three fights in Toccoa – two wins and a draw) and pitching for the Toccoa baseball team. He remembers throwing a no-hitter the day after his marriage to a good Baptist girl named Velma Warren who'd heard him sing with his group, the Ever Ready Gospel Singers. After a few months, Brown joined Bobby Byrd's nameless secular group, which became the Flames, then James Brown and the Famous Flames, with a record on the King label, 'Please, Please, Please', that would sell over a million copies. By then – the record was released in 1956 – Brown had two sons; another would be born the next year, during which Brown played Harlem's Apollo Theatre and saw his mother, who'd been absent from his life for twenty years. When she smiled at him, he saw that she had lost her teeth. 'I'm going to get your mouth fixed for you,' he told her.

In 1958 Brown had another million-seller, 'Try Me', and another, 'Think', two years later. When his musical success began, he had been allowed to play Augusta as long as he spent less than twenty-four hours in town. In 1964, after integrating the Macon City Auditorium, Brown integrated Augusta's Bell Auditorium, both before the passage of that year's Civil Rights Bill.

In 1965, in the midst of a popular-music revolution, Brown cut his first international hit, 'Papa's Got a Brand New Bag'. At thirty-two years of age, Brown – known by then as 'the hardest-working man in show business' – had become an institution. But he saw himself as just getting started. 'I wasn't content to be only a performer and be used by other people; I wanted to be a complete show business person: artist, businessman, entrepreneur.' He also had higher societal ambitions of a statesmanlike sort: he joined the NAACP, and visited Africa. People started calling him 'Soul Brother Number One', which to Brown meant that 'I was the leader of the Afro-American movement for world dignity and integrity through music.'

He expanded in business, buying radio stations in Knoxville, Baltimore and Augusta. In Boston the night after Martin Luther King was shot, Brown saw to it that his concert was televised, and counseled blacks to stay home. 'Let's not do anything to dishonor Dr. King,' Brown told the audience, at one point adding, 'I used to shine shoes in front of a radio station. Now I own radio stations. You know what that is? That's Black Power.'

After that President Johnson invited Brown to dinner at the White House, and sent him to entertain US troops in Vietnam. Another epoch-making hit followed, 'Say It Loud – I'm Black and I'm Proud', ending a year of characteristically contradictory apotheosis. In January 1969 he sang at President Nixon's inauguration; in February he attended James Brown Day in Augusta, an event promoted by the principal of the grammar school he'd left without graduating. Following this, Brown, who'd lived since the early 1960s in Queens, New York, decided to return to Augusta. Buoyed by a B'nai B'rith Humanitarian Award and a cover story in Look headlined 'Is This the Most Important Black Man in America?', Brown – though plagued with divorce and paternity suits and IRS problems – went home.

Some of Brown's white neighbors were still protesting about his moving into a house on Augusta's exclusive, expensive Walton Way when, the following year, a sixteen-year-old black boy was killed in the jail, and blacks rioted. Georgia Governor Lester Maddox found Brown at a gig in Flint, Michigan, and told him what was happening. Brown returned the next morning; on the air, in the streets, he pleaded for non-violence. Amid rumors of an invasion by Ku Kluxers and Black Panthers, the Augusta airport and bus terminal were closed for a week.

A few months later, Brown got married to a woman from Baltimore named Deedee, by a probate judge in Barnwell, South Carolina, who had never heard of Brown and told *Jet*, 'I married them out there on the front porch. I got a real nice front porch. I marry most of my colored couples out there unless it's raining, then we come inside.'

In the 1970s, Brown's life, like many American lives, seemed to suffer from the 'malaise' of which President Carter spoke. Brown played Vegas, visited Nigeria, recorded his third *Live at the Apollo* album, but he seemed to be searching for significance; he played a rock festival for crippled children, was honored by then-Governor Carter for his work with state drug programs, and released an anti-abuse song called 'King Heroin'. His tax problems continued; the Apollo closed, his oldest son died in a car wreck, and Brown went into semi-retirement. His decision to spend more time with Deedee and their two daughters resulted in a second divorce. In 1978 the Apollo reopened; on July 16, Brown had just finished his second show there when he was arrested on a contempt charge arising from a civil suit against one of his radio stations. 'I'd come out of prison to do right,' he said, 'and still wound up in jail.' Brown sank into a, *comme on dit*, funk – ended, he says, by a rededication of his life to God.

The 1980 film *Blues Brothers* brought Brown back to public attention. He toured parts of Europe and did club and television appearances.

On Groundhog Day 1982, Brown was on *Solid Gold* and met Adrienne Rodriguez, who would become the third, and possibly the last, Mrs. Brown.

'It wasn't love at first sight,' Brown said, 'it was recognition at first sight. Our souls had met a long time before.'

Brown followed the *Blues Brothers* success with the films *Dr. Detroit* and *Rocky IV*, the latter containing a new James Brown top-ten pop hit. In January 1986, with that song, 'Living in America', still on the charts, Brown was inducted into the Rock and Roll Hall of Fame. He spoke of it as the culmination of his career. Just over two years later, on the day after Easter, 1988, Brown was wanted by the police for trying to kill his wife.

My Augusta radio news friend had mentioned a woman who represented Brown in organizing a charity concert ordered by an Augusta judge as part of a sentence against Brown for a traffic offense. Though the concert was to benefit an agency for abused children called Helping Hands, the Leukemia Society and the Fraternal Order of Police, it was boycotted by the police and very negatively portrayed in the local media.

A few days after Brown went to prison, I spent an evening in Atlanta talking with his friend, Jacque Daughtry, who wore, as I'd heard, one pink and one blue cowboy boot and blonde hair down to the tag on her Levi's. Her story started over a decade before, with a young girl, bald from chemotherapy and pale, looking younger than her sixteen years, meeting James Brown at the Atlanta airport and telling him, 'I want to be a singer and songwriter like you, but the doctors say I'm dying,' and James Brown saying, 'You don't have to do what they say. You can be anything you want to be if you believe in yourself and what you're doing.'

Flash forward ten years: the girl, now a singer and songwriter, was working on a charity recording project with the Atlanta Falcons football team, none of whom knew that she, Jacque Daughtry, was the sick girl members of the Falcons had once visited in cancer wards. At this point the healthy Daughtry had a sick recording project — after two years and $25,000 worth of studio time, the record wasn't finished, the Falcons kept losing, no one could agree on which charity to endow, and the whole thing appeared a bottomless pit. Then Daughtry had a dream about James Brown, got in touch with his attorney, sent him a tape, and received a call from Brown, who said he'd sing the song and set a date for a recording session in Augusta.

So it happened that in 1987, on a stormy spring night 'like something out of a horror movie', Jacque Daughtry found herself at a sound studio on Peach Orchard Road waiting for James Brown, who was over six hours late (detained in Atlanta, unbeknownst to Daughtry, by dental surgery). Close to despair, standing outside the studio so the musicians and personnel inside wouldn't see her crying, Daughtry saw two headlights 'like Rudolph the Red-nosed Reindeer coming through the fog'. When the car stopped, out stepped James Brown. 'I told you I'd be here,' he said.

Without another word, Brown went into the studio, put on headphones, listened, then asked, 'Who *wrote* this song?'

Daughtry, in the control room, closer now to outrage, said, '*I* did. What's wrong with it?'

'If you wrote it, get out here.' With Daughtry beside him at the microphone, Brown said, 'Don't ever let anybody tell you there's anything wrong with your song. I just wanted to be sure *you* knew there was nothing wrong with it. You have just learned one of the most valuable lessons of your career.'

The morning after the session, Daughtry, back in Atlanta, answered the phone.

'Jacque, it's me, James. What do you think about the record? Is it all right? Should we change anything?'

'He was just making me feel like somebody,' Daughtry said, 'like he did ten years before at the airport.'

Far from being a *fait accompli*, the record still lacked a charity to benefit and a sponsor to pay for it. Finally the Leukemia Foundation was selected; Coca-Cola, that conspicuously affluent Atlanta phenomenon, donated expenses; and then came the idea to release the record at the half-time show of the Falcon's first 1987 home game, with James Brown performing. Brown agreed, but when Daughtry asked the Falcons to pay traveling costs for Brown and his musicians, they refused. Soon after that, Daughtry, at home and crying again, answered the phone. 'Whassaproblem?' James Brown asked, and offered – though he'd refused to play Nixon's second inauguration when the Republicans wouldn't cough up expense money – to pay the half-time show expenses himself.

On the day of the show, September 20, Brown made it from Florida, where he and his band were appearing, to Fulton County Stadium with seconds to spare, sang with Jacque Daughtry, and received a standing ovation. The Falcons won, something they would do only twice more that season. 'It was magic,' Daughtry said. 'Sunny, seventy-two degrees, a breeze was blowing, there wasn't a cloud in the sky.' But in the distance a thunderhead was forming.

It would take over a year for Daughtry to tell me the reason for the storm: that on the day of the Falcons show, after going from the stadium to Scottish Rite Hospital to visit a little girl, she and James Brown became lovers. 'You and me were made for each other,' she remembered him saying.

The night we met, Jacque Daughtry and I talked for eight hours. Some of what she told me I found hard to understand, but that was because I'd never been to Augusta. Driving into Augusta from where I lived, on the Georgia coast south of Savannah, along the scenic route from Garnett through Estill to Fairfax and so on, one encounters a roadblock with guards dressed like a cross between state troopers and storm troopers. This is the Savannah River Project, the nuclear-trigger factory, where they have been dumping toxic waste in cardboard boxes into shallow landfills for over forty years, a place evacuated by strontium-90 laden turtles. In the daytime one sees giant tubes belching steam from what must be a big, angry core. At night one sees mysterious flashes of light like glimpses into the door of Hell. Whole towns were destroyed to create this spectacle. Each driver is issued a pass, each car's number of occupants is recorded, and for the next 17 miles one drives above 35 miles an hour until reaching the exit roadblock and surrendering the pass. High spirits on the highway anywhere near this place are like bomb jokes in an airport. James Brown found the wrong neighborhood to put his business in the street.

On July 5, 1987, Brown, in Augusta, had backed into a car and received a ticket for not having insurance papers. In September, a week before the Falcons' half-time show, he was charged with speeding and attempting to elude the police. That incident occurred a few days after Adrienne Brown's arrest on Washington Road near the Augusta National Golf Club. Stopped for speeding, she struck and kicked the doors and windows of a police car, incurring a charge of criminal trespass. Early in November James Brown was jailed in Aiken, South Carolina, for running into two parked cars, leaving the scene of an accident and resisting arrest. People in the Augusta–Aiken area, many of whom already disliked Brown, began to think of him and his wife as public menaces.

Not long after the Falcons' show, James Brown listened to more of Jacque Daughtry's songs, asked if she'd like him to manage her, and was accepted. 'He worked me to death, but he gave me balls, he gave me strength,' Daughtry said. 'And I saw this strong man become an exhausted, beaten child. He changed from a cocky, arrogant man to a pitiful child, begging for his life.'

Brown's arrests shocked Daughtry, but she found more disturbing his fears for his own sanity: 'I can't think straight,' she remembers him telling her. 'I'm afraid I'm losing my mind.' At other times Daughtry said Brown seemed convinced that 'somebody's tryin' to do me in,' telling her 'be careful what you eat and drink', and insisting that his phones and office were bugged.

Meetings were held with Brown, his manager-attorney Buddy Dallas and veteran band members like guitarist Ron Lassiter and saxophonist St. Claire Pinckney. In these meetings the idea surfaced that Brown, who had been regarded in the music business as, if anything, too much of a disciplinarian, fining musicians for playing wrong notes, being unshaven, or needing a shoeshine, was being drugged, and he agreed.

On April Fool's Day, 1988, Daughtry, in Augusta at Brown's invitation as she often was around this time, staying in a room at the local Marriott Courtyard suites, went for a ride with Brown in his van. They stopped at a Washington Road car dealership, where some work was being done on a Volkswagen Rabbit Brown was buying for one of his daughters, and at a convenience store for soft drinks and candy. Then, driving down a South Carolina expressway, Brown asked Daughtry for a cigarette, declined one of her Winstons – 'too strong' – and asked Daughtry to give him one of his wife's Kools from a package he'd seen behind the front seat. Before the cigarette was finished, Brown began to hear voices in the van. 'They're comin' to get me,' he told Daughtry. Wheeling away from the expressway into dense pine woods, Brown bounced the van off trees, knocking the back doors off, getting stuck as night fell. 'He had a sawed-off shotgun pointed at me,' Daughtry said.

'That van was an arsenal. It was like Fort Knox. He didn't know who I was. He kept hearing things outside the van and talking about Vietnam, he thought he was in Vietnam. He told me to get in the back. What would you have done? I got in the back. I thought if I could make love to him I could get him calmed down.

'It would have been one thing if I'd said, "James, take me out, bounce off of trees, let's have a hair-raising, death-defying ride and sex romp in the woods and see if we come out alive. And then spend the next three fucking hours trying to figure out how to get out of the woods.' Because it was past midnight, it was twelve-thirty or one o'clock in the morning. I don't to this day know how he got us there without killing us, but it was pitch black. When you turned your lights on, you couldn't see anything except pine trees, and he'd run over a sort of low cliff and flipped the van over on one side . . . you know, the thrill was kind of gone.

'That was the point when I realized that he was not a violent man. Anybody else would have fucking wrung my neck. Because I'm sitting there crying and screaming in fear and he looks over at me very calmly and he goes, "Jacque. Shut up. Please. We gotta get out of here." I'm thinking, Oh my God, we're gonna die, I'm gonna die with this man and they're gonna find out later that we died out in the middle of the woods. I didn't think, number one, that the man could get the van up. But he did. He's a hell of a driver, I must admit. Anybody else would never have gotten out of there. But he did it. He got his act together. He said, "They did this to me. They did this to me, and they almost killed you."'

April Fool's Day that year was on Good Friday; Brown did not return to his Beech Island, South Carolina, ranch until early morning, Easter Sunday. Before that day ended Brown had, according to his wife, shot holes in her mink coat and her white Lincoln and beaten her with a metal mop handle. She had the Sheriff's department issue warrants for aggravated assault and assault with intent to kill, but later declined to testify, as she had once before following an alleged incident in December 1984. She also filed for divorce, then changed her mind, as Brown had done twice. The Saturday after Easter, Mrs. Brown was arrested at Augusta's Bush Field airport and charged with illegally possessing

8 grams of phencyclidine, an animal tranquilizer nicknamed PCP, a substance that is tasteless, odorless, and can be absorbed through the skin. The next month she was arrested in Bedford, New Hampshire, for setting fire to the Browns' hotel room and for having 7 ounces of PCP. Nine days after that, James Brown was jailed in Aiken, South Carolina on charges that included possession of 7 grams of PCP, possession of a weapon, and assault on an officer after leading police on a high-speed chase. According to the Sheriff, the PCP was in a nasal-spray bottle that fell out of Brown's coat. Two days later police arrested Mrs. Brown at the Augusta airport with half a pound of PCP in her bra.

During the summer of 1988, Jacque Daughtry worked on plans for a charity telethon, and James Brown went to Europe on tour. When he returned he seemed clear-minded and in good general health, but after being hospitalized for further dental surgery – Jacque Daughtry met Adrienne Brown for the first time in Brown's hospital room – James Brown 'feeling funny from the medicine', went to an Athens, Georgia, drug-treatment clinic, staying only one night. He was still suffering from his operation, but also seemed to be depressed. On one occasion he asked Daughtry to come to Augusta and then said he couldn't make it to the office. 'I'm washed up,' she remembers him saying. 'I'm finished.' Close associates observed a marked deterioration in Brown's condition when he came off the road; Brown, the master of control, found it impossible to deal with home life in a reasonable, restrained manner – a task at which other great men have failed.

In July, Brown, tried for the offense involving PCP possession, received a sentence of two and a half years' probation and was ordered to give a charity concert within the year. (That same month, a white police officer in the roll-call room at the Augusta Police Department shot a black officer dead at point-blank range and was charged at first with nothing, at last with involuntary manslaughter. A University of Georgia management study of the APD was ordered.)

On Saturday, September 24, James Brown, visiting his suite in an office park on Augusta's Claussen Road, found to his displeasure that some unauthorized person or people had been using his rest room. Indoor plumbing has a heightened significance for those raised without it. That may account in part for what happened next. Carrying an inoperative antique shotgun, Brown walked into a nearby room where an insurance licencing seminar was in progress and asked two women there to come with him to lock the rest rooms. Although Brown threatened no one, a sheriff's deputy who happened to be attending the seminar slipped out and called the police. According to news reports, Brown left in his red-and-white pickup truck as Richmond County Lieutenant Overstreet arrived, lights flashing. He followed Brown a mile down Interstate 20, where Brown stopped, driving away again when Overstreet got out of his car. Brown went to North Augusta, South Carolina, where he was pursued by police officers and Aiken County sheriff's deputy Donald Danner. Testifying in Brown's defense at the resulting trial, Danner said that Brown obeyed the command, given over his patrol-car loudspeaker, to pull into an abandoned lot at the corner of Martindale and Atomic Roads. According to Danner, he went to the truck, spoke to Brown, and reached in and turned off the engine. At this point the other officers arrived and started breaking out the truck's windows. Brown restarted the vehicle, backed up, then drove forward past the officers as they unloaded at least seventeen, maybe two dozen, hollow-point ·45 bullets into the truck, flattening its front tires. Fearing for his own life, Danner said, he left the scene. Fourteen police cars followed Brown at a speed of about 30 m.p.h. back to Augusta, where he drove into a ditch in front of a friend's house and was taken into custody.

At 7.25 the next morning, Brown, who had been released on a $4,100 bond, was again arrested in Augusta, driving his Lincoln Continental down Ninth Street. Arresting officer T.J. Taylor said that Brown 'just had his hands up in the air while he was driving down the street. He was incoherent and couldn't hold his balance.' Blood tests on Brown revealed the presence of PCP.

A few days later, Jacque Daughtry took James and Adrienne Brown to Anchor Hospital in Atlanta. ('Actually,' Daughtry said, 'I took them several times, because James had to go home for clothes, he was drooling, foaming at the mouth, it was awful. We kept stopping at McDonald's, at the Burger King, the Western Sizzlin'. At one place a little boy asked for an autograph and James pulled a gun on him. It was a nightmare.') Brown told admitting doctors that he might have a brain tumor, but insisted he had no drug problem, and the hospital physicians agreed, allowing him to leave after four days. 'Take care of my wife,' Brown said. He left for a tour of Europe, and Mrs. Brown returned to Beech Island.

The next day, Daughtry took Mrs. Brown to Atlanta's South Fulton Hospital, where she was confined for a month.

On October 26, an Aiken County grand jury indicted James Brown on two counts of assault and battery with intent to kill (because of his driving forward past the police who were shooting at the truck) in connection with the September chase. Jacque Daughtry, asked to put together the charity concert ordered back in July by the Augusta court, devised Wrestle-Rock, a combination sports (if wrestling is a sport) and music event. The *Chronicle* said that a more appropriate punishment for trash like Brown would be to have him clean trash from the highway in a prison road gang, and at first Augusta Civic Center officials refused to allow him into the building.

On October 31, Augusta police came to James Brown's second cousin's house – Melvin Glenn, Willie Glenn's son, lived there with his family – on a domestic dispute call. When police arrived, no dispute was in progress, but at least five officers took Melvin Glenn into a back room, decided to arrest him, and were unable to do so without killing him. Augusta Police Chief Freddie Lott explained the death by saying that Glenn had been drinking and fighting with his wife and that he struggled with the officers. The night Glenn died, Buddy Dallas called Jacque Daughtry – curiouser and curiouser – and sent her down into the ghetto in a white limousine to see what she could do for Glenn's wife and family. 'I saw the room where they killed him,' she said. 'There was blood all over, on the walls, the mattress, on the bed. They said he had a nosebleed. Must have been a hell of a nosebleed.'

The Civic Center officials finally agreed to give Daughtry a date for the charity concert – Sunday afternoon, December 2, when everything would cost triple scale – although there was nothing else scheduled at the Center that weekend. 'Augusta gave me a thorough education in racial prejudice,' Daughtry said.

'During November, I got death threats, somebody called up and offered me $150,000 not to have the concert, the police called me a niggerfucker, they'd come in my motel room when I was out, they knew everything I did. I found cocaine in my room and flushed it down the john.' On the eve of the concert, the *Chronicle* reported sales of only 56 tickets. Daughtry, sensing disaster, took some of the musicians who'd be playing the next afternoon to an Augusta hospital so they could see a few of the children their work might help. There she met a fifteen-year-old black girl named Katina Bryant, who said she wanted to be a singer but couldn't because she was too sick. 'Don't you believe it,' Daughtry said. Later that evening, at a country church with James Brown, Jacque told him that she was the little girl he'd spoken to at the airport years before.

The concert was scheduled for two o'clock on that cold Sunday afternoon, but at 1.30 the Civic Center officials still had the front door locked. Daughtry opened the back door, letting in Boy's Club members and children's ward residents to whom she'd given tickets. That boosted attendance at the 7,500-seat arena to under 400. The police stayed away, but a line of them, drawing triple-time pay, stood in front of the stage, scowling. Musicians from the Atlanta Rhythm Section, Hall and Oates, Lynrd Skynrd and other bands, played bravely into the gloom, until Daughtry stopped the show. 'I couldn't stand it,' she said. 'I asked, "Could you turn up the house lights? There's a little girl here." Nobody knew what I was talking about, because there were many little girls there. I brought Katina Bryant on stage, asked for two chairs, put my hand-mike in my lap, asked her if she'd sing, and she said yes. I thought if the whole thing was going to hell anyway, why not let a little girl's dream come true? She'd sung for me in the hospital, so I knew she had a beautiful voice. She'd had a blood transfusion less than an hour before, but she said she'd do it.

' "Aren't you afraid?" I asked her. She said, "Why should I be afraid?" She told the audience, "This is my friend. We're here for the children." I'd told her about the boycott, and she asked, "Why are they boycotting the children?" I said I couldn't answer that, and asked her to sing. She did the Whitney Houston song that goes, "I believe the children are the future . . ." Then I asked her to sing "Amazing Grace", and she got a standing ovation. "Katina Bryant has cancer," I told the crowd. "People like her are what this show's all about." I looked down at those cops in front of the stage and there wasn't a dry eye among 'em.'

James Brown, dancing as if he had no troubles, sang 'Papa's Got a Brand New Bag', and the small crowd stood and cheered. Afterwards he said, 'We got to try . . . for those who can't help themselves. It's the children of the world that we have to help. That's the most important thing . . . it's the children that count.'

Ten days later, a chilly Tuesday, James Brown awaited trial in the Aiken County jail. On Thursday he was convicted of aggravated assault and sentenced to six and a half years in prison.

'After he got me back to my car, that Friday before Easter,' Daughtry said, 'I started back to Atlanta, and I was several miles out of Augusta when here came James like a bat out of hell, blowing his horn, motioning for me to pull over. I did, and he ran up to the car. "You forgot to tell me you love me," he said. I had to laugh. My clothes were torn, I was a wreck, but he made me laugh. The next morning he called and said, "My God, what have I done to you?"

'He called after that to say that he was wearing denims – he couldn't even say *denim* – and tennis shoes, because that was what I liked to wear. When I went back to Augusta, he had the radio set on this easy listening station, because he thought I liked it. I'm sitting there listening to "Somewhere My Love", wondering what is this man going to do for me next?

'I know what he did for me – he went to jail. I really believe if he had gotten to court, and he had just turned around and said, "I know this is going to be very alarming to everybody in this courtroom, but I was set up," it would have opened up the whole case. It really hurt me, because I realized then that there's no justice.' Daughtry was utterly convinced of James's innocence.

'He's under a lot of medication and a lot of craziness,' Brown's wife told the court in his defense, and they can hardly have doubted her. With Brown in jail, Mrs. Brown's lawyers and the court arranged for her a sentence of probation. 'Justice Was Done', the ever-severe *Chronicle* titled its editorial on James Brown's sentence, but the one about Mrs. Brown's asked the musical question, 'A Squishy-soft Deal?'

Jacque Daughtry found herself spending time with her new friend, Katina Bryant.

'At first it was partly a way of staying close to James, because children mean so much to him,' Daughtry said. 'I told Katina she could live and be a singing star and help other children, because James Brown showed me anything was possible if you really believe. I asked the judge who sentenced James, "Why would you take all the good this man does out of the world?" I believed too much – one day Katina called and said she had something to tell me, and she wanted me to be calm. "You're a very emotional person," she told me. I asked her what it was, and she said "I'm going to Heaven. Soon. The doctors told me." I started saying all over again how they'd told me that, but she stopped me and said, "Just remember, around my mama, right up to the end, we have to pretend I'm gonna get well."

'I wrote "Katina's Song" and she used the last strength in that little body to sing it. The Kroger grocery stores helped put it out with all the proceeds going to children's hospitals, and the song was used in the Miracle Network telethon in 1990.'

A year after the Wrestle-Rock show, the mayor of Augusta, Georgia, honoring Daughtry for her charity work, specifically 'Katina's Song', gave her the key to the city.

On July 17, 1991, the governor of Georgia issued a proclamation honoring James Brown, who was described as a 'personal friend'. 'It's just a pleasure to celebrate in the comeback of the legendary Godfather of Soul,' Governor Zell Miller said, and denied that there was any irony in Brown's being honored by a state that had imprisoned him. 'I know the inner man of James Brown. The inner man is a man who's compassionate, a man who's strong, and a man who's not going to stay down. Here he is, bigger and better than ever.'

Miller asked Brown how he felt, and James Brown sang one of his best known lines: 'I Feel Good'.

Burnt Fort, Georgia, 1991 (© Stanley Booth)

Of Beale Street, Thomas Pinkston said, 'I seen things come up down there that you be surprised at.' So had I, having been in Memphis more than once when it was on fire, but I knew that Georgia held an ignorance, a depth of depravity, an excess of evil — a wildness — to be surpassed nowhere. If Stendahl was correct in describing the novel as 'a mirror dawdling down a lane', there existed around the Okefinokee Swamp lanes the likes of which civilized people knew nothing about. As a child I had watched the fleshy, sparkling, sundew plants devour blue-bottle flies, looked on as shapely pitcher plants swallowed honeybees. Once again I drew near, became still, silent, and settled down to observe.

ACKNOWLEDGMENTS

These pieces first appeared as follows:

Standing at the Crossroads in *Rock and Roll Disc*, Furry's Blues in *Playboy*, Situation Report: Elvis in Memphis, 1967 in *Esquire*, The Memphis Soul Sound in *Saturday Evening Post*, Blues Boy in *Eye*, The Memphis Début of the Janis Joplin Revue, The Gilded Palace of Sin: The Flying Burrito Brothers and Blues for the Red Man in *Rolling Stone*, Elvis's Women in *St. Petersburg Times*, Wiregrass in *Atlanta Weekly*, Psalmist of Soul: Al Green, That's Why They Call it the Blues: Stax in Atlanta and The Burden of the Blues: ZZ Top in *Musician*, Keith Richards at Forty-Five in *Smart* and Fascinating Changes in *Village Voice*.

The author and publishers are grateful for permission to quote extracts from lyrics:

'Hound Dog' (Jerry Leiber, Mike Stoller) used by permission of Carlin Music Corporation, Iron Bridge House, 3 Bridge Approach, London NW1 8BD and © 1956 Gladys Music & MCA Music Publishing (Renewed) All rights reserved. Used by permission.
'Sittin' On The Dock of The Bay' reproduced by permission of Warner Chappell Music Ltd
'I'm a Hoochie Coochie Man' © Jewel Music Publishing Co. Ltd; reproduced by permission of Warner Chappell Music Ltd, written by Willie Dixon © 1957 (renewed) Hoochie Coochie Music (BMI)/administered by Bug. All rights reserved/used by permission
'Soul Man' © Warner Chappell Music Ltd; reproduced by permission of Warner Chappell Music Ltd
'How Blue Can You Get' © Leonard Feather, reproduced by permission of Model Music Company
'Sin City', 'My Uncle', 'Juanita' composed by Gram Parsons and Chris Hillman; published by Rondor Music (London) Ltd
'Heebie Jeebies' reproduced by permission of MCA Music Ltd

Every effort has been made to trace copyright holders. The publishers apologise if inadvertently any source remains unacknowledged.

INDEX

'All God's Children', 143
Afterburner, 174
'Amazing Grace', 155, 245–6
American Studios, 69, 82–4
Atlanta Weekly, 138
Atlanta, Georgia, 112, 159, 168
Atlantic Records, 112, 123, 160, 172, 190–2, 206, 213–14, 219
Augusta, Georgia, 230–47
Avalon, Mississippi, 40–5

Bailey, Buster, 15
Bad & Worldwide (Deborah Faust), 171
Bar-Keys, The, 69–73, 87, 109, 161
Bartram, William, 2, 231
Basie, Count, 21, 196, 203–4
Beale St., Memphis, 15, 17, 21–4, 31, 36, 39, 44, 72, 89, 94, 100, 169, 197–9, 203, 225, 249
Beard, Frank, 171, 173
Beatles, The, 74, 78, 87, 180, 183
Bell, William, 167
Bergman, Jo, 106, 181–2
Berry, Chuck, 76, 124, 184
Big Brother and the Holding Company, 107–10
Bishop, Elvin, 90–1
Bitter Lemon, 24, 27, 29, 39
Bland, Bobby, 86, 148
Bloomfield, Mike, 110
'Blue Suede Shoes', 15
Blues Brothers, The, 236

Booker T and the MGs, 73–9, 91, 121, 160–3
Brando, Marlon, 60
Brewster, Rev. Herbert, 50, 153
Brown, Adrienne, 230–46
Brown, Charlie, 23–36
Brown, Gatemouth, 147, 202
Brown, James, 95, 228–47
Bryant, Katina, 245–7
Byrd, Bobby, 234
Byrds, The, 111, 113

Cannon, Gus, 15, 30, 84
Carter, President J., 237
Cash, Johnny, 15, 22
Centrepiece, 218
Charisma Project, 83–4
Charles, Ray, 16
Circle G Ranch, 56–7
Civil Rights Bill, 234
Civil War, 17, 29
Clapton, Eric, 90, 171
Clayborn Temple A.M.E. Church, 21, 32, 69–72
Cleveland, Mississippi, 13, 15
Club Handy, 33, 190
Club Paradise, 102–5, 110, 192, 218
Cooder, Ry, 148–9
Cooke, Sam, 88, 152
Coolidge, Rita, 124–5
Crews, Donald, 82–4
Criteria Recording Studio, 123
Cropper, Steve, 74–5, 107, 119, 121

Crump, E.H. ('Ed', 'Boss'), 20, 31, 48, 50
Cuoghi, Joe, 151–3

Dallas, Albert H ('Buddy'), 230, 240, 244
Danner, Daniel, 243
Daughtry, Jacqueline, 229, 237–47
Davis, Miles, 144, 204, 229
De Guello, 174
Dean, James, 60
Depression, The, 31, 51, 72
Dickinson, James, 83–4
Dickinson, Jim, 148, 171–2, 177, 215
Dirty Work, 185–6
Dixie Flyers, The, 123–4
Do The Popeye, 121
Doors, The, 171
Down Beat, 191, 206–7
Dunn, Donald ('Duck'), 75, 78–9, 107–8, 119

Edison, Thomas, 20
Eisenhower, President D., 48, 60, 204
El Loco, 174
Eliminator, 174
Ellington, Duke, 15
Elvis and Gladys (Elaine Dundy), 131–4
Elvis and Me (Priscilla Presley), 131–4
Emancipation Proclamation, 15, 136
Ertegun, Nesuhi and Ahmet, 194
Esquire, 52, 69, 203
Eye, 89

Fabulous Phineas, 207
Fandango!, 173
Faust, Deborah, 171, 173
Flames, The Famous, 234
Floyd, Eddie, 161–2, 166
Flying Burrito Brothers, 111–15
Ford, Fred ('Daddy Goodlow'), 128, 190, 192–4, 213, 218–19
Ford, Isaac, 231
Fortas, Alan, 61
Franklin, Aretha, 95, 107, 114, 124, 163, 225
Freeman, C.F., III ('Charlie') 117–30, 190, 193
Freeman, Sonny and the Unusuals, 90–105
French Quarter (Herbert Asbury), 141

Full Gospel Tabernacle, 151, 157
Fun in Acapulco, 67

G.I. Blues, 67
Gibbons, Billy, 169–79
Gilded Palace of Sin, The, 111–15
Glenn, William, 229, 232, 244
Glenn, Melvin, 244
'Good Rockin' Tonight', 63
Graceland, 58–9, 67–8
Green, Rev. Al, 150–8
Green, Herman, 16
Green Is Blues, 151
Godfather of Soul, The (James Brown), 231
Greenwood, Mississippi, 40–5
Green's Collection of Voyages, 180
Gumbo, 145

Haley, Bill, and the Comets, 60
Hampton, Lionel, 15, 199, 210
Ham, Bill, 172
Handy, W.C., 13, 15, 20, 24, 29, 31–2, 69, 204
Hansen, Patti, 186–9
Harrison, George, 74
Hayes, Isaac, 80–2, 107, 165, 167–8
He Is The Light, 151
'Heebie Jeebies', 76
Hendrix, Jimi, 73, 153, 171
Hill, Dusty, 170–1, 173
Hooker, John Lee, 33, 39
'Hound Dog', 65, 202
'How Blue Can You Get', 92–3
Hurt, Mississippi John, 37–45
Hurt, Theodore Roosevelt ('T.R.'), 42–5

Jagger, Mick, 180, 182–5, 187
Jenkins, Johnny, and the Pinetoppers, 76–7
Johnson, Johnnie, 187–8
Johnson, President L., 235
Johnson, Robert, 2–3, 4–12, 15
Johnson, Tommy, 10–12
Jones, Brian, 143, 160, 182–3, 189
Joplin, Janis, 106–10
Jordan, De Witt, 154
'Juanita', 114

Kennedy, President J.F., 139, 149, 170
Kennedy, Robert, 89, 139

King, Albert, 91–4, 109, 147, 176
King, B.B., 89–105, 199–200, 222–3
King, Martin Luther, 15, 21, 51, 89, 95, 111, 139, 159, 161, 164, 235
Kristofferson, Kris, 124

La Belle, Patti, 82, 151
Lady In Satin, 206
LaRue, Lash, 59, 117
Last Night, 121
Laird, Woodrow C., 229
Lennon, John, 51, 90
'The Letter', 82–3
Lewis, Furry, 15, 23–36, 37–45, 89, 170
Lewis, Jerry Lee, 15, 22, 50, 53, 122
Lewis, Versie, 27–36
Little Richard, 76
Lord Will Make A Way, The, 151
Look Out! Phineas Is Back!, 218
Lorraine Motel, 110, 111
'Love Me Tender', 64
Lunceford, Jimmy, 15

McDowell, Fred ('Mississippi'), 38, 170
Maddox, Governor Lester, 235
Manning, Terry, 173
Mar-Keys, The, 73–5, 78–9, 120, 160–1
Marsalis, Ellis, 146
Marsalis, Wynton, 144
Mayall, John, 172
Memphis, 15–19, 21–2, 47–9, 51, 72–4, 83–4, 89, 157
Miller, Governor Zell, 247
Mingus, Charles, 206
Mississippi Delta, 38–9
Mitchell, Willie, 151–2, 156–8
Moman, Lincoln ('Chips'), 82–4
Moorhead, Mississippi, 39
'My Uncle', 114

New Orleans, 23, 30, 138–49
Newborn, Calvin, 15, 197–208, 219–22, 225
Newborn, Phineas, Jnr., 21, 169, 190–227
Newborn, Phineas, Snr., 15, 194–7, 200–4
Newborn, 'Mama Rose', 196–227
Night Before Last, 121
Nixon, President R., 235, 238

'Ode to Billy Joe', 82
Okefinokee Swamp, 2, 112–13, 135, 249
Overstreet, Lieutenant, 243
Orbison, Roy, 15, 146

Pallenberg, Anita, 182–3, 188–9
'Papa's Got A Brand New Bag', 235, 246
Parker, T.A. ('Colonel'), 53, 63–4, 133–4, 172–3
Parsons, Gram, 111–15, 116, 149
Peebles, Ann, 158, 167
Penn, Dan, 83–4
Performance, 182
Perkins, Carl, 15, 21, 50
Perrin, Leslie, 106, 181
Phillips, Dewey, 47–51, 53, 61, 63–5, 69
Phillips, Sam, 15, 22, 47–51, 53, 62–3, 134, 172, 176, 180–1, 200
Pickett, Wilson, 112, 160–1
Pierce, Webb, 62–3
Pinkston, Thomas, 249
Plantation Inn, 117–19
'Please, Please, Please', 171, 234
Porter, David, 80–2, 107, 167
Posey, Sandy, 82–3
Presley, Elvis, 15, 21–22, 46–51, 52–68, 69, 73, 131–4, 153, 179, 202
Presley, Gladys, 61, 64, 66–7
Presley, Lisa Marie, 132
Presley, Priscilla, 56, 67, 131–4
Presley, Vernon, 62, 67
Profile of Primitive Culture, A (Elman R. Service), 116

Raitt, Bonnie, 148
Ray, Danny, 229
RCA Victor, 50, 63, 72
Rebennack, Mac ('Dr John'), 145–6
'Red Hot and Blue', 47–50, 62
Redding, Otis, 69–88, 89, 153, 159–63
Reed, Jimmy, 33
Revolver, 78
rhythm and blues, 72–3
Rich, Charlie, 15, 22
Richards, Keith, 124, 135, 179, 180–9
Rolling Stone, 106
Rolling Stone Record Guide (Dave Marsh), 174

Rolling Stones, The, 106, 116, 120, 129, 160, 173, 179, 180–2, 187, 214
Roosevelt, President F., 7, 20
Roy Rogers Fan Club, 117, 123, 130

Safe at Home, 113–15
Sam and Dave (Moore and Prater), 80, 85, 87, 161, 167
Sam the Sham, 120, 123–4, 128–30
'Say It Loud – I'm Black and I'm Proud', 235
St. Louis, 30
segregation, in Memphis, 47–9
Shade, Will, 15, 30, 84
Shadows, 206
Sherrill, Robert, 52
'Sin City', 114
Sinatra, Frank, 154
'Sittin' On the Dock of the Bay', 77, 79, 153, 161–2, 166
Solo Piano, 213–14, 218
'Soul Man', 80, 85, 87, 165, 167
South Carolina, 229, 231
Smith, Travis J., 55–7
'Stagolee', 28
Staples, Roebuck, 145
Stax/Volt Recording Company, 69, 73–82, 87, 107–8, 120, 159–61
Stewart, Jim, 107, 161
Sullivan, Ed, 64
Sun Records, 15, 49–50, 62, 73
Sweetheart of the Rodeo, 113–14

Talk is Cheap, 187
Taylor, Cyclone, 4–12
Taylor, T.J., 243
Teen Town Singers, 86–7
Tejas, 173
'That's All Right, Mama', 49–50
'Think', 234

Thomas, Carla, 74, 85–7, 109, 120, 160–8
Thomas, Rufus, 49, 87, 109, 160–7, 199
Touissant, Allen, 144–5, 149
Tres Hombres, 173
Truman, President H., 48
'Try Me', 234

Vaughan, Sarah, 146
Vaughan, Stevie Ray, 147
Village Voice, 190

Walker, Polly, 97
'Walkin' the Dog', 87, 160, 163, 166
Wallace, Sippie, 145
Waters, Muddy, 86, 175, 178–9
Waycross, Georgia, 111–15
WDIA, 85, 87, 100
Weeks, Bill, 229–30
Wells, Junior, 102–4
Wexler, Jerry, 112, 123, 191–3
WHBQ, 47–50
While My Lady Sleeps, 207
White, Bukka, 99
Who, The, 73
Wild One, The, 60
Wilson, Jackie, 154
Wilkins, Rev. Robert, 15, 38
Williams, Nat, 100
Williamson, Sonny Boy, 99–100, 103
Wilson, Kemmons, 48, 50
Wiregrass, Georgia, 112–13, 135–7
Wolf, Howlin', 22, 33, 180–1, 203
Woods, Johnny, 169

X-pensive Winos, The, 185–8

Young Men From Memphis, 206

Zeppelin, Led, 173
ZZ Top, 169–79

10241210R0

Made in the USA
Lexington, KY
08 July 2011